Eunice Hunton Carter

EUNICE HUNTON CARTER

A Lifelong Fight for Social Justice

Marilyn S. Greenwald and Yun Li

EMPIRE STATE EDITIONS

AN IMPRINT OF FORDHAM UNIVERSITY PRESS

NEW YORK   2021

Fordham University Press has no responsibility for the persistence or accuracy of URLs for external or third-party Internet websites referred to in this publication and does not guarantee that any content on such websites is, or will remain, accurate or appropriate.

Fordham University Press also publishes its books in a variety of electronic formats. Some content that appears in print may not be available in electronic books.

Visit us online at www.fordhampress.com/empire-state-editions.

Library of Congress Cataloging-in-Publication Data available online at https://catalog.loc.gov.

Printed in the United States of America

23 22 21   5 4 3 2 1

First edition

for Tim

CONTENTS

If there is no struggle, there is no progress.

—Frederick Douglass, 1857

INTRODUCTION

EUNICE HUNTON CARTER first came to our attention in 2014 when we visited the Mob Museum in Las Vegas. As part of an extensive exhibit about the first significant mob prosecution in this country in the 1930s, the museum posted a series of large black-and-white photos of special prosecutor Thomas E. Dewey and his legal team of "mob busters." All but one of these talented attorneys looked exactly as one would think: stern and intimidating, they conveyed a sense of danger and glamor. It was no wonder they ventured into territory even J. Edgar Hoover's G-men feared to tread.

But one member of Dewey's team didn't fit the profile, and the reason was apparent: she was a kindly looking Black woman.

Anyone with even a passing knowledge of US history and civil rights could guess that Carter was an anomaly among the group of young White men who surrounded her on that wall. We knew without investigating that there were few female or Black attorneys in the 1930s, and certainly few Black women attorneys. And we suspected there were few Black prosecutors.

A year or so later, we began looking into the background of Carter: who was she, how did she get the job as mob buster, and how did she thrive in this professional environment in an era of rampant racial discrimination and sexism? What we found was far more interesting than we could have imagined. Carter's decade working for the ambitious Dewey—who would become the Republican Party's presidential nominee twice—made up a relatively small part of her fascinating and trailblazing life. Equally as impressive were the lives of her family. Her grandfather was a slave who bought his freedom, fled to Canada, and became a successful businessman. Her mother was an early peace and women's rights advocate who traveled to France during World War I to aid the Black troops there. Her father nearly single-handedly integrated the nation's YMCAs at the turn of the century, spending much of his time traveling and organizing in the Jim Crow South. The first generation of Huntons began their lives as slaves in Virginia; the second generation lived in Chatham, Ontario, and became part of a small enclave of former slaves who became prosperous; and the third generation, including Eunice and her brother Alphaeus, became key players in social justice and racial equality movements in the United States and overseas. Eunice's son, Lisle, continued the tradition of civic involvement. Among many accomplishments, he was the first president of the University of the District of Columbia, legal counsel to the National Urban League, and a high-ranking official of the federal Department of Health, Education, and Welfare.

Eunice's accomplishments go on: the first Black woman to serve in the New York Prosecutor's Office; the first Black woman to simultaneously earn a bachelor's and master's degree at Smith College at a time when that college was almost exclusively White; and one of the first women to earn a law degree at Fordham University

We hope that by telling Eunice's story, we can place the era in which she lived in a cultural and historical context and shed light on a crucial period in American history.

PERHAPS FATE INTERVENED when the lives of Thomas E. Dewey and Eunice Hunton Carter became linked. At first, it would appear that the two could not be more opposite. Dewey, who was born three years after Carter and raised in a small town in Michigan, came from a White middle-class and Republican family. His grandfather and father were both newspaper publishers—his father ran the hometown paper—and he, too, became active in journalism in college when he worked at the University of Michigan *Daily*. Dewey achieved few "firsts" as a young man—one of the reasons he traveled to New York to attend Columbia law school was to follow his girlfriend—later his wife—to New York. He did not graduate at the top of his class.

Ironically, though, Dewey and Carter had more in common than one would think. Both were writers and communicators at heart. Carter as a young woman published reviews, opinion pieces, and fiction in the respected and lively National Urban League publication *Opportunity*, and she once was viewed by members of the Harlem arts scene during the Harlem Renaissance as an up-and-coming young writer. Dewey wrote for his college newspaper and was an accomplished orator who was one of the first politicians to make extensive use of radio addresses to communicate information and inform voters. Both were Episcopalians, and both were lifelong Republicans. Eunice remained in the party of Lincoln long after many Black Americans abandoned it. (Years after their successful prosecution of the New York mob, Carter joined Dewey's first few political campaigns.) Although neither was a native New Yorker, both embraced their adopted city with a vengeance—Dewey was a known fixture in Manhattan, as Carter was in Harlem. They both became famous faces and names in these venues.

Furthermore, both were devoted to their jobs. They were tireless workers who did not let barriers, criticism, or initial failures deter them. Indeed, work was a crucial aspect of their lives, sometimes to the detriment of their personal relationships. But the ongoing long workdays were the least of it—neither was happy unless they were working or thinking about work.

Carter and Dewey were both innovative thinkers who didn't always embrace accepted dogma or existing beliefs. Carter's master's thesis at Smith was a rethinking of the structure of local governments, written in minute detail. Dewey used public relations and the cultivation of the media to help beat the mob and further his political career to become within a hair's breadth of the presidency. Previous politicians and government officials had done this to a limited degree. Still, Dewey perfected it—this was a man who persuaded the publisher of the *New York Times* to temper that newspaper's coverage of the mob investigation until he, as special prosecutor, finished it. After all, publicity and "leaks" could hurt or paralyze the probe.

Most important, Dewey recognized a strategic thinker when he saw one; it was Carter, with her sharp mind and knowledge of the streets of Harlem, who provided the final puzzle piece that ultimately clinched the case for the prosecution.

It is impossible to determine what makes the professional relationship between two people gel. In the case of Carter and Dewey, however, it might have been a combination of their similarities and differences. Carter had a razor-sharp mind and could cut someone with a quip, but she was low-key and subdued in public interactions. Dewey was charismatic and dramatic, personality traits that were shaped in part by his long training as a professional singer. Carter was happy to work behind the scenes; Dewey usually took center stage. And both were fearless—not everyone would take a public stance against one of the most brutal and organized criminal networks in the country. Both traveled with bodyguards before and after the trial.

Interestingly, journalism, particularly newspapers, played vital roles in the lives of both, although in different ways. Dewey cultivated the editors and publishers of some of New York City's leading newspapers to conduct his mob investigation and, later, to court voters during his runs for public office. While many of Carter's achievements throughout her life were not recorded in the mainstream press—they were given scant attention there—the nation's thriving Black press paid extensive attention to her, following her achievements and activities in detail for decades. She became a fixture in these national publications, which were largely ignored by White readers, and they treated her as a pioneer, a "doer," and someone who could serve as a role model for their mostly Black readers.

In actuality, the famous trial of Charles "Lucky" Luciano and his fellow mobsters ultimately played only a minor part in the lives and careers of Dewey and Carter, although that episode was one that was the most publicized and even fictionalized decades later. After the trial, Dewey, almost overnight, earned the reputation as a heroic crime fighter, and his colorful prosecuting techniques were illustrated in newsreels, movies, and fictional accounts of him. Ultimately, Carter, too, achieved the status of minor celebrity more than half a century after the Luciano trial, when a fictionalized version of the dogged Black female assistant prosecutor emerged in the popular Home Box Office television show *Boardwalk Empire*.

Still, much of the individual legacies of Carter and Dewey have been lost to history. Carter's decades-long commitment to organizations that furthered racial equality in this country and overseas has long been a footnote in the story of the nation's civil rights and feminist movements. And Dewey, whose impressive political career included three terms as New York governor and two stints as the Republican nominee for president, has become an iconic figure in popular culture not for his accomplishments but because of a spectacular journalistic gaffe: the famous *Chicago Tribune* headline proclaiming that "Dewey Defeats Truman" in the 1948 presidential race.

But as their story here reveals, both made contributions far beyond their few years prosecuting killers, prostitutes, and drug dealers. That job served as merely the launching point for much more important work, especially in Carter's case. She emerged as a role model, activist, and energetic advocate for social justice.

The dogged determination, fearlessness, and devotion to hard work that first drew Eunice Hunton Carter and Thomas E. Dewey to each other would ultimately determine their legacies in other fields and allow them, in their own way, to shape this nation's history.

THROUGHOUT THIS BOOK, we refer to Eunice Hunton Carter by her first name for reasons of clarity. We do this because many of her relatives with the same last name are an integral part of the story but also because she had two last names in her life—Eunice Hunton, her maiden name, and Eunice Carter, her married name.

1

Heirs to the Struggle

It takes rare courage to fight a fight that more often than not ends in death, poverty or prostitution of genius.... But it is to those who make this fight despite the tremendous odds ... that we must look for the breaking of the bonds now linked together by ignorance and misunderstanding.
—Eunice Hunton, in *Survey*, March 1, 1925

AS SHE SAT IN HER OFFICE at 137 Centre Street in Manhattan in the mid-1930s, few would peg Eunice Hunton Carter as the crime buster whose work would ultimately nail the notorious and glamorous Charles "Lucky" Luciano and many in his gang. As the first Black woman to be named to the prosecutor's office in New York City, she stood out from the White men in her office, both in physical appearance and demeanor. The low-key Carter, who usually dressed in conservative loose-fitting dresses and often wore a hat, achieved much of her success not on the streets, but behind her desk, working the phones and painstakingly reviewing thousands of documents. Soft-spoken, she didn't boast about her accomplishments and certainly didn't exaggerate them. And she never complained about the long hours that often led to many frustrating dead ends.

Eunice was not just another member of the twenty-person team of attorneys who busted the mob and revealed its illegal activities to the public. She was the one who linked prostitution in the city to the work of mob head Luciano, a seemingly far-fetched connection that would ultimately crack the case. Her knowledge of the streets of Harlem, combined with her innate common sense and her willingness to review thousands of pages of legal documents and testimony, led to her discovery. And even then, she had trouble persuading her boss of its importance. She managed to do so only because her colleagues respected her, so they trusted her instincts.

This finding would become Carter's legacy and would ultimately garner more attention than the many "firsts" she achieved throughout her life: one of the first Black women to earn a law degree at Fordham University and to pass the New York bar, and the first Black person to be awarded an honorary doctorate of law at Smith College, first Black woman to pass the New York Bar, and more. And her association with the glamorous world of Luciano and other mobsters could not have been more ironic for the woman who had always buried herself in solitary work: first as a young college graduate who wrote gentle and descriptive short stories about her vague memories of early childhood in the sunny and lush South, and later as an attorney and bureaucrat who devoted herself to social-justice causes.

As with many people, Eunice's personality was, in some ways, contradictory. She was a talented writer who gave up hopes of that creative pursuit for social work and the law, and she became a dedicated scholar and dogged attorney for whom family would be one of the most important aspects of her life.

Eunice was a third-generation member of a family of social-justice pioneers who struggled against slavery and segregation and bias. To attempt to understand her persistence, motivations, and way of thinking, one must first turn to her mother, Addie Hunton.

EUNICE SEEMS to have inherited her strong work ethic, single-minded determination, and creative, independent way of thinking from her father, William Alphaeus Hunton. William Hunton was the first top Black YMCA administrator whose pioneering work established YMCA facilities for both "colored" people and Whites. He devoted much of his life to that exceedingly difficult task, traveling around the world and spending many years in the American South during the era of codified segregation known as the Jim Crow years.

But it was her mother, Adelina "Addie" Hunton, who served as the lifelong role model for her two children, Eunice and William Jr. (known as Alphaeus), in her actions, beliefs, and determination. Addie Hunton's life revolved around her activities as a civil rights and suffrage activist whose goal was to fight for equality and improve the lives of those who followed her. Addie spent much of her early adulthood assisting her husband in his role as a YMCA executive and activist. Throughout her life and her extensive travels, she made sure to record her activities and beliefs on paper. She was a student of the world around her, leaving behind countless writings in the form of books, journal and magazine articles, essays, and newspaper stories. Addie Hunton had a strong sense of history and early on recognized the importance of documenting the struggles—and victories—of Black people in their quest for equality. Her daughter would share this penchant for writing and recording observations, even though she would make her mark in the world as an attorney, crime fighter, and club woman.

IN 1917, ADDIE WAITES HUNTON was a widow with two teenage children: a daughter, Eunice, 18, and a son, Alphaeus, 13. Her husband of twenty-three years had died the previous year after a lengthy illness, and his care had depleted much of the family's savings and had worn down Addie emotionally. But now she had started to get on her feet again, even though she was never one to remain stationary and tend to the home—not before she married and not as she raised her two children. Now, in the middle of World War I, she and two other Black women used their membership in the National Association of Colored Women (NACW) to contribute to the war effort through rallies, war bond campaigns, and emotional support for Black troops. In their book, *Two Colored Women in World War I France*, she and Kathryn Johnson described the thrill and apprehension they felt that day in June 1918 when they were called to begin a journey to the coast of France as part of the American Expeditionary Forces. The two women worked for the YMCA and under the auspices of the NACW to sail to France to provide aid and moral support to the two hundred thousand racially segregated Black troops there. The two women were moved by the "great thrilling, throbbing spirit of war." As they indicate in the detailed memoir about the thirteen-month mission, the excitement and trepidation were palpable—even the weather that day was foreboding:

> One dark afternoon, as the rain came down in torrents, the buzz of the telephone at our elbow told us our time had come. We asked no questions, for those were days of deep secrecy, but looked for the last time at the war map in the office wondering where in that war-wrecked country across the Atlantic, we would find our place of service. We breathed a little prayer, said good-bye to our fellow workers, knowing that tomorrow we would be on the ocean eastward bound. . . . There was no sleep that night for us.

The participation in World War I of Black troops was in itself controversial: while many Blacks at the time advocated resisting military service for a country they believed denied them basic rights, Black media organizations, the National Association for the Advancement of Colored People (NAACP), and leading intellectuals of the era, including prominent author and scholar W. E. B. Du Bois, advocated their participation in the military, believing that such service could ultimately alleviate the racial prejudice in the United States. The 92nd Division—composed of draftees and officers—and the 93rd Division—made up primarily of National Guard units—were created for Black Americans. Yet most Black soldiers were assigned to service units, based on the belief that Blacks were more suited for manual labor than combat. And, initially, only a dozen or so Black women were recruited to work with the four hundred thousand Black soldiers in Europe. Addie was sent first to a supply center in St. Nazaire, and later to the town of Aix-les-Bains in the southeast of France.

Hunton's and Johnson's 1921 memoir about their shocking, dramatic, and fulfilling time in France was the first of two full-length books Hunton wrote about her and her husband's lives. Both books differ in style from what many readers would characterize as conventional memoirs because they overflow with primary source material that includes poems, letters, and memos and, in the case of *Two Colored Women*, written summaries of real-time conversations and excerpts of Hunton's own thoughts of events shortly after they happened. Hunton apparently realized that because of the marginalization of Blacks of her era, direct accounts of experiences and thoughts would likely be overlooked and lost to history if they were not documented in detail as they happened. Ironically, in the foreword to *Two Colored Women*, Hunton and Johnson own up to the idea that their own opinions and emotions about their time in France may be biased in some ways due to their unbridled admiration and respect for the soldiers with whom they worked: "We have not refrained in our story from a large measure of loyalty and patriotic service, performed oftentimes under the most trying conditions." Still, they say modestly that "we have no desire to attain to an authentic history but have rather aimed to record our impressions and facts in a simple way." Yet Hunton and Johnson's account of their time in France during World War I *is* a history that vividly recounts the struggles of a disenfranchised group who fought for their country but ultimately were let down by the government they supported. As the women imply in their book, their time in France was fulfilling to them but also became a disillusioning experience that prompted them to redouble their efforts on fairness and justice after they returned to the United States.

AS YMCA PROGRAM DIRECTORS, known as secretaries, Hunton and Johnson were tasked with teaching literacy classes, running kitchens, leading

Bible study classes, arranging athletic events, and, in general, providing moral and emotional support to the Black troops stationed at or near the Western Front. In *Two Colored Women*, they describe in detail their exhaustive but rewarding months in these efforts. But the mistreatment, neglect, and general lack of humane treatment of the Black soldiers on the part of the American Command as well as YMCA officials shocked them, leading them to believe that America's Jim Crow laws extended informally to France. Further, although the YMCA pledged equal treatment of the Black soldiers, the women were spread thin, and, at one point, three women were responsible for aiding one hundred fifty thousand men. (The YMCA ultimately sent a total of eighty-five Black social workers to France to aid in the war effort.) The terrible treatment of Black soldiers overseas enraged Blacks in the states and, for many, erased any optimism that their service in the military could ultimately alleviate racism back home. In an essay published in the NAACP journal, *The Crisis*, which was devoted to Black troops in World War I, Du Bois wrote that the lack of more Black welfare workers like Hunton and Johnson was intentional and designed to demoralize them so they would return home. What Du Bois did not know at the time was that Hunton and Johnson, as well as Helen Curtis and two other Black YMCA workers in France, were being investigated during their trip by Military Intelligence and the National War Work Council of the YMCA after an American heard Curtis urging Black soldiers to protest their abysmal circumstances. Investigators allowed the worker to stay overseas but urged the YMCA not to send any similar "radicals" to France.

Addie Hunton was no babe in the woods when it came to the realities of discrimination, nor was she easily deterred. A native of Norfolk, Virginia, she had traveled extensively and had spent much of her life in the South. Johnson, a field agent for the NAACP in New Orleans, also was a seasoned traveler and social worker. But the two were taken aback by what they saw in France, and they recount throughout the book individual cases of harassment of Black soldiers, inadequate housing, and propaganda by military officials about the supposed cowardice of Black soldiers. The women were quick to praise the work of some of the YMCA officials who came to France, but they also noted that many of them exhibited racist behavior. They describe an all-too-typical instance when an all-Black band led by a white bandleader came to a hut to entertain the soldiers: "Several colored soldiers followed the band into the hut. The secretary got up and announced that no colored men would be admitted." Signs prohibiting Black soldiers from entering some areas were common, the women write, as were recommendations by American officers that the French prohibit Black soldiers from entering hotels and restaurants for fear they would interact with White women. To show Black soldiers common courtesy, some officers indicated, "not only would be dangerous, but . . . would be an insult to the American people." Ironically, the French, for the most part, respected and admired the Black soldiers and treated them warmly. "The relationship between the colored soldiers, the colored welfare workers, and the French people was most cordial and friendly and grew in sympathy and understanding, as their association brought about a closer acquaintance," the women write. That warm treatment was in direct contrast to what many of them experienced in their home country: "It was rather an unusual as well as a most welcome experience to be able to go into places of public accommodation without having any hesitations or misgivings; to be at liberty to take a seat in a common carrier, without fear of inviting some humiliating experience; to go into a home and receive a greeting that carried with it a hospitality and kindliness of spirit that could not be questioned."

Even the Germans recognized this irony: In August 1918, they dropped leaflets over the 367th Infantry in the 92nd Division, suggesting they "come over to the German lines." "Do you enjoy the same rights as white people do in America, the land of Freedom and Democracy, or are you treated over there as second-class citizens?" the leaflet said, asking, sarcastically, if the Black soldiers can go into restaurants "where white people dine" or "get a seat in [a] theater where white people sit" or "get a seat or a berth in a railroad car," or "can you even ride, in the South, in the same street car with white people?" The leaflets were brutally candid: "You have been made the tool of the egotistic and rapacious rich in America, and there is nothing in the whole game for you but broken bones, horrible wounds, spoiled health, or death. No satisfaction whatever will you get out of this unjust war."

That the soldiers would be treated with more respect and hospitality in a foreign country than in their own was, of course, noted throughout *Two Colored Women*. "There was being developed in France a racial consciousness and racial strength that could not have been gained in a half century of normal living in America," they write. "Over the canteen in France we learned to know that our young manhood was the natural and struggling guardian of our struggling race. Learning all this and more, we learned to love our men better than ever before."

Hunton and Johnson became maternal figures to the Black soldiers they met, and many of the anecdotes in the book convey the warmth and camaraderie among them. They worked to make huts and living quarters as hospitable as possible and were quick to note that their generosity was returned. "We learned to know our own men as we had not known them before, and this knowledge makes large our faith in them," they write. The men reminisced about the women they left at home and had "an attitude of deep respect, often bordering on worship" toward Hunton and Johnson. The two note the joy many of the soldiers took through the "salvation" of music: "Those who know the native love and ability of our race for music will not marvel at the statement that colored soldiers sang, whistled, and played their way through the late war" and through days of "hunger and thirst . . . deathly fatigue . . . days filled with dense smoke and deafening uproar of battle; days when terrible discriminations and prejudices ate into the soul deeper than the oppressors knew."

The end of the war did not ease the discrimination and ill-treatment of the Black soldiers, Hunton and Johnson imply: Black soldiers were not permitted to participate in a victory parade in France, even though many had been cited or decorated for bravery. The French did not understand the reasons, but "they gradually discovered that the colored man was not the wild, vicious character that he had been represented to be, but that he was kind-hearted, genteel and polite."

The women's trip home from France during the humid August of 1919 may have been emblematic of what they found when they reached American shores: Hunton, Johnson, Curtis, and sixteen Black nurses were housed in poorly ventilated second-class cabins on a deck below White nurses and secretaries making the same trip. When they asked why the assignments were segregated, they were told that some of the workers on the ship would be insulted to have Black people in the same dining room where they ate. But Hunton and Johnson focused on their work and were not sidetracked by the kind of treatment they could have predicted. Their response was to meticulously record their experiences and hope they would one day become public. Yet the two women seem oddly optimistic at the end of *Two Colored Women*, as they write that the war experience of the Black soldiers demonstrated what their lives could be like in their home country: "Thousands had a contact and association [with the French people] which resulted in bringing for the entire number a broader view of life; they caught the vision of a freedom that gave them new hope and new inspiration. . . . Some of them received the rudiments of an education through direct instruction; a thing that would not have come to them in all the years of a lifetime at home."

Hunton and Johnson write eloquently of the importance of culture and beauty—even during an era of war and hatred: "Many hundreds had the opportunity of traveling through the flowering fields of a country long famed for its love of the beautiful, and seeing its wonderful monuments, cathedrals, art galleries, places, chateaux that represent the highest attainment in the world of architecture and art." And, perhaps even more important to these soldiers, "While they traveled they learned that there is a fair-skinned people in the world who believe in the equality of races, and who practice what they believe," the women write. "They also had an opportunity to give the truth a hearing before . . . the civilized world; the truth with regard to their conduct, their mental capacity, their God-given talents, and their ability for the leadership of men." What the men gained, Hunton and Johnson write, "[was] quite enough to offset whatever came to them of hardship and sacrifice, of war and suffering, of mean prejudice and subtle propaganda, of misrepresentation and glaring injustice."

Johnson and Hunton wrote *Two Colored Women* to quickly get on the record the first-person accounts of what they viewed as history in the making. But their motives may have also been a bit slyer than that. The advent of *Plessy v. Ferguson*, the 1896 Supreme Court decision that essentially codified the concept of "separate but equal" treatment in public facilities, in many ways legalized discrimination, declaring that Fourteenth Amendment protections—granting citizenship to all people born in the United States—applied to political and civil rights, but not social rights. In her book about the activism of Black women in the early and mid-twentieth century, Nikki Brown writes, "[The women] critiqued Jim Crow in an international context as race women and cultural ambassadors. Few African Americans utilized an international forum to debate American race relations. . . . [They] became both commentators and critiquers of white supremacy and racial discrimination in the United States. Hoping for widespread embarrassment with an international condemnation of Jim Crow, they essentially asked, how can America treat her loyal blacks this way?"

The terrible treatment of the Black soldiers in France by their own countrymen drove home to many of them the virulence and ubiquity of racial prejudice. In fact, the success of the program in which Hunton and Johnson participated may have been threatening to some Americans because it succeeded, sociologist Susan Kerr Chandler wrote decades later: "The program stood out as a fundamental challenge to the maintenance of a system of white supremacy, and white YMCA leaders were deeply threatened by it and by the growing racial pride that would in time challenge the segregated basis of social services." To W. E. B. Du Bois, who had initially encouraged Black participation in the war, the racism displayed overseas may have exacerbated the divisions between Blacks and Whites: "This war has disillusioned millions of fighting white men—disillusioned them with its frank truth of dirt, disease, cold, wet and discomfort; maiming and hatred. But the disillusion of Negro American troops was more than this, or rather it was this and more—the flat, frank realization that however high the ideas of America or however noble her tasks, her great duty as conceived by an astonishing number of able men, brave and good, as well as of other sorts of men, is to hate 'niggers.'"

Still, Du Bois believed that patriotism was a value that could not be diluted; he maintained that Black soldiers did not regret their service to a nation that treated them so poorly: "There is not a black soldier but who is glad he went—glad to fight for France, the only real white Democracy; glad to have a new, clear vision of the real, inner spirit of American prejudice. The day of camouflage is past."

HUNTON AND JOHNSON RETURNED to a country where racism and inequality were intensifying, but the advent of World War I marked a turning point of sorts in Black history, coinciding with the Great Migration—the mass movement between 1914 and 1920 of nearly half a million Black southerners to large Northern cities, including Chicago, New York, Cleveland, Pittsburgh, and Detroit. In addition to the injustices brought about by the brutal and oppressive Jim Crow legislation in the South, a boll weevil infestation at the time that ruined crops threatened the livelihood of the many laborers, sharecroppers, and farmers who already lived in extreme poverty. Meanwhile, as industry grew in the North and the war led to a reduction of European immigrant labor, northern businesses increasingly turned to Black southern workers. The Great Migration turned into a social movement, with influential Black leaders and the Black newspaper the *Chicago Defender* urging Black people to leave the South for a new life in the North. Testimonials and correspondence by those who made the move triggered others to do the same. Informal networks of family and friends were organized to facilitate the moves.

Even before her experiences in France, Addie Hunton had traveled widely, and her parents instilled in her a sense of patriotism and optimism that she could do anything she put her mind to. Born in Norfolk in 1866—although her exact birth date remains somewhat of a mystery and is on her tombstone as 1875—to Jesse and Adelina Lawton Waites, she was the oldest of their two daughters and a son. Her mother, Adelina Lawton, was born in 1845 in Beaufort, South Carolina, to enslaved parents who named her after the White daughter of her owners. Jesse Waites, who moved to Norfolk with his wife shortly after the Civil War, had been a porter, a retail worker, and, ultimately, the owner of a successful wholesale oyster and shipping company. The Waites family belonged to the African Methodist Episcopal Church and were avid churchgoers. Adelina Waites died when Addie was a teenager, and she was sent to Boston to be raised by a maternal aunt. Addie completed high school at Boston Latin School, and then went to Spencerian College of Commerce in Philadelphia, where she became the first Black person to graduate. By this time, Addie had already traveled overseas to Western Europe and had become fluent in French and German. She taught school briefly in Portsmouth, Virginia, and then became a principal at State Normal and Agricultural College in Alabama.

Interestingly, in all of Addie Hunton's writings about her life and experiences, she focuses little on her personal life. In an extensive biography of her husband, *William Alphaeus Hunton: A Pioneer Prophet of Young Men*, she delves into great detail about the life, contributions, and sacrifices of her husband, including much information about how she dedicated a portion of her life to help him in his struggle to extend YMCA services to Black Americans. It was a position that allowed them both to travel around the world, but one that required great sacrifices. Other than passing references and in a poignant section of the book outlining the last few years of Hunton's life, she writes little about herself or her family. For instance, after four chapters describing William Hunton's early life—including a brief biography of his father, Stanton Hunton, a former slave who bought his freedom—she mentions in passing that she began her decades of helping him in 1891, the year after they first met. William Hunton had been living in Norfolk, and Addie was still working in Alabama when Addie's father introduced them. The year 1891 had been a turning point in both their lives, she said, because William was the first Black person to be named a secretary of the International Committee of the YMCA, and it was the year they met. "From 1891 to 1898 he worked continuously with a steady surveillance, a keen watchfulness and an unabated ardor, also necessary in the first steps taken in any worth-while cause," she writes. "From this period until his death [in 1916] I had the privilege of a most intimate touch with him in his work and I knew how earnestly he labored." She recounts very briefly the story of their initial meeting. Jesse Waites, who had been an early supporter of William's work with the YMCA, told him that his daughter, Addie, had planned to travel from her home in Normal, Alabama, to Wilberforce University in southern Ohio to visit her sister. William told Jesse that he hoped to head to his home country of Canada during the same period that Addie had planned her trip. He offered to accompany Addie from Alabama to Xenia, Ohio, "as girls rarely traveled alone at that time," Addie writes. "My father was glad to accept his offer, and thus began the friendship that resulted in our marriage." Before their marriage in 1893, the two had embarked on a two-year long-distance romantic relationship. Addie had been working in Alabama, and while William spent much of his time in Norfolk, his travels took him around the South and as far north as his hometown of Chatham, Ontario. (Interestingly, Addie quotes his letters to her extensively in her book, but relates little about the content of her letters to him). Those years were tough, Addie writes—and not only because the two were physically separated. At this point in his life, Addie implies the Canadian-born and well-educated William was still somewhat naïve when it came to race relations in the United States and particularly in the South. When he first moved from Ottawa to Norfolk, for instance, he might have experienced a bit of culture shock: "Coming from the environment of Ottawa to that of Norfolk was much like being transferred from the charm and advantages of a great university to a humble rural school," Addie writes. It would be wrong to say that racism did not exist in the Canadian cities where William had lived, but it had not been codified into law as it had in the American South, and race riots there were unheard of. Still, in Norfolk, he had not experienced the virulent racism he would experience in the deep South later in his career. "At Norfolk he had, comparatively speaking, felt but slightly the shock of segregation and its attendant evils," she writes. "Street cars and railroads in the state had not yet come to have their infamous 'Jim Crow' laws." One of his first tastes of the prejudice he would soon experience came as he boarded a small train headed from Norfolk to Portsmouth—accommodations were the same, Addie writes, but separate sides were used by Black and White patrons. At that time, she adds, railroad cars were not required by law to segregate the races.

IT WAS FATE that united Addie Waites and William Alphaeus Hunton. The two were raised in two different countries—and under different financial and social circumstances. Hunton was the sixth of nine children born in 1863 to Mary Ann Conyer and Stanton Hunton, a former slave who managed to purchase himself and move from Virginia to a small town in Southwestern Ontario called Chatham, an enclave where many former slaves had gathered in the mid- and late nineteenth century. Chatham was a rich agricultural district that had been settled in 1830, and it grew rapidly. The little river that flowed through it, named Escunispe by the Indians, was later called the Thames in homage to the British homeland, Addie writes. Interestingly, the residents of Chatham, many of whom came from the United States, apparently chose to honor Great Britain, perhaps because federal law at the time made it dangerous for even freed slaves to travel in the United States, forcing the Underground Railroad to find a direct route across the border to Canada; Chatham was a stop on the route.

As the daughter of a successful businessman, Addie wanted for little growing up. William Hunton loved his life growing up in the small, close-knit community of Chatham and had hardly any desire or opportunity to leave Canada. But these two people who lived on opposite sides of the North American continent also had much in common: a love of learning, a strong spiritual leaning, and the ability and desire to work hard—qualities that had been instilled in them by their fathers. (Both Addie and William had mothers who died when they were young. William and his siblings were raised primarily by their father.) Each also had a love of and talent for writing, a pastime that would sustain them throughout their lives and allow them to leave behind vital records of their experiences and of the historical times in which they lived.

In her extensive research into the Hunton family, Christine Lutz examines three generations of Huntons in relation to their devotion to Pan-Africanism, an ideology of Black political, cultural, and intellectual thought that centers around the belief that a brotherhood of African people around the world share a common history and destiny. This sense of shared identity, defined by Pan-Africanism in the early twentieth century, was the focus of several major conferences held around the world. Lutz maintains that the concept of Pan-Africanism in the Hunton family originated with Stanton Hunton, and was carried on through the work of Addie and William Hunton and then by their children, Eunice and Alphaeus. It was this sense of mission and shared identity that attracted Addie Waites to William Hutton. And, ultimately, they became part of a network of activists around the world who worked to reverse the ill effects of the slave trade and colonialism and to counter discrimination.

The two shared yet another value: religion. Addie was raised in a devout African Methodist Episcopal household, and William's spirituality was one of his most distinctive lifelong traits, and he raised his own children as Episcopalians. During much of his childhood and adolescence, William had been a devout Christian and member of the British Methodist Episcopal church, and he infused his decades-long YMCA work with a strong Christian component. William taught Sunday school as an adolescent, continued to teach Bible school classes for most of his adult life, and carried a Bible with him at all times. After his graduation from Wilberforce Institute of Ontario in 1883, he took a job teaching public school in Dresden, Ontario—even though he hadn't planned to make teaching his permanent vocation. After two years of teaching, he passed a government exam and was named a clerk in the Canadian Department of Indian Affairs in Ottawa. It was in Ottawa where his life took a dramatic and fateful turn: he became an active member of the Ottawa YMCA and took an interest in that organization's attempts to serve Blacks. As Addie described it, his life in Ottawa and his activities with the YMCA were extremely fulfilling to him. He established at the YMCA facility a Bible Study group, choral society, debating group, and a library. Still, she writes, something was missing from his life: "In many respects, it was the most ideally satisfying period of his life. And yet he was not completely satisfied there. He still longed for the service that would answer his soul's chief desire to be altogether used by the Master for the spread of his kingdom here on earth." After three years working as a Canadian civil servant, William's dream would be fulfilled, Addie writes, although at first he was ambivalent about his choices. In 1888, the YMCA's record in equality was decidedly mixed. Its self-described mission—to encourage Christian brotherhood—apparently did not always extend to Blacks, who could be denied membership at local facilities. The YMCA was founded in London in 1844 by George Williams, a twenty-two-year-old department store worker who was troubled by the negative influences and poverty among young men that he saw in industrialized London. He believed that a gathering place for them would fulfill a social need and provide a haven for men of all social classes. The YMCA in the United States opened in Boston eight years later, when retired sea captain Thomas Valentine Sullivan noticed a similar need for a safe haven for sailors and merchants. As Nina Mjagkij notes in her extensive history of the relationship between the YMCA and Black citizens, during much of the first century of its existence, the YMCA followed the lead of the United States in its treatment of Blacks. Anthony Bowen, a freed slave, established the first YMCA for Blacks in Washington, DC, in 1853, but until the late 1880s, little if anything had been done by the YMCA to serve them. By then, the YMCA had begun to encourage Blacks to form their own "separate but equal" associations, a push that Blacks embraced. International Secretary Henry Edwards, a former abolitionist, determined that the best way to do this was to visit Black colleges and universities in the South to introduce students to the YMCA in hopes that they would continue their association with it throughout their lives. It was a strategy that would pay off in the short run and prove effective for decades to come. H. E. Brown, the YMCA official who was in charge of recruiting Blacks to the organization, had become aware of William's participation in the Ottawa YMCA—which at the time had few Black members—and recommended

William be hired as the organization's first Black secretary. The naming of William Hunton would prove to be one of the key appointments in the YMCAs early history; it not only indicated that the organization was serious about serving Blacks, but it ultimately launched the efforts of an innovative and tireless leader whose work would indirectly shape the direction of the YMCA for years to come.

Initially, William's main job was to transfer the primarily Black YMCA in Norfolk, Virginia, from White to Black leadership. Although he may not have realized it at the time, William, who was then twenty-five, was well-suited for that job, which required enthusiasm, determination, and a smooth manner: "He was handsome, cultured, and very definitely earnest," Addie writes of her future husband. And, indeed, the tall, lanky William was always impeccably dressed and elegant with his open face and downward curving mustache. But low salary was very nearly a stumbling block when it came to the job switch: while Brown had finally persuaded the International Committee of the YMCA to devote funds to encourage Black leadership in local YMCAs, much of its funding was still contingent on donations. William was torn about whether to take the job, which paid $800 a year (the equivalent of about $22,500 in 2020)—less than what he was earning in his government job, and certainly not as secure a job in the long term, he believed. And it would, of course, require him to leave his home country to travel extensively in the United States—especially the South. But ultimately, he decided it would be "God's will finding fulfillment in the life of the Young Men's Christian Association and in the life of this pioneer prophet," Addie writes. (W. E. B. Du Bois once referred to William as a "pioneer prophet of young men," the appellation Addie used in the title of her biography of her husband.)

Those with whom he worked were shocked and saddened when he said he was leaving them—and so confident that he would return home soon that they refused his resignation and instead granted him a leave of absence. "I really had no choice," he said. "It was God's leading and I could but follow." William would never return to Canada to live, and would stay at his first posting in Norfolk for three years. After that, he became a true citizen of the world who would eventually spend most of the rest of his life traveling the globe.

ADDIE HUNTON WROTE her biography of her husband in 1938, twenty-two years after his death at age fifty-three. "Wherever I have moved since his 'Great Adventure,' there has been an insistent demand that the facts of his life be recorded for authentic future reference," she wrote. Addie insists, however, that despite their intense love for each other, her intent in writing the biography was not to focus on their marriage or family but on William Hunton's enduring accomplishments as an activist, executive, and role model. "I had [in writing the book] to adjust myself for the very difficult task of evaluating Mr. Hunton impersonally as a man rather than as a devoted husband and comrade for many years," she wrote. "It was necessary to come to the realization of the fact that his value to his times and to posterity was not merely in the undisputed fineness of his character . . . but more exactly in his permanent influence through the great movement with which he was long associated." Both Eunice and her brother, Alphaeus, inherited from both their parents their lifelong dedication to equality and to what they perceived as their mission to help society and encourage similar generations to do the same. It is apparent through their activities, their writings, and their longtime associations that seeking publicity or kudos for their work was not of great importance to them. Instead, as Alphaeus wrote as an adult, their most important task was long-term effectiveness of their work and the importance of others to carry it on: "Men die, but their ideas and movements live on. We who carry on the struggle are the heirs to those who went before us."

It was apparently this philosophy that led the Huntons to play the role of historians or chroniclers of the times. In the years before she began writing her book about William, Addie wrote: "I have re-read hundreds of letters that had their beginning three years before our marriage that continued twenty years after. . . . They are very precious documents. . . . They are very human, and in them I have found revealed, with an intimacy unequaled elsewhere in his writings—the heart throbs, the patience, the dauntless courage of a crusader."

Both Addie and William were eloquent and graceful writers; William, also, was an eloquent and persuasive speaker—a talent that contributed to his success as a YMCA executive and crusader. Addie quotes at length his speeches, and notes throughout *A Pioneer Prophet* the care and time he took when writing each one.

To Addie, William (or "Mr. Hunton," as she refers to him throughout the biography) was almost Christ-like, and indeed those with whom he worked used similar analogies when they spoke about him. (In a memorial speech, his friend and coworker Jesse Moorland said that when he left home to take the job with the YMCA, "He took upon himself, like his Master, the form of a servant in Jim Crow Country. . . . His whole soul revolted at times . . . yet he summoned his courage, he took counsel with God, and persisted on at the end to die a martyr to these conditions.") Before the two were married, Addie wrote, he seemed so different from other men his age "in his general manners and his earnestness of purpose that [her] girlfriends used to say that [she] might see him depart much in the way that Elijah had disappeared from the earth." During his first few years as a YMCA secretary, he barely discussed the loneliness, discomforts, and indignities he experienced while traveling, in part, she speculates, because he found solace in his faith. "In all the intimate years of our life, he made no comment on the hardships and loneliness of that period [the late 1880s and early 1890s]. . . . When questioned about it, he would laughingly reply, 'It was all in the day's work.'" William Hunton endured buggy rides in torrential downpours; rides in freight cars; rail delays that meant he could not eat for a day; and, once in rural Mississippi, travel in an ox cart. But the ever-optimistic William always sought the bright side: "I had traveled a hundred and twenty miles in three rains, two hacks and a bus, with cheese and ginger wafers as my only rations," he wrote Addie from Jefferson City, Missouri. "I did finally reach here and slept well in a comfortable bed." He rarely mentioned the indignities he suffered traveling in the deep South, but occasionally would allude to them. In one letter to Addie, he wrote, "You and I will travel together as little possible in the far South. I can endure many things myself for the work's sake. . . . But I am sure it would go infinitely harder if we together were subjected to indignities. But never mind, we'll not borrow trouble." Addie and her husband did travel together periodically early in their marriage, including one trip between Birmingham and Decatur, when William persuaded a train conductor to allow them to remain in a Pullman car even though they were Black. At the time, they were traveling with their baby, who soon died. "When we were taking our dying baby northward to Asheville, [William's] quiet determination again won. . . . Justice, humane conditions and enlightened thought were pathetically, tragically missing. But he was never bitter."

The three years he spent in Norfolk establishing YMCA facilities for Blacks were an unqualified success; as it turned out, William Hunton and the YMCA were a good fit. He also worked at facilities in Washington, Richmond, and Baltimore, helping to establish literary and debating societies, choral clubs, athletic activities, and educational classes, all against the backdrop of what he referred to as "practical Christianity." After his first year on the job, Brown proclaimed his appointment such a success that he recommended that the organization seek out more Black men in the South to train as leaders in the YMCA—a task that he undertook himself. Ironically, William did such a good job that he eventually replaced Brown, his mentor. In 1891, Brown had become ill and could no longer travel extensively. William was named to succeed him as secretary of the staff of the International Committee. He was now the first Black secretary to engage in supervisory work in the YMCA organization. Addie saw the promotion as a turning point in her husband's life, but it would prove a blessing and a curse for the couple. It was a fulfilling position that ultimately allowed him, in the short run, to help improve the lives of thousands of Black youths and, in the long run, many more, but it would take a toll first on his family life and, ultimately, on his physical well-being.

ADDIE HUNTON ACKNOWLEDGES that William's tenure in Norfolk was probably meant to test his fitness as YMCA director, and to determine if he could overcome the physical and emotional hardships of a job that required him to work in the South in the Jim Crow era, and to establish facilities for Blacks in an environment of overt racism. When Addie and William married in 1893, he was in the midst of a job that had required him to travel throughout the southern and northeastern portion of the country to oversee the establishment of more facilities for Blacks. At times, Addie traveled with her husband, she writes, helping him with secretarial work, editing some of his writings, and "looking after details and advising and inspiring him." It was through this work that she said she learned about his character and source of strength: "He had the habit of serenity that could not be easily disturbed. . . . He also had a faith to the end of his life that reality, however crude or even cruel, could by patient effort be somehow lifted to the realm of idealism. . . . He had the faculty of making other men feel this faith of his. . . . He spurned narrowness and pettiness." But she also acknowledges that he enjoyed solitude even when he was at home with his family. William's travel schedule was a brutal one; letters he wrote to Addie and Moorland indicate that during a normal month, he would travel to four or five cities, spending four to five days in each one. Also typical is his description in a letter to Moorland that "It's nearly 10 p.m. and I have been at it since six this a.m. Hence this scrawling."

Shortly after their marriage, William was given one of the YMCA's greatest honors: he was named to the American delegation to the Gold Jubilee of the YMCA in London. It was after this conference that William's career and reputation soared, and he was seen as one of the top leaders of the YMCA, responsible for helping to launch "colored" facilities across the United States. But it was shortly after this time that the relationship between the Huntons was conducted largely through correspondence, because he was rarely home. But his almost-daily letters to his Addie, and later to his family, were extensive and detailed. She describes one in particular when he returned triumphantly in 1898 for a visit to his beloved Ottawa: "There was unbounded joy" on the part of his friends, who gave him "a triumphal entry because he had conquered the unknown and returned as their brave warrior."

William seems uncharacteristically jubilant and almost giddy. In many other letters to Addie, his enthusiasm is directed largely toward his work; this letter focuses on his friends and the region as a source of happiness. And it also reveals that despite his success in the United States—and his stoicism about racism there—he missed the color blindness of his Canadian compatriots. As he wrote, "I am here. It is like a dream. I know of no place that I would rather live." After what he considered a royal welcome by friends and officials of the local YMCA, he and a friend attended a session of the Canadian House of Commons: "I presume that a talk about the colored people as a class is not heard in Parliament once in two or three years. Sweetheart, I wish you were here to see how different these people are from many white people we know." William, of course, would not be the only one in the family to feel more welcome as a Black person outside the United States than in it. During her trip to France with the Expeditionary Forces, Addie made it clear that she and the Black soldiers did not experience the cruel prejudice there that they felt in their own country. William would maintain his love for his native Canada throughout his life even though he never carried out a plan to bring his family there for a visit, Addie said: "A visit to Ottawa together was one of the unfulfilled dreams of our united life."

DURING THE LAST DECADE or so of his life, William wrote hundreds of letters to Addie. Still, one of his closest friends and colleagues was Jesse Moorland, a former minister who became a secretary, fundraiser, and administrator in the Colored Men's Department of the YMCA. Moorland had joined the YMCA administration in 1892 and became a secretary in the Colored Men's Department in 1896, when he became William's partner—and ultimately his closest confidante, even though the men were based in different cities, with William in Atlanta—and later Brooklyn—and Moorland in Washington, DC. It is fair to say that his work with Moorland had a profound effect on William's life and career, and the men developed a deep professional and personal bond. William expressed many of his inner thoughts to Moorland by letter, including the great weariness he felt during some of his travels, brought on by overwork and the continual degradation of segregation and racism. Interestingly, about the only times the two men were together was at conferences and YMCA-related conventions. William's letters indicate that Moorland came to the Hunton home in times of need—for instance, when the Huntons moved from Richmond to Atlanta and during William's severe and ultimately fatal illness. (Addie and Moorland's lives would intersect again after William's death when Addie traveled to France to help Black soldiers during the war. Moorland, at the time, worked through the YMCA with the Department of Colored Troops to coordinate the program in which Addie and Kathryn Johnson participated.) Moorland was a tireless worker and organizer who contributed greatly to William's success with the YMCA; among many other accomplishments, they recruited Black students from the South to staff YMCA missions in Africa. One of the most notable and enduring achievements of the two men was securing a contribution in 1910 by Chicago businessman and philanthropist Julius Rosenwald, the founder of Sears, Roebuck and Co., who pledged $25,000 toward the cost of a YMCA building in any city that could raise $75,000 on its own. ($25,000 in 1910 would be worth about $706,000 in 2020). The two used the pledge as a springboard to begin a campaign that would ultimately raise thousands of dollars and launch thirteen YMCA facilities. (William, over the years, had established an international presence with the YMCA. He had been selected to give an address at its 1907 World Student Christian Federation conference in Tokyo, and he later traveled from there across Asia.)

The hundreds of letters William wrote to his friend Moorland during the two decades they worked together show a powerful bond between the men. William's salutation of "My dear Brother Moorland"—a standard greeting—could be taken literally. Although those letters discuss mostly travel schedules and other YMCA business, many of them touch on William's home life, his thoughts while on the road, and other intimate issues. Based on Addie's written recollections of her husband and these letters, William was not an emotional person, and his passion manifested itself primarily when he spoke of God and his faith. To Moorland, however, he often tiptoed around key happenings in his life; his letters, while personal, were somewhat formal. For instance, he refers to Addie in them as "Mrs. H," and in his constant invitations for Moorland to visit his family in Atlanta, he refers to Moorland's wife as "Mrs. Moorland." He mentions his children occasionally, often summing up their activities in a sentence. Poignantly, in one letter, he talks about his second-born baby, William, who later died in infancy: "You would laugh to see our baby kicking and rolling all over the floor and begging me to take him. Just like his father, you know." He later writes about the death of that baby in two sentences: After telling him about the death of his brother in October 1896, "a heavier blow came to us in May when it pleased the Lord to take away our sweet baby also. O Moorland, I cannot tell you about it. The other world is far more real to me now than formerly." He ends this note mentioning the solace he takes from Moorland's friendship: "How I would enjoy having a long talk with you. I thank the Lord for the bonds of real friendship which unites us."

Three years later, William also shares with Moorland some good news: his great joy in the birth of Eunice, even though his letters indicate that he had not mentioned Addie was pregnant until a month before the birth: "I must tell you a secret. We are daily expecting a 'newcomer.' But Mrs. Hunton's weakness gives us great anxiety." In a letter to Moorland four days after the birth of Eunice on July 16, 1899, he wrote, "You will be pleased to learn that I have an heiress, born early Sunday morning. Mother and daughter are doing nicely. Of course we are very proud." As Eunice grew, he occasionally mentioned her temperament and health: when she was one, for instance, she had a temperature of 103, but soon recuperated. "Glad at the prospect of seeing you," William told Moorland, apparently in reference to an upcoming conference. "But very sorry to have to leave my little family."

It is unknown whether Moorland shared William's religious devotion. Although Moorland makes occasional references to his spirituality, William's references to God and his own "mission" are mentioned much more frequently. William's devout Christianity played only a minor role in his YMCA duties. When he and Moorland recruited Black secretaries, they required applicants to belong to the Protestant church, but otherwise stressed inter-denominationalism in all other aspects of the organization. They were careful not to step on the toes of local clergy and assured them that the YMCA was not "competing" with local churches. They knew community support and donations depended on the idea that they favored no specific denomination.

Of course, it could be said that the success of Hunton and Moorland in finding Black leaders and in encouraging the growth of Black YMCA facilities cut both ways. Some critics, including Du Bois, felt that YMCA policy indirectly encouraged segregation, both within the YMCA's own organization and in the country. Even Rosenwald's donation drew the ire of Du Bois, who felt that the money would be better spent to combat YMCA policy that permitted the exclusion of Blacks in some facilities. William had made peace with the idea that instead of direct confrontation, the way to help overturn the nation's racist environment was through self-help. That meant the organization would continue to focus on employing top Black leaders to carry out the mission of the YMCA and to reach disenfranchised and poor Blacks. He had even taken steps throughout his tenure as secretary to strengthen ties among Black YMCA facilities through the regional conferences and the launching of a monthly newspaper, the *Messenger*. Earlier in his career, he had argued that by being complicit with the prevailing unchristian terrain, the YMCA was an institution that indirectly sanctioned it—but he had come to change his mind about a strategy that he felt would ultimately benefit Black citizens.

Despite his professional success and the subsequent recognition by YMCA officials of his efforts, all was not well within the Hunton family. Christine Lutz notes that while they made sure to save money for the education of their two children, a lack of money and overspending had long been an issue for the family, and they sometimes received financial help from Moorland in the form of loans, a phenomenon that angered Addie, as she had maintained a cool relationship with Moorland. Further, the seemingly robust William often hid the fact that he periodically suffered from various ailments, including colitis, malaria, and respiratory problems. And throughout their marriage, they suffered through the deaths of many relatives, including three of William's siblings—Robert, Augustus, and Stanton—and Addie's beloved father, Jesse Waites. More devastating, however, were the deaths of two of their children who died as babies before Eunice and Alphaeus were born. Their first child, Bernice, died in 1895, and baby William died a year later. In the 1890s, "death stalked us for several years," Addie wrote. William dealt with his grief through poetry: he wrote one poem after the death of Jesse Waites and another after the death of his infant son. He sent the latter to Addie while he was traveling:

Lo, eyes were made for the light
And souls were made for joy.
But eyes must be blinded by the night,
And souls must be burdened by grief.
That alike they may find relief,
Relief from the strain of the light
and strength from the strain of joy.

Addie mentions the existence of these two infants only twice in her biography: when she quotes her husband's poem, and, earlier, when she quotes a letter in which he mentions their son, the infant William, during his joyful visit to Ottawa.

In an uncharacteristically emotional passage, Addie Hunton writes of another terrible twist of fate during the late 1890s—it happened a few months before the birth of Eunice. In 1898, the family had decided to move to Atlanta where they settled in early 1899. By most accounts, they were happy there, living in a big house on 418 Houston Street, with some domestic help. William's YMCA work with college students continued to accelerate, and he believed it would be practical for him to supervise student work in a large city. When she was old enough to go to school, Eunice attended one of only three primarily Black schools in the city; and the family, like others affiliated with the school, took pride in the fact that their children were taught by others of their race. Shortly after they moved to Atlanta, however, in the spring of 1899, a Black man named Sam Hose was lynched in a town nearby, his body burned, and body parts distributed for "souvenirs." William and Addie were so horrified, she writes, that they drew away from their friends and even questioned the introduction of a new baby into the world: "The wisdom of having our expected child born to us in such an environment seemed quite doubtful, but after prayer and deep thought, we decided to remain." Fortunately, she writes, the birth of Eunice came "and bound our love more closely, and later, our second, Alphaeus took the place of the first, whom we lost."

William and Addie's children would ultimately provide them with the greatest fulfillment of their lives. Still, the horrific lynching near Atlanta shortly after they moved there would not be the only time they or their children would be exposed so closely to racial hatred and violence. Soon, they would move north in search of a more peaceful life. But William never returned to his childhood home of Canada, and Addie never got a chance to visit Chatham or Ottawa, two cities her husband loved.

2

Free But Not Equal

Name: Stanton Hunton
Age: About 30 years old
Stature: 5 feet 7 inches
Colour: Bright Mulattoe [*sic*] Man
Description: With long hair and dark eyes[,] an aquiline nose, tolerably large, small hands and a little knock kneed—no other marks visible.
How Freed: Emancipated by Wm. H. Gaines
(Copy delivered 28th February 1937)
—Stanton Hunton's emancipation papers

IN LESS THAN FIFTY WORDS, Virginia slave Stanton Hunton was granted his freedom and thus given the opportunity to travel north to start a new life in what was—literally—a promised land. Hunton didn't know it at the time, but he would represent the first of three generations of Huntons to make long journeys in attempts to improve their lives and those of their children. Stanton Hunton—who was then probably twenty-seven and not thirty as listed on his emancipation papers—made his way alone to Chatham, Ontario, to begin a new life in a community of like-minded people who were not welcome in their own country. The further north he traveled as a free man, the more ambivalent he may have grown about his identity—was he, at heart, still an American, or would he become a Canadian, or possibly even loyal to Great Britain? At least he now had a choice.

ADDIE WAITES HUNTON begins her biography of her husband, William, with a brief recounting of the early life of her father-in-law, Stanton

Hunton. And it's a natural starting point—he not only raised Addie's husband and his eight siblings, but Stanton's life story reads like fiction. Born in Virginia in 1815, he and his brother, Benjamin, were the slaves "of a most humane maiden lady of the Virginia aristocracy who taught him to read and provided him with an education," Addie writes. Addie Hunton notes in passing that the ties of slave to mistress may also have been "those of blood." It is possible that his owner was Elizabeth Hunton, who may have been his aunt, and that the name "William Gaines" on the emancipation documents belonged to one of her employees. (Census records also note that he had lived on the "Eppa Hunton Plantation" in Fauquier County.) "Slavery, more often dehumanizing to both master and mastered than otherwise . . . had overspread the nation like a black cloud that grew more and more ominous with time," Addie writes. Despite the so-called "humanity" of his owner, Stanton tried to escape three times before his mistress relented and allowed him to buy his freedom, apparently with money she had paid him in wages. In the second paragraph of her book, Addie notes that all of Stanton's attempted escapes had been risky thanks to federal laws that required all states to return escaped slaves to their owners.

Stanton Hunton first traveled to Washington, DC, and eventually made his way to the Ontario community of Chatham, a small community about fifty miles north of Lake Erie. It was in Chatham where Stanton Hunton became an active abolitionist, raised a family almost single-handedly after the early death of his wife, and, ultimately, became a wealthy man. It was in Canada where several of his nine children remained for the rest of their lives. Addie Hunton believes it was Stanton Hunton's adopted country of Canada that nurtured her husband's sense of mission, his pioneering spirit, and his single-minded determination.

THE FUGITIVE SLAVE ACT of 1850 triggered an influx of escaped and former slaves to Canada. Because the legislation required that all escaped and captured slaves be returned to their masters—even those caught in free states—no portion of the United States was deemed safe for escaped slaves. Once slaves passed over the border between the United States and Canada, the law, of course, did not apply.

In some ways, the small towns of Kent County in the southwestern Canadian province of Ontario would seem a perfect refuge for the oppressed in the United States. Chatham, in particular, was one of several Canadian river towns that began to thrive in the early nineteenth century as railways began replacing ships as modes of transportation, thus connecting disparate regions of Canada and promoting economic growth in the country.

Further, it was the only urban center between London and Windsor. In short, it was a rich agricultural area that benefitted from railway lines that passed through it and was located on a river. And, perhaps most important, it was sufficiently inland to provide security for escaped slaves. By the mid-nineteenth century, Chatham and nearby Buxton were viewed as ideal settlement locations for Blacks hoping to escape the oppression of the United States. As time went on, close-knit communities began to develop in those areas. And, as the cities grew, so did the need for skilled and unskilled labor. The Black newspaper in Chatham, the *Provincial Freeman*, encouraged Blacks to immigrate to Chatham, where they could find employment and would have equal protection under the law. (Chatham was seen as a haven for artisans, businesspersons, and, to a lesser extent, unskilled laborers. Buxton was a rural region where the main occupation was farming.) From 1851 to 1861, the Black population of Chatham increased from 353 people to 1,259, about one-sixth of the total population. About half were skilled or semi-skilled workers—many were shoemakers, carpenters, and blacksmiths—and 41 percent were unskilled workers.

After his brief stay in Washington, DC, Stanton Hunton migrated northward, entering the seemingly hospitable environment of Chatham in 1843. Stanton, a brick mason and carpenter, stayed in Chatham for one year so he could establish himself; but he was lonely. He returned to Natchez, Mississippi, to buy the freedom of his brother, Benjamin, and the two returned to Chatham. Soon, Benjamin "succumbed to the severity of the life and climate," Addie writes. The ambitious Stanton was thriving personally and professionally in Chatham, but he was still lonely. As Addie tells it, he had apparently traveled through Cincinnati, "where he had seen many lovely colored girls," and decided to return to the city. He met and soon proposed to local resident Mary Ann Conyer. The two moved to the east side of Chatham, home to many of the city's Black residents, built a house on the corner of King and Wellington Streets, and had nine children before Mary Ann died in 1869. Stanton never remarried and, for the most part, raised his younger children—including William—by himself.

Still, it would appear that Stanton and Mary Hunton led a contented life together in Chatham. He eventually joined a small circle of Canadian abolitionists in the region—Chatham had become a stop on the route of the Underground Railroad—and came to own a two-story brick building on one of the city's main avenues, King Street. The structure housed three stores, a large gathering hall, and three offices. He thrived as a carpenter, brick mason, and businessman, but the focus of Stanton and Mary's lives were their children, religion, and learning.

The Huntons were devout members of the British Methodist Episcopal Church, which was known for its evangelical zeal. (By 1851, 55 percent of Chatham's Black residents belonged to a denomination of the Methodist church; 36 percent were Baptists, 3 percent were Catholics, and the rest were Presbyterians or had no religious affiliations.) Addie notes that religion and tradition were extremely important to Stanton: "He had a fixed faith in religious tradition and custom, and would, if need be, vigorously defend the faith against any mixture of newer theories of 'isms.'" Above all, he instilled in his children the value of industriousness and self-reliance; each child had his or her own chores, and Stanton assigned them more if the tasks were completed early. Idleness was prohibited. Going hand in hand with the focus on religion and industriousness was, naturally, education. Stanton knew that was key to his children's success, and he stressed its value throughout their childhood. In a brief oral history voiced by an actor that was based on his writings, Chatham's Black Mecca Museum displays a life-size Stanton Hunton declaring that his children are his greatest pride and joy: "Augustus followed me into the carpentry business. George became a schoolteacher; William Alphaeus started out as a teacher and rose to become the Secretary of the International Committee of the YMCA. The baby, Robert, became the managing editor of *Protest*, a newspaper for the coloured race in St. Paul, Minnesota."

Still, some of the details of a pivotal event in Stanton Hunton's life remain murky—his association with abolitionist and martyr John Brown. Chatham and its surrounding communities played a key role in the history of American slavery, and part of this role is graphically illustrated today in an exhibit in the Black Mecca Museum, operated by Chatham's Black Historical Society. The harrowing activities of escaped and freed slaves from the United States are told through relics such as the harrowing front pages of Black newspapers, first-person accounts by former slaves in the form of transcripts, "reenacted" recorded conversations, quilts and other handiwork of Chatham residents, and displays of leg irons and shackles.

Brown became a crucial character in the city's history when he decided in 1858 to visit with some of the city's antislavery activists and possibly garner support for a planned attack on Harper's Ferry. Stanton Hunton was among the handful of Chatham residents who met with Brown—one time in Hunton's home—although the precise details of the meetings are still somewhat vague. Brown's visit represented a turning point in Hunton's life, though, and his family kept as a souvenir a table where Brown sat when he visited the Hunton home. According to Addie, Brown had visited several cities in Ontario where ex-slaves lived but had decided to make Chatham the base of his preparations because of the rapid growth of the city, its central location, and its "intelligent citizenry." He and some of Chatham's residents formed a provisionary organization to consult with Brown, and meetings were held in April and May of that year, some in churches and some in the office of the *Provincial Freeman*.

The Huntons also treasured a brief note from Brown to Stanton, inviting him to a meeting at the local firehouse: "My Dear Friend: I have called a quiet conference in this place, May 8, and your attendance is earnestly requested. Your Friend, John Brown." Little else is known about the meeting, other than what was said in some notes taken by a participant who indicated that there was little ceremony at the opening proceedings: "[The participants] were of two colors but one mind [and] all were equal in degree and station here," he wrote, adding that the mission of the group was unadorned yet of utmost importance: "No civic address to this Canadian town; no beat of drums; no firing of guns was heard. . . . Yet the object of this little parliament was the freedom of four million slaves." In her history of the Hunton family, Christine Lutz writes that twelve White and thirty-three Black men attended the meeting, which was the culmination of a series of discussions held at locations along Chatham's King Street East. Little else is known about Brown's visit to Chatham or residents' possible participation in the October 17, 1859, Harper's Ferry raid. But the visits are etched in the memories of those who lived through them. When Addie met her father-in-law for the only time when she was a bride—apparently in 1893—"he was still keen in his memory of the scenes and events in Chatham at that important period that thrilled to the dynamic power of John Brown." And, near the end of his life when he was ill, William Hunton made sure to make a pilgrimage to Brown's grave in upstate New York.

Unlike many other former slaves who moved to Canada before the Civil War, Stanton Hunton's loyalty to his adopted home and its ruling country of Great Britain was absolute. He remained in Chatham for the rest of his life, even after he could have returned safely to the United States as a free man. After the Civil War, Blacks left Chatham in large numbers, in part because of increased economic opportunities in the industrialized northern United States. Census figures indicate that Chatham had only 315 Black residents in 1871 compared to 1,259 in 1861. Further, about 45 percent of Chatham's Black males held skilled occupations between 1861 and 1871; that number declined to 38 percent by 1882. Part of this decline may have been due to an influx of White residents in the years following the Civil War. A similar pattern in nearby Buxton, whose racial composition had also changed by the late 1860s, with many Blacks leaving for economic opportunities in the northern United States. Whites were buying land in higher numbers, and fewer Blacks were coming in to replace the ones leaving.

Still, the end of the Civil War was not the only reason many Black residents returned to the United States. Despite the success of Stanton Hunton and other former slaves who moved to Canada, Chatham was hardly an egalitarian paradise devoid of racism. Its public schools were segregated, in part because of district gerrymandering that ensured the separation of races in the schools, and they remained so despite decades of attempts by Blacks to integrate them. And general anti-Negro bias did exist among some Whites, as it did in the northern United States. Schoolchildren such as William Hunton and his siblings were used to hearing epithets applied to the areas of town that housed much of Chatham's Black population: "Coonsville," "Africa," and "Nigertown" [sic] were the most common. Still, William and his siblings did not experience or witness racial violence, and they were granted the same rights under the law as other Canadians.

Stanton Hunton would come to consider Canada his home, and he instilled his patriotic feelings in his children, who, like William, loved their parents' adopted country. As Christine Lutz notes, "identity" for people like Stanton Hunton could be a fluid concept—abolitionism was an international movement, and some of Chatham's residents' loyalty to Canada stemmed from their resentment of a country that allowed legal enslavement. Because Canada was a territory of Great Britain, Hunton and others also considered themselves loyal to the mother country. Stanton and Mary Hunton named their first daughter Victoria after the British Queen. When the adult William Hunton visited London on YMCA business in 1894, he was particularly thrilled to be there "having acquired a cherished knowledge of British traditions and customs" and "stirred by the knowledge that he would for the first time visit the seat of the British empire." But Stanton's loyalty to Canada also stemmed from his personal experiences. He valued the camaraderie of like-minded former slaves whose goals mirrored his: they sought to achieve economic independence by working hard; they wanted to raise children who were safe and well-educated; and, in the case of some, they wanted to participate in antislavery activity without fear of recrimination.

As Addie Hunton implies throughout her biography of William, many of his values were shaped by his father and his allegiance to Chatham, William's birthplace. "It was into this environment, so rich in its pioneer influences, strong humanitarian principles, and Christian faith that, on October 31, 1863, Stanton Hunton's sixth son, William Alphaeus Hunton, was born," she writes. "He was to inherit not only the pioneer and far-visioned qualities involved in this background, but also the quiet reticent, but stalwart character of his father."

THE BIRTH of Eunice Roberta Hunton brought Addie and William great happiness, feelings that were particularly deep because she would become their first child to survive infancy; four years later, William Alphaeus came along—he was the namesake of their second child who died as a baby. (A daughter, Bernice, also died as an infant.) But William's job duties and travel schedule only accelerated after Eunice's birth. Addie says little in William's biography about her personal life after the couple's move to Atlanta in 1899. Still, she does note that his exhausting job, the associated travel, and the dispiriting social environment—"traveling over the South under conditions unfavorable to both body and spirit"—were taking a toll on him. "One realizes that he must have experienced at times great yearning for the companionship at home and the nursery hours of his children, where he could find relief from problems and cares." Although William had suffered from some minor ailments in adulthood, five years after the move to Atlanta, he exhibited the first signs of serious illnesses that would dog him for much of the last nine or ten years of his life. In 1899, he wrote to Moorland to tell him that he had been bedridden due to malaria, and Addie writes that he was stricken after a trip to the Gulf states. "His heart weakened under the strain and he was desperately ill for some time," she wrote, adding that a summer vacation with relatives in Michigan and Ontario helped him gain back his health.

Although she was devoted to her young children, Addie was not one who could devote all her time to domestic activities and child care. She soon began work as a secretary and later bursar at Clark College. Even more important to her, however, was the start of an activity that would occupy her for much of the rest of her life—the women's reform movement. The women's club movement was a significant reform movement in the United States and one that remains active today. In July 1896, at a convention in Washington, DC, the National Association of Colored Women (NACW) was formed as a result of a consolidation of several other similar groups with Mary Church Terrell as its president. Terrell was a prominent reformer whose father, a former slave, became wealthy in the real estate business in Memphis during Reconstruction. Terrell was a teacher, both in college and in public schools, and the first Black woman to be offered the position of registrar at a White college, an offer she declined to get married. Addie had been an enthusiastic supporter of the NACW since its inception. The NACW, whose motto, "lifting as we climb," defined itself as an organization to "promote equality and justice for all women and girls and ensure they are represented and empowered in their communities." Much has been written about the purpose and mission of the NACW and similar organizations, and they were established for a variety of purposes, including to gain the vote for Black women, to fight against discrimination and racial violence, and to provide aid and educational resources for poor Blacks and poor families. Between 1900 and 1920, more than 50,000 women became involved with women's clubs and similar organizations that fought for social justice. The women's club movement underscored the social status of Black women as they evolved from slavery to domestic workers and keepers of the hearth and home, to underground crusaders. Addie knew firsthand about the importance of Black people sharing information and stories, and the power of organizations to create unity. Similarly, she and others knew of the vital importance of education as a tool for upward mobility. Black women during this era of Reconstruction were in a "no woman's land"—they lacked the legal status of their White counterparts and the social status of Black men.

Obviously, race dominated discussions of these women's clubs, but it is important to note that issues of class also played a role in their formation. The NACW was an organization of middle-class women and, as Lutz writes, that concept might seem antithetical to its purpose: "Like many other reformers in turn-of-the-century America, [the NACW leadership] accommodated the class, race and gender hierarchies of a now-powerful capitalism even as they protested its inequities." The NACW shared many of the values and goals of White women's clubs of the era. Paula Giddings writes in her chronicle of Black women and power in the United States that the history of slavery naturally had a dramatic and immediate effect on the outlook of Black women of the era, many of whom were daughters of former slaves. In that way, racism and feminism were intertwined. Because they had a history of fighting for freedom and even for their lives, Black women learned to fight battles the same way men did, earning them a status that transcended feminism: "[Black women] redefined the meaning of what was called 'true womanhood,'" Giddings writes. Because of this history of savagery under slavery, "her participation in the workforce, her political activities, and her sense of independence made her more of a woman, not less of one."

By the time her children were toddlers, Addie Hunton had begun navigating this byzantine power structure in a society where Black women had faced a form of double discrimination—and, in her case, as an educated woman with a successful husband, class entered the picture. By this point in her life, she began taking advantage of her writing ability to submit essays to some widely read journals designed to provide a forum for Blacks. Included in this group a bit later were *The Crisis*, the widely read magazine of the National Association for the Advancement of Colored People (NAACP) that was founded in 1910 by W. E. B Du Bois, and, at this point in Addie's life, a new monthly called *Voice of the Negro*. Founded in 1904 in Atlanta, *Voice of the Negro* was considered the leading Black periodical in the country, and its eclectic content consisted of serious political and cultural essays as well as poems and some arts reviews. Most important, the magazine offered a glimpse into the thoughts, concerns, and opinions of Black people of the era—only four decades after the end of slavery. At ten cents an issue, each publication opened with several pages of a news review called "Our Monthly Review." During its first year, the magazine focused heavily on current events, international and education issues, and the activities and goals of organized groups like the NACW. During its first year, for example, it devoted its September issue to politics and the upcoming presidential race; it gave a resounding thumbs up to incumbent Theodore Roosevelt and overwhelming support to Republicans. That party, according to one article, "proposes an honest investigation into conditions in the Southern States," where there is likely suppression of the Black vote. Democrats, on the other hand, advocate taxation without representation, limited education, and disenfranchisement of people of color, the writer says.

Addie contributed several essays and opinion columns to *Voice of the Negro*, and she was in good company. Prominent authors, educators, and intellectuals of the era—including Du Bois and Mary Church Terrell—were also contributors. Through her bylines, Addie gradually became a known and respected figure in social justice circles. (*Voice of the Negro*, which later was renamed *The Voice*, stayed in Atlanta for only two years, moving to Chicago in 1906 after the Atlanta riots. It folded a year later.)

Addie's writing often had a distinctive tone, and she had developed a style that was clear and concise, but also a bit flowery at times and often full of vivid imagery and allusions. For instance, in the July 1904 column in *Voice of the Negro* titled "Negro Womanhood Defended," she discusses what she believes are unwarranted negative sexual stereotyping of Black women and attacks on their morals, and she ventures into the area of class differences among Blacks. "Whence come these base aspersions to blight and dwarf the spirit of the Negro woman? Who . . . can be so forgetful to her service and servitude as to seek to crush her already wounded and bleeding soul." In this essay, she begins by making references to class differences among Black women, noting that criticisms and "base aspersions" against Black women in society are often made by those who "know little or nothing of that best elements of our women who are quietly and unobtrusively working out the salvation of the race. . . . The Negro women with whom they [critics] come in contact exhibit none of those higher qualities that are based upon virtue." But Addie is brutally direct when bringing up the horrors and indignities faced by women who were once slaves, noting that their history of slavery would affect their lives and the lives of their relatives for years to come: "For two centuries, the Negro woman was forced by cruelty too diverse and appalling to mention. . . . She was voiceless and there was no arm lifted in her defense. . . . There is an unwritten and an almost unmentionable history of the burdens of those soul-trying times when . . . the Negro woman was the subject of compulsory immorality." Addie ends her essay on an oft-repeated note in her life and in her writings—the idea that it is the role of Black women to maintain homes, provide stability for families, and work to improve the lives of their children: "With her deeper interest in her people, her larger knowledge of their needs, with the culture and character that education give, she is constantly at work for the uplift of her race." This article in *Voice of the Negro* came as part of a special issue of the magazine about women and by women. The female contributors were identified by short descriptive phrases before their names. Addie was called "the calm and equitably poised Mrs. Addie Hunton," who at the time was president of the Atlanta Women's Club.

Addie's work with the NACW and other reform organizations addresses the intersection of gender and race equality. Upon the fifteenth anniversary of the NACW in 1911, she spells out very specifically in *The Crisis* the activities and successes of the group up to that point, writing that its forty-five thousand members had come from a variety of backgrounds and ages to unite for common goals: "This unifying process in the spirit and aim of the intelligent colored women has been one of her strongest blessings in the past decade." Among its many accomplishments is organizing divisions that focus on disparate subject areas such as literature, temperance, domestic science, music, art, and others; organizing state federations of the group and sponsoring local conventions; fighting for the end of segregation in public facilities; and lobbying for anti-lynching laws. Five years earlier, she had written a similar article for *Voice of the Negro* summarizing the accomplishments of the Atlanta chapter of the NACW—a chapter of which she was president. By this time, Addie headed a state federation of affiliated women's clubs, including the NACW, and she did some traveling within the South for the group. This article is an upbeat and optimistic summary of the accomplishments of the NACW nationwide. As was characteristic of Addie, the article opens poetically: "Somewhere it has been written by a poet-singer of the race: 'The harvest is great/let the reaper be many/May you sow and beautifully reap.'" Addie continues, "The colored women of the country have caught the spirit of this stanza and have gone forth to sow. Right earnestly have they toiled, and there is promise of a bountiful fruitage for the reaping by and by."

During her first six years in Brooklyn, Addie traveled across much of the country as a NACW organizer, giving dozens of speeches, soliciting members, and urging women to form regional NACW-affiliated organizations. In some ways, Addie's efforts with the women's club movement mirrored her husband's—both became part of existing organizations that fought racial inequality, and both hoped to enrich the lives of middle-class and poor Blacks while, ironically, indirectly working within a society that tacitly promoted some of the institutions they opposed.

WILLIAM HUNTON's first few years with the YMCA were filled with highs and lows. By the first decade of the twentieth century, he had, by any measure, provided great leadership with the YMCA and surpassed any expressed or implicit goals the International Committee and its Colored Men's unit might have had. He and Jesse Moorland worked together well as a team; ultimately, William focused on gaining participation on college campuses, and Moorland organized branches in cities. By 1911, more than one hundred student associations had membership near seven thousand in twenty states, and the two made sure that all YMCA conventions and conferences were integrated. But ongoing frustrations dogged William through most of his tenure with the YMCA, the most serious being the lack of money and manpower that the organization was willing to invest in its Colored Men's Department. Hunton and Moorland were reasonably successful at soliciting donations during their travels, and William's letters to Addie frequently mention how grateful he was to the donors, whom he consistently labeled as generous and kind. His success with the organization is particularly impressive, given that he succeeded with limited resources.

Both William and Addie believed that the YMCA's Christian leadership could gradually help to end segregation in the United States. William was encouraged by the fact that not all YMCA facilities in the South were segregated, and he believed college students, who were young and open to new ways of thinking, could help reverse culturally induced racism. In retrospect, one might conclude that their optimism at the turn of the century was overly idealistic. As Addie writes, her husband "learned that real understanding and appreciation of values could create an *esprit de corps* that could transcend the traditions of centuries, and he kept his faith that in the brotherhood of man was found the true norm of life." During the latter part of his tenure with the YMCA, William's activities gradually contained international components. Under William's supervision, the YMCA had hoped to staff its African missions with Black students from its branches in the South, and as time went on, William worked to fulfill this goal. In her husband's biography, Addie writes at length about his trips to London early in his career for the Golden Jubilee of the YMCA, and about his trip to several Far East nations when he visited Japan for the Conference of the World Student Christian Federation in Tokyo in 1907. He also traveled throughout western Europe to cities, including Edinburgh, Paris, and Brussels. As Addie writes, a continuing theme running through most of his visits overseas was, ironically, acceptance and egalitarianism. As both Addie and William realized, Black people were sometimes treated with more dignity and respect internationally than they were in their own country. Addie fills a dozen pages of her biography with excerpts of William's speeches and anecdotes indicating how the mixed-race groups he addressed often applauded William enthusiastically and indicated their agreement with his comments about the scourge of segregation and the cruelty of European colonialism in parts of Africa.

Still, by the turn of the century, with Atlanta as their home base, the Huntons appeared to be living a conventional middle-class existence—or as conventional as it could be considering they were Black people living in the Jim Crow South in an era of legal segregation. By 1906, Eunice was seven years old; her brother, Alphaeus, born on September 18, 1903, was three. It is not known how much William was paid by this point, but some of the correspondence between William and Moorland indicate that finances in the Hunton household were tight; a few letters and telegrams indicate that William occasionally requested short-term loans from Moorland—particularly when his children were young. "Dear Moorland," he wrote in 1903, "Can you let me have $20 until next Monday. . . . I enclose check in payment which you are not to put in bank until Monday. You will greatly oblige me." Moorland responded in a telegram that he had just sent the check.

The family lived on Houston Street, which was considered the unofficial border between White and Black residential areas in the city. And although only five schools in the town would allow Black children, one of those was located near their home. Addie acknowledges in her husband's biography that the family was reasonably content when, one day, a catastrophic event would shatter their complacency and forever change their lives. A violent race riot that erupted in Atlanta in the fall 1906 was "one of the most tragic incidents of our married life," she writes, and prompted their immediate relocation North. Over four days, beginning on September 22, a group of men, inflamed by erroneous newspaper reports about Black sex crimes, began attacking Black men at random. Twenty-five Black people and four Whites were killed and 150 injured. Addie's recollection indicates she was still devastated decades later: "After eight contented years in Atlanta, the pent-up hate and envy of a dominant group broke upon us suddenly, though not without some previous rumblings. In a moment all our sense of security was gone, and we had to realize that we, as colored people, had really no rights as citizens whatsoever. It left us very empty, for we knew in that hour that all for which we had labored and sacrificed belonged not to us but to a ruthless mob." The riot triggered a severe physical reaction in William—he had a recurrence of colitis. This condition had dogged him a few years earlier, but this attack was so severe that he considered canceling or delaying the long-planned trip to the Far East. "His spirit for the first time lost its resilience," Addie writes, adding that in hindsight, she believes that the shock of the event indirectly contributed to William's much more severe illnesses a few years later. The family moved out of their home in December 1906, with Addie and the two children heading north to Brooklyn while William traveled to Asia during the first months of the year. Addie acknowledges that the move from their beloved Atlanta home didn't seem real. "We did not realize that we were taking final leave," she writes. (Indeed, even Eunice, who was seven when the family left Atlanta, would write decades later about her memories of the gentle beauty of her childhood home and city). The family moved permanently to Brooklyn the following year.

Relocating her home must have been a culture shock to Addie, who was well-traveled but who was accustomed to living in the South. Still, the economic opportunities and good schools in Brooklyn made it a magnet for immigrants and Black people. Moreover, there were plenty of opportunities for men and women who were willing to work hard and establish their roots there. Also, Addie's new home offered her proximity to New York City and its people and resources. She soon joined the National Board of the YWCA, a move that would pave the way for a more significant role in that organization a few years later. She also became a member of a group called the Cosmopolitan Society of Greater New York, which she described in an article in *Voice of the Negro* as a "socialistic" group comprising people of all colors and races who gather to become acquainted and learn to understand and appreciate each other and to take "strong issue with those who believe in the inferiority of any race." As time went on, she became more active in this group.

A few years after the move from Atlanta, William's health declined even more. Still, he remained an energetic and devoted advocate for the YMCA, and by this time he had established himself as a beloved and respected figure. Howard University had conferred upon him an honorary degree, and, in 1913, the YMCA honored him for twenty-five years of service—three in Norfolk and twenty-two with the International Committee. His continued travels drove home this reputation. But he was spending even less time at home and had established the Washington, DC, headquarters of the YMCA Colored Department, as his home base. However, he continued as a prolific letter writer who wrote almost daily to his wife.

Interestingly, Addie and her two children did some extensive traveling themselves in 1909 and 1910—the three spent much of those years in Europe, mostly in Alsace-Lorraine and Strasbourg, Germany, where Addie attended Kaiser Wilhelm University. Addie writes little about this trip in William's biography, other than to note that she and her husband "felt very close [in this period] despite the ocean between and his letters teemed with interest." Christine Lutz and Stephen Carter, Eunice's grandson, imply that she gathered her children and took them overseas out of sheer loneliness and possibly estrangement from William, but to Addie, traveling had always been an eye-opening experience, and she may have wanted her young children to live in another part of the world. Addie, Eunice, and Alphaeus returned home in 1910 as William's health took a downward turn. Addie writes that it was her husband's poor health that led to the family's return to Brooklyn "before I had fully finished the studies I had undertaken." She did not elaborate on the specific nature of those studies—but she did enroll in the College of the City of New York shortly after her return. William had begun to have severe respiratory problems by now and had developed a chronic cough that two minor surgeries could not alleviate. Addie knew he was quite ill when "his spirit was not quite so tranquil" as usual. Once again, William took a vacation—this time to a quiet rural area on Long Island, where, she said, he fished, "loafed," and read—and apparently felt substantially reenergized that he returned to work full-time. But by this time, William's health had declined precipitously, even though he managed to continue most of his strenuous travel.

By fall 1913, William acknowledged in letters to Addie that he felt ill much of the time—a complaint that was uncharacteristic—and within a year of that time, he was unable to work.

Meanwhile, Addie had expanded her network of activism. In her role with the YWCA, she was asked to do what her husband had done for the group's counterpart, the YMCA: encourage the agency to provide facilities and services for Blacks. Addie was successful in persuading the YWCA to hire a Black field secretary, and she introduced the organization to Black female leaders in New York City and officials of the NACW. It was during this period that she began volunteering with the NAACP, becoming that organization's point person for women's equality. Her activities here became a springboard for what would prove to be one of Addie's lifelong missions: obtaining the vote for women.

Addie's biography of her husband is an homage to his hard work and to what she felt was his determination and selflessness; in fact, she and her family are, indeed, only minor "characters" in the book. In most cases, she mentions herself and her children only in terms of how they affected or reacted to him. It is only in the last three chapters of the twelve-chapter book that her tone becomes emotional and poignant. These chapters focus primarily on the last two-and-one-half years of his life after his respiratory illness was diagnosed as tuberculosis. The diagnosis soon became known to those with whom he worked at the YMCA, and Addie fills several pages with portions of the heartfelt letters his coworkers sent to him, wishing him a speedy recovery. Based on the examples she gives, these were hardly brief pro forma get-well wishes but instead were detailed, sincere, and full of genuine concern. Some contained newsy tidbits about YMCA administrative events, and many were full of spiritual references. Most were eloquent and touching.

What is particularly stirring about these last few chapters, however, is Addie's recounting of their physical closeness. For what is apparently the first time in their marriage, they spent uninterrupted months together, some of them traveling to areas considered more hospitable to William's health. William's health had deteriorated to the point where he often had trouble speaking, and, alarmingly, he would sometimes suddenly start to hemorrhage after long fits of coughing. Still, he managed to help plan a major national YMCA-related event: a Negro student congress to be held in Atlanta in the spring of 1914. Addie gives the reader a detailed record of the ups and downs of his illness and finally, the gradual decline that forced him to curtail his job duties completely. Sadly, immediately before the long-planned Atlanta student congress, he hemorrhaged and lost consciousness for days, so he was unaware of the stream of concerned letters and telegrams that arrived in the Huntons' home when his friends and coworkers heard the news. (Addie, however, did address the 665 participants of the Negro Christian Student Conference, talking mostly about the importance of the YWCA and women.) After three of his siblings came to visit—George from Montreal, Victoria from Detroit, and Mary from St. Louis—Addie admits that she was overcome with emotion and sadness: "It was often necessary in those trying days for me to find privacy to fight my emotions and to gain strength to match my faith with that of my husband."

At the urging of William's doctors, he and Addie spent much of the last two years of William's life in rural Saranac Lake in the Adirondacks, home to a respected clinic that treated tuberculosis. By this time, Eunice, who was a high school student, lived with her maternal aunt in Brooklyn to continue her schooling; Alphaeus moved with his parents. Addie implies that their time in Saranac Lake was among the happiest of their marriage and referred to it as "those shining uninterrupted hours that God gave us together in that glorious setting." He had gained a little strength during their second trip there, and one of its highlights was a visit to John Brown's grave near Lake Placid. It was important to him that the two make that trip, Addie writes, "to the shrine of this martyr whose life had touched so closely that of his own father, and when we returned . . . we tried to describe the little cemetery, the house, and every detail of that sacred spot."

But correspondence among Hunton, Moorland, and Addie indicates that—perhaps unsurprisingly—those last two to three years of William's life were also filled with stress and tension for Addie. She not only had to witness the almost daily physical deterioration of her husband's health but also deal with the unrelenting financial strains caused by his treatment and the costs of their living quarters. A constant stream of letters between Addie and Moorland indicates Moorland had advised Addie on the subject of their family's finances and, to a limited degree, William's care. The letters suggest that the Huntons had rented their home in Brooklyn to help pay for living expenses in Saranac Lake. Doctors at the clinic had recommended special equipment and medication for William as well as a full-time nurse, and the couple accrued bills they could not pay. Further, there appeared to be some confusion as to whether William would continue to be paid by the YMCA as a full-time employee, whether he would get sick pay, or whether he would not be paid at all.

Dozens of letters between Addie and Moorland show a gentle tug-of-war between the two, with Addie implying that it would be impossible for the family to juggle the costs of their daily living (and expensive medication) with what she indicates is the tremendous expense of a full-time nurse. Yet she also writes numerous times that caring for such a sick person was exhausting, and she was often physically ill and, as she writes, close to a breakdown. But those last two years of William's life illustrate the devotion both Addie and Moorland felt for William—and how Moorland and William were far more than just colleagues, but instead more like close brothers. The letters sent among Addie, Moorland, and a few other top officials of the YMCA show that William's health, by the start of 1914, had declined so precipitously that he could no longer work, thus triggering the temporary move to Saranac Lake. And although Addie notes in William's biography that their time there allowed them to be together uninterrupted for the first time in their marriage, clearly all was not well. First, the costs associated with the move and daily expenses combined with William's medical expenses dogged them constantly, and some came unexpectedly. The clinic in Saranac Lake recommended that the Huntons employ a private nurse for William, and Moorland advocated this to Addie, despite the high cost. In one letter in late 1914, Addie asks for a temporary fifty-dollar loan that she would repay him in two weeks. William had incurred $88 more than expected that month in nursing care and medication, she wrote, and she had no money for repairs for their home: "I don't know how I am going to make it at this rate but God will find a way and I don't dare let the nurse go under [the] circumstances. . . . Pray for us." Some tension developed between Addie and Moorland—the former worried that they could not afford the long-term services of a private nurse, while the latter stressed that a nurse was necessary. "I would be willing to go to the ends of the earth and do anything to bring Mr. H back to health but I think you will see that I can't do the impossible," she wrote him a week before Christmas in 1914. Addie noted in several letters that she felt ill due to stress—and in January 1915, she had asked Eunice to leave school for a week for a visit to help her. "I am all nerves myself but I am holding them down by absolute force," she wrote to Moorland. Two months later: "I feel stronger now than for some time, but realize I am in danger of a mental collapse, but I am using all precautions and will fight it out. Pray for us that we may have strength and courage in this severe battle."

Naturally, the combination of William's inability to draw a regular paycheck, combined with the added medical and housing expenses, forced a financial crisis. The Huntons apparently sold their Brooklyn home before they moved to Saranac Lake, but Addie owned a home in Washington, DC, at 919 South S Street NW that she had inherited and one that was used periodically by William and his family, as well as a brother, Benjamin. But it still carried a mortgage and needed renovations and repairs, according to letters between her and Moorland. Together, these factors caused a perfect storm of sorts for the Huntons; and to Addie, it was more than just a financial crisis. The fact that the family had trouble making ends meet distressed her immensely, and she felt it demeaning to ask Moorland for loans. (Interestingly, she did note in one letter that the couple had maintained a small savings account for their children that she apparently did not want to access.) Yet, by the start of 1914, Moorland also worried that his sick friend William would not be able to afford the medical attention he needed, nor would he be able to support his family. After receiving another panicked letter from Addie about finances in spring 1914, he sought financial help from the YMCA for his friend, even though he knew he could not get financial assistance through conventional methods. For instance, in April of that year, he sent a candid letter to Frederic Shipp, secretary of the International Committee in New York, describing William's dire financial straits. He needed $600, he wrote, "to clear up a number of obligations"—such as property taxes and insurance premiums, "which would have been taken care of had he not been stricken." (That amount did not cover medical costs, he added.) "This is a delicate matter," he added, and a crisis "which has come upon him like a thief in the night." Shipp replied that he could arrange for the money to be sent to William as a salary bonus, and "his [regular] salary would be continued." ($100 in 1914 would be worth about $2,500 in 2020 dollars.) But Moorland and Shipp knew that this financial arrangement was unorthodox: "You can assure Mr. and Mrs. Hunton that no one, not even the members of our [International] Committee, will be apprised as to his bills," Shipp wrote. In a response letter to Shipp, Moorland wrote that William was grateful when he told him of the financial arrangement but "he did not want to be put on a basis of charity. . . . I explained to him that there was no such thought." The conversation showed the deep bond between William and Moorland. "He expressed his deep appreciation of my loyal friendship . . . and said he did not know how he could ever repay me and what would he do without my constant presence," Moorland wrote. "I never had a more pleasant conversation in my life . . . I have always been Hunton's best personal friend in every way and will stand by him to the end."

And Moorland continued to "stand by" his friend, and for the first time in their friendship, William addressed Moorland by his first name in letters. ("My dear Jesse") and signed his letters with his childhood name of "Billie." Moorland had to realize that the family's budgetary short-term fix was just that and that as long as William was ill, the family would continue to have financial problems. By late 1914, Moorland sent a mailing to all YMCA field secretaries across the country seeking donations to cover some of the costs of William's medical care; three months later, after only seven responded with small donations, he sent another donation request: William's poor health and living expenses in Saranac Lake "make it incumbent upon those who love Mr. Hunton as we do, to bear some of the burdens, not as a duty but as a sweet privilege." Moorland's efforts to raise money for his friend may have proved controversial, with some YMCA officials apparently questioning the solicitation. A letter from a YMCA official in Philadelphia alludes to the fact that several people objected to the solicitation. "It seems to me that it is grose [sic] ingratitude on the part of any fellow who knew Mr. Hunton's sacrificing life given entirely to Association work and then not do something to make him happy in his last moments."

William Hunton left Saranac Lake in September—after a temporary rally of his medical condition—but sent Addie home four months earlier, fearful that she would break down if she stayed longer, he told Moorland. He spent the last year of his life at a home in Greene Street in Brooklyn, receiving many visitors, including W. E. B Du Bois, the prominent author and opinion leader. The fact that Du Bois visited him speaks to William's stature within the Black community of the era—and to the fact that Du Bois considered him an important person. In a letter to Moorland describing his visit—which came less than a week before William died—Du Bois described him as "greatly emaciated" and looking ten years older than his age of fifty-three. By this time, Du Bois writes, he was on strong opioids for pain, and he lapsed in and out of consciousness. Interestingly, Du Bois in the letter mentions Moorland's solicitations for donations, noting that it was in some ways a public relations issue: "It would be very unfortunate all around to have the impression get abroad that there was misunderstanding or lack of sympathy and unity between two men [William and Hunton] who are the historic figures and the chief representatives of Association work among colored men."

On Wednesday, November 26, 1916, before his two children left for school, he asked Addie, Eunice, and Alphaeus to kneel at his bedside so he could pray for them. He lapsed into a coma that afternoon and died later that day. "I am not embarrassed to write, nor do I make any apology for so doing, that in his death those who were at his side as well as myself saw the passing of a saint," Addie wrote. But perhaps even more telling are Addie's comments that the two grew very close as William's disease progressed: "I think that God willed it that we should have almost three years of unbroken companionship before our earthly ties were broken." Evidently, her husband's years of traveling for a noble cause had taken their toll on the strong and resourceful Addie, who was ultimately grateful that in his final years, she finally had her husband to herself. But she probably realized that after his death, her life would change dramatically.

3

One Vision in Her Eye, One Cry in Her Soul

TRIBUTES STREAMED IN immediately after the death of William Hunton, and dozens of YMCA facilities across the country arranged memorial services. Addie writes that a "quiet service" was held at their home three days after his death, but a large and well-attended memorial service took place on January 7, 1917, at St. Mark's Church in Brooklyn. Based on Addie's description, a large crowd of people, most of whom had known or worked with William during his twenty-five-year career with the YMCA, attended, spoke, or served as pallbearers. He was buried in Cypress Hills Cemetery in Brooklyn. His family received many notes and condolence cards from all over the world, including one that arrived three months later from Shanghai. Many of these were far from pro forma messages of condolences; indeed, some were long and filled with emotion. Taken as a whole, the messages show that William Hunton had undeniably been an inspiration, a sounding board, and a symbol of hope for many people. Unsurprisingly, Jesse Moorland delivered one of William's eulogies, a transcript of which was found among Moorland's personal papers. ("His greatest gift was his Christ-like character," Moorland said. In his decades of travel, "he summoned his courage, he took counsel with God, and persisted, only at the end to die a martyr.") Moorland's private words to W. E. B. Du Bois immediately after William's death—as Moorland prepared a public statement—were equally as poignant but more personal. Moorland described in a letter his last visit with William: "It was the saddest moment I have ever experienced when I looked in his emaciated face, his eyes closed. . . .

I cannot tell you how near it comes to breaking my heart to be engaged in preparing this statement on my return to the office today."

In the last chapter of William's biography, Addie attempts to summarize some of the lavish and heartfelt praise, thoughts, and views of his coworkers about how and why he succeeded at his job, and the legacy he would leave. Interestingly, Addie writes that one of his unfulfilled goals was to help establish a YMCA movement in Africa. But she adds that a current YMCA employee whom William had mentored, Max Yergen, had begun work there. Yergen, as she described him, was a new "pioneer prophet." It is particularly telling that the last sentence of her book, which is taken from an essay by one of his friends and coworkers, Frank K. Sanders, notes that the legacy of true pioneers lays not necessarily in brick-and-mortar buildings or material items, but in their contributions to generations yet unborn: "We cannot but rejoice in the life of our brother. He did his work well. Our memorial to him will be, not new Associations, or even new buildings, but our sincere dedication to the great unfinished tasks, social, religious and racial, to which he gladly gave his life."

ADDIE'S WORK with the National Association of Colored Women (NACW), the National Association for the Advancement of Colored People (NAACP), and the YWCA began to expand before William's death, and it intensified after he died. Her children now did not require daily care—within a year of their father's death, Eunice graduated from high school and Alphaeus from grammar school. The family still owned the home in Washington, DC, that generated rental income, and Addie wrote Morehouse College president John Hope, a good friend, that her financial situation had eased due to the rental income, some money William left, and some investments that she had. In 1907, the board of the YMCA named her secretary for work among Negro students with the charge of assessing the participation of Black women in the association; in addition, she helped to organize a national convention the NACW held in Brooklyn the following year. In the two years before William became severely ill, she had traveled extensively around the country on NACW and YMCA business. Her trip to France during World War I had been arranged through the YMCA and the NACW and came about a mere two years after he died. In the short time between William's death and that trip, however, she devoted much of her time to NACW activities and spreading the word about the importance of that organization. It is essential to understand that the mission and goals of Black women's clubs of this time extended far beyond social ones. Members of these groups developed specific and intricate goals to exert pressure on legislators and private citizens to affect change that had broad ramifications for both Blacks and Whites. To Addie, club work held a special appeal—in addition to providing great service to society, the clubs offered a type of camaraderie and inclusiveness that was new to Black women, and these alliances endured for the rest of the lives of many of them. The friendships they developed were intense, and club work allowed them to travel to expand their horizons and network. As Paula Giddings writes, Black women's familiarity with both racism and sexism separated them from both men and White women. The end of the Civil War did not mean the end of sexual exploitation of Black women, many of whom still worked in the Jim Crow South in the early twentieth century and suffered through a different type of unspoken enslavement (although many were too ashamed to admit it). The gatherings and activities of the NACW energized many participants because it gave them a forum to discuss openly the many economic and social problems that were a part of their lives. They had common goals, an opportunity to be recognized outside of the boundaries of race, and a shared sense of mission. Still, Giddings writes, the Black women's club movement and its White counterpart were similar in some ways: both were made up primarily of middle-class, educated women, and both believed that home and family were the anchors of society.

The vast differences between the worlds of Black women and White women came into play in the women's reform movement. While White women may have taken for granted their access to established pillars of society such as access to lawmakers, education facilities, and other public institutions, Black women in the early twentieth century did not have equal access to these resources. Further, many of the era's public reforms had the most significant effect on urban areas, but by the end of the century, many Black people still lived in the rural South. As historian Linda Gordon notes, the overall disenfranchisement of Blacks of the era forced Black women reformers to focus their efforts on education and preventative health care—institutions and services that Whites took for granted. Inevitably, to Black women reformers, social welfare and civil rights went hand in hand: even women who were well-educated had trouble finding jobs for which they were prepared because of their race. Ironically, their status in society forced leaders of the Black reform movement to become trailblazers ahead of their time in some ways. For example, because of the sexual exploitation of many Black women, rape prevention became part of the education programs of some Black reform groups, but not of White ones. And, unlike their White counterparts, some of the Black reform groups gave particular emphasis to the importance of women establishing their own economic independence outside of marriage. (Interestingly, a study of the top women's club reformers from 1890 to 1945 indicates that the majority of the women who led Black women's clubs were married, while the majority of their White counterparts were unmarried.)

Addie Hunton and other reformers continually emphasized the notion that Black women's experiences and thoughts were separate from both White women and Black men of the era. And they frequently sought to extend their organizational networks. As early as 1914—when William's health had begun to deteriorate rapidly—Addie was named a featured speaker at the Negro Christian Student Conference in Atlanta, a large gathering of students and activists. William played a significant role in planning this conference, which included 288 college students, 182 YMCA regional secretaries, thirty college presidents, and a handful of social workers and clergy. He had planned to attend the event until he suffered a massive seizure days before it began. But Addie was there, and in a speech, she emphasized a recurring theme of the meeting—the importance of ties of Black Americans to Africa. She also called for unity among the many discrete reform organizations comprised of men and women. The YWCA, with its five thousand Black female members, represented an "insignificant fraction of the 4.5 million colored women in the United States," she said. She pointed out in descriptive and vivid terms that Black women have probably given up more than their male counterparts: "The colored woman has perhaps been the most misunderstood, the most misrepresented element of American society. She has remained within the veil and the world has not been conscious of the deep aspirations of her sorrow-laden soul. Her sacrificial instincts, greater by far than in the men of the race, have almost been overlooked." Addie ended her talk dramatically, with a cry for unity and freedom: "With an enthusiasm matchless in its power to withstand cruel shocks of adversity, the colored woman has moved forward these fifty years. There has been in her eye one vision, and in her soul one cry; that vision and cry are freedom—freedom from ignorance, prejudice and poverty, and above all, the freedom of opportunity."

With her experience working in the women's reform movement, it is natural that Addie and many of her contemporaries took on what they considered another pressing issue of that era: women's suffrage. Many of these women, including Addie, worked as abolitionists, and, after World War I, they also helped to wage anti-lynching campaigns. Also, the women worked not just for racial equality, but gender equality; and they sought direct political clout independent from that of their husbands, fathers, or brothers. Both the NAACP's journal, *The Crisis,* and *Voice of the Negro* devoted many column inches to the discussion of women's power, their social and financial status, and their suffrage efforts during these first two decades of the century. *The Crisis* devoted its entire August 1915 issue to "Votes for Women: A Symposium," which consisted of twenty-six essays by what editors called "leading thinkers of colored America." Each contributor represented an organization or movement, including Addie Hunton, who wrote as a former advisor to the board of directors of the YWCA. In her short essay, she writes about the widespread popularity of the YWCA, which then had three hundred thousand members nationwide who had as their objective "the advancement of the physical, social, intellectual, moral and spiritual interests of young women." Naturally, the "spirit" of the YWCA would advocate the vote for women, she writes. "The colored woman within the association . . . is animated by a fine spirit of idealism— an idealism not too far removed from everyday existence to find expression in service."

Leaders of the Black women's club movement knew it was crucial to build alliances with other groups and with young women who they believed represented the future of their organizations. At the time of her father's death, Eunice was seventeen. As an adult, she, too, became active in the women's club movement and carried on much of her mother's work. The early life of Eunice, however, remains somewhat of a mystery. Addie Hunton does not write extensively about her children in her husband's biography. Still, she indicates that both she and her husband may have been closer to Eunice's younger brother, Alphaeus, than they were to Eunice. For example, Addie describes at length the bond established by her son and husband during the last few years of William's life when the family stayed at Saranac Lake. William helped his son with his studies—an activity that was impossible when he worked—and the two spent much time outdoors as both were nature lovers. Eunice spent the last few years of William's life living with a relative in Brooklyn so she could attend high school there. In her husband's biography, Addie periodically refers to Eunice, who was away, or "at school in Brooklyn." But she also notes that Eunice wrote her father frequently when they were separated because of his illness and that she "kept her father cheerful."

When Eunice enrolled in Smith College in 1917, the United States had just entered World War I. In February of that year, Congress passed a $250 million arms appropriation bill and, in April, declared war. Addie Hunton, through Moorland and other contacts she had with the YMCA, volunteered to travel to France as part of the American Expeditionary Forces. As she prepared for that trip, she wrote later, she knew that it might be one of the pivotal events of her life.

Eunice was one of the few Black students at Smith College when she started her freshman year, and one of a handful in the college's history—the first Black student, Otelia Cromwell, graduated in 1900. The second and third, Ethel and Helen Chestnut, graduated in 1901. But Eunice's decision to attend the college was hardly unpredictable. Two generations of Huntons and Waites—led by William's father, Stanton, and Addie's father, Jesse Waites—valued education and family over all else. Naturally, Addie Hunton would give top priority to making sure that her daughter got an excellent education at one of the nation's most respected colleges. Through her activism, Addie had become friends with NAACP cofounder Mary White Ovington, a social worker and activist based in Brooklyn. Christine Lutz writes that Eunice became close to Ovington, apparently after Addie introduced them, and Ovington, in turn, introduced the young woman to other prominent people in social work and activist circles. To women like Addie and Ovington, the camaraderie and what we now call "networking" were crucial both personally and professionally. Addie Hunton instilled in her daughter the necessity of establishing friendships and alliances in her personal and professional lives. In fact, it might have been Ovington who financed all or part of Eunice's education at Smith, according to Stephen Carter, who wrote that even though William's YMCA salary was paid to the Huntons for a brief period after his death, money had been tight for the family.

Records at Smith list her as directing inter-college debates and having a small role in "False Gods," a French play written by Eugene Brieux. The play, presented by Smith's senior class shortly before their 1921 graduation, is set in Egypt and, as a review notes, is largely a morality play and a psychological study of one character, Satni, who has abandoned his faith in any god and instead believes in the power of truth and the inherent good of mankind. The five-act play has a large cast of nearly sixty, including leading and minor characters, dancers, and about two dozen characters who appear to be townspeople or a chorus. The play's program lists Eunice as "A Nubian Fanbearer," seemingly a minor role. The play drew raves from the *Smith College Weekly*, which praised the company for presenting it for the first time in the United States; the review noted that some controversy arose from the decision by the seniors to produce such a "deep and heavy" play, but such criticism turned out to be unfounded. Nearly every aspect of its production was excellent, from the acting to the lighting, to the set, the review stated: "'False Gods' had a brilliant introduction to the United States and the seniors may well cherish their laurels as their audience will cherish the memory of 1921's glorious success." A story about her graduation that appeared in the *Chicago Defender* said that as a Smith student, she served as a "hostess" to Marie Curie and Vice President Calvin Coolidge when they visited the college.

Eunice graduated *cum laude* in 1921 with a bachelor's degree in sociology and a master's degree in political science; earning the dual degree was a rare feat, according to the *Defender*, which mentioned she was the only one of five hundred students at Smith to receive two degrees at the same time, and the only one "of her race" to graduate that year.

Eunice and Addie Hunton were fixtures in the Black national press for decades, becoming well known in these weekly publications that were widely read nationwide. The history of the Black press during the first half of the twentieth century makes it clear that most Black people were not getting the information they wanted from the primarily White mainstream press, and they disdained their news judgment—the interests and activities of Black people were largely ignored by the White press unless they committed crimes against Whites.

During the early twentieth century, most Black weeklies followed the lead of Robert Abbott, who founded the *Chicago Defender* on May 5, 1905. Abbott at first printed three hundred copies of the weekly *Defender*, modeling its style after the yellow journalism practiced by William Randolph Hearst and Joseph Pulitzer. Abbott's approach—which was much more sensational and lively than the type of journalism practiced at the time by other regional Black weeklies—was often strident in its criticism of racism and its focus on inequality.

After some initial success, Abbott realized that to become truly successful, the newspaper had to extend its reach beyond Chicago. By 1915, the *Defender* had a circulation of 230,000 nationwide, and others that followed its lead—for example, the *Pittsburgh Courier* and the (Baltimore) *Afro-American*—were also growing in circulation. Black papers gave audiences what they wanted: a denunciation of racial inequalities. But those papers did far more than just rail against racism. They covered events and news stories, published society and religion stories, and covered cultural affairs. They ran extensive stories about the accomplishments of Black people across the county—stories that were often full of praise for their subjects. Both Addie Hunton and her daughter, Eunice, became well known to readers of these newspapers, which covered both their accomplishments and their foibles (for instance, the *Pittsburgh Courier* published a story about Addie's second marriage, which ended in divorce after only one year, and gave coverage to a hospital stay of Eunice). So the Black press played a vital role in the fight for equality. As historians Armistead S. Pride and Clint C. Wilson II write, it "was an indispensable tool in Negro attempts to improve the quality of life for African Americans."

Eunice's master's thesis about reform in state government was titled, "Reform of State Government with Special Attention to the State of Massachusetts." The fact that she earned two degrees in a four-year span is remarkable—she was, of course, one of the few Black students enrolled at Smith during that time, but also one of the few Black people of the era to attend college at all. Fewer than 1 percent of Blacks in 1921 had graduated from college. In an interview for the *Smith Alumnae Quarterly* magazine in 1935, Eunice explained that she had practical reasons for earning both a master's and a bachelor's degree simultaneously: she had taken every course she could in sociology, so she began taking government and political science classes for graduate credit. She also belonged to the Debate Club while at Smith.

After she graduated, Eunice, like her mother and father, became a schoolteacher, probably in Louisiana. She taught for only one year before moving to New York City to start a career in social work. It is not known for sure where Eunice taught school during that year, but a fictional story she wrote in 1924 for the literary journal *Opportunity*, features a protagonist who spends a lonely Christmas Eve and Christmas at a Louisiana boarding school. ("Christmas isn't Christmas when you're marooned in a boarding school in the far South in Louisiana. It's just one more day. Moreover, it couldn't be Christmas Eve. It was too hot.") Other than the few years she spent in Atlanta as an infant and young child, she had lived full-time only in Brooklyn and in Northampton, Massachusetts, so this account was likely autobiographical. Eunice's move to Harlem after her year of teaching would become an important one for her personally and professionally. It would set the stage for her activities throughout the rest of her life. Her life there would change dramatically as she became an engaged member of an established community that embraced her; in short, her move to Harlem can be compared to her grandfather Stanton Hunton's move to Chatham, Ontario, and her father's move from Canada to Norfolk. All three Huntons would ultimately prevail in these new worlds, and their environment would have lifelong influences on them.

EUNICE HUNTON was born six months before the dawn of a new century, and she came of age in a time of cultural turbulence and societal change.

Her first jobs after graduating from college were with social service agencies—first in Harlem with the Charity Organization Society of the City of New York, an umbrella organization designed to link independent organizations formed to fight problems associated with poverty. Then, in 1928, she coordinated activities of the Social Service Bureau of Newark, New Jersey—services which, one writer noted, were "varied, confused, and in many cases, inadequate." In 1932, she became a casework superintendent for the privately funded Gibson Fund that had been organized during the Depression and was later taken over by the city's North Harlem Relief Bureau. Still, working full-time for agencies and organizations that were often understaffed and disorganized did not fill all of Eunice's time. While she worked full-time, she began law school at night at Fordham University in 1927 and graduated in 1932. For the most part, Eunice's time at Fordham was uneventful. Still, her grandson, Stephen, writes that although the Fordham curriculum was designed to be completed in three years, it took Eunice five years to finish; he speculates that the delay was due to an illness she suffered, or illness of her young son, Lisle Jr. After she passed the bar exam nearly a year later, after two tries, the *Chicago Defender* wrote in glowing terms how she and another New York woman got "high marks on the exam": "Among the 645 out of 1,800 examined for the New York state bar examination were two outstanding young Race women who studied law after business hours and both of whom passed the hard test." The article praised Eunice and businesswoman Lucille Edwards for the passage of the exam and included paragraphs about their personal and business backgrounds. Eunice, the story said, completed two degrees at Smith College in four years, became a successful social worker and maintained a household with a seven-year-old child: "By talent, background, and training, she is considered excellent material for the practice of the law."

After being admitted to the New York bar two years later, she opened a law office and, once again, was one of the few Black women to join a profession made up almost exclusively of White men. As an attorney, first, in private practice and, later, for the city of New York, the low-key, soft-spoken Eunice Hunton, who had always avoided the spotlight, would soon separate herself from the pack to become one of the most high-profile attorneys in the city.

Eunice may have inherited from her mother a strong work ethic and quiet persistence, but she also had a love of and talent for writing. In the mid-1920s, shortly after graduating from Smith but before entering law school, Eunice contributed articles to *Opportunity: Journal of Negro Life*, a publication of the National Urban League that began publishing fiction, reviews, essays, and commentary in 1923. Like *Voice of the Negro, Opportunity* was founded to provide a forum for discussion of topics of interest to Black Americans of the era and served as both a source of information and a sounding board for its readers. Much of Eunice's writing provides a hint of her thoughts and feelings, as well as her vague memories of her roots in Georgia. The focus often was on class, race, and the lushness and romanticism of the South. Her writing, like that of her mother, is clear and concise, yet vivid and expressive. For instance, in one short fictional essay, "Replica," she describes a scene of Black children playing in rural Georgia:

> Noonday sun scorched a treeless ribbon of brick red road; a breeze hot and languid stirred fitfully; angry red dusts rose in great puffs only to settle back heavily on all who dared the road. . . . In the cool shadow of the mammoth trees, the heat of the road was forgotten. Life was a pleasant bustle—shouts of merriment from youths in holiday attire, shrill cries from romping children, mellow peals of laughter from slim brown girls, whose comely bodies stood silhouetted as streaks of light pierced thin and clinging garments.

In a longer story, "Digression," she writes in the first person about the pleasant surprise three young Black women from the North experience when they stumble upon a party in rural Georgia. She opens the story with detailed description: "It was April and the sickle of a new moon hung low in a star-studded day as our car sped through the soft-scented stillness of a southern night. Past miles of ghostly peach orchards in full bloom, through a sweet, cool wood of cedar, down a hill, and through a gully cut in a bank of damp red clay."

Eunice then describes the scene as couples dance for hours, until most eventually leave the floor exhausted. Finally, one couple was left dancing to the beat of the intoxicating music: "There never was, nor will there be again, music like that; it stirred the blood; it blinded reason; it stripped away the veneer of civilization; and laying the senses bare and unprotected." Her short story set in Louisiana, "Who Gives Himself," relies heavily on using nature to describe the narrator's feelings: "I have seen dawn in all its mysteries and promise breaking over shadowing mountains and limitless plains, over peaceful deep and turbulent streams; I have seen it creep upon the crowded skylines of the great cities of the world and gild the steeple of a village church. But to these dawns, dawn in the swamplands of Louisiana is as Hades to Heaven—antithesis. . . . Dawn in Louisiana is not a lovely thing, dew-pearled or even dew-drenched. It is sullen and soggy; gnarled and groggy."

But, like her other fiction, this short story has a happy ending—the narrator (presumably Eunice) stumbles upon a celebration and absorbs the happiness and spirit of others. She is awakened from a nap by the sound of carolers distributing baskets of food. She joins them and is rejuvenated by their energy and generosity, and the gratitude of those who received the gifts. She describes one recipient: "The cabin door flew open and a gaunt black woman in a drab and faded gingham dress, clasping a newborn babe to her breast, stared wonderingly. Then, seeing that we came to her, she cried 'Christmas gift' in a voice that trembled with excitement and emotion. She received our gifts regally but her thanks were broken and breathless . . . silent tears coursed down her cheeks."

Overall, Eunice made five contributions to *Opportunity* in 1923 and 1924, including a book review. The journal, which apparently began as a forum for social scientists and educators, soon changed its focus to a more literary one, gradually publishing more fiction and poetry. In his biography of W. E. B. Du Bois, David Levering Lewis describes in detail a literary gala in New York held in 1924 by Charles Johnson, the publisher of *Opportunity*, for established writers such as Eugene O'Neill, H. L. Mencken, Oswald Villard, and others to celebrate the talents of up-and-coming Black writers and poets. The exclusive guest list included Eunice Hunton, her father's YMCA colleague Jesse Moorland, writer and activist Arthur Schomburg, and Crystal Bird, who would become the nation's first Black female state legislator. Eunice's invitation to the event indicated that she was viewed as a serious writer—and indeed, her writing appeared to be the result of hard work and much thought. Interestingly, the fictional stories Eunice contributed to the journal all had one thing in common: they ended on an optimistic note, and they describe in great detail the joy their characters take in nature, friendship, and music.

WHEN SHE MOVED to Harlem in her early twenties, Eunice's life changed almost immediately, and she soon became involved in Harlem society and mores and customs. As Stephen Carter describes it, middle-class Black women who were active in that city formed unofficial "rules" for the ways young people should act, how they should dress, and what they should prioritize in their lives. The women who had the status to monitor and control these practices unofficially were "czarinas," he notes, and their activities—which often included large and lavish weddings and grand societal events—were widely chronicled by the Black press.

Eunice's scholarly and professional accomplishments were certainly extensive even by the time she reached her late twenties. In this way, she can certainly be considered a "career woman" who gave top priority to her career. But she still straddled the line of wanting a successful career and a fulfilling home life that included a husband and family. Eunice's desire, in modern parlance, "to have it all," probably stemmed from her close but sometimes fraught relationship with her mother. Addie, too, was an extraordinarily accomplished and sophisticated career woman, yet she valued domesticity and the critical role of a woman as wife and mother. (The platform and focus of the National Association of Colored Women, in addition to stressing self-reliance, always also prioritized the importance of motherhood and the duty of women to keep the home fires burning.) Stephen Carter writes that Eunice continually tried to please the strong-willed Addie, particularly when it came to issues of hearth and home.

It was probably this desire to settle down and begin a conventional family life that led to Eunice's marriage on November 26, 1924, at age twenty-five, to Lisle Carleton Carter, a dentist from Barbados who was seven years older than she. (Harlem at the time had a large population of West Indies immigrants, who had an impact on the area's culture and politics—particularly the appeal of socialism and Black nationalism.) Eunice met him a year before the marriage when she volunteered to solicit funds for Harlem's first free dental clinic. The *Chicago Defender* carried a four-paragraph account of the wedding in its society section, with the headline, "Dr. L. C. Carter Marries Popular School Teacher," calling the ceremony, which took place in St. Augustine's Episcopal Church in Brooklyn "very impressive": "Both the bride and groom are widely known and the wedding is the topic of discussion among society folk. . . . The church was beautifully decorated . . . and befitting music was elegantly rendered. The bride's gown was elaborate, as were those worn by her attendants. . . . They received many handsome and costly presents." The story also noted that Dorothy Tuck Parsons of Cleveland was the maid of honor, and Jacqueline C. Hairston was the flower girl. The bride was given away by her brother, Alphaeus, and the groom's brother, Cecil E. Carter, was the best man. The wedding announcement itself—and the fact that it was published in the widely read *Chicago Defender*—indicates the stature the couple had in the Harlem and Brooklyn communities.

Like his wife, Carter was accomplished professionally and active in social welfare causes. He graduated from the City College of New York and the Columbia School of Dentistry. He began his practice in 1921 in Upper Manhattan, with offices at 2255 Fifth Avenue. With Harry Hopkins, who would later become an aide to President Franklin D. Roosevelt, Carter opened the first free dental clinic in New York City at 102 West 136th

Street. The couple moved into an apartment at 90 Edgecombe Avenue. Their only child, Lisle Jr., was born on November 18, 1925.

Harlem in the 1920s had to be an exciting place for a young and ambitious woman like Eunice—for what may have been the first time in her adult life, she was surrounded by like-minded people who were hardworking, socially conscious, ambitious, and Black. From 1920 to 1930, the New York uptown neighborhood of Harlem had grown to become the largest and most diverse urban Black community in the country. Its Black population had increased by nearly 160 percent to 186,000 people in that period. Prominent authors, philosophers, educators, musicians, and activists made their home there, and it was seen as a symbol of liberty to Blacks of the era and a "race capital," according to one writer.

It was also the changing post–World War I social and cultural environment in the United States that drew many Blacks to Harlem. Like many other Black Americans, Addie Hunton had believed that Blacks should serve in the armed forces during World War I, concluding that such service would elevate their standing and alleviate racism at home. She and others discovered they were wrong. Addie and others who had witnessed the shoddy treatment of Black soldiers in World War I were energized—some have said radicalized—in their fight for peace and against racial discrimination. Those who served overseas saw Black soldiers treated with more dignity in France than in their own country, and they had viewed actions and policies intended to deliberately demoralize and vilify Black soldiers. These realizations combined with dramatic increases in membership in hate groups and a startling rise in hate crimes ignited a wave of civil rights activism after the war.

In 1919, there were seventy-seven lynchings in the United States—including the lynching of eleven soldiers—and membership in the Ku Klux Klan was soaring, exceeding two million by 1925. Pundits dubbed the year 1919 the "red summer" because of the blood that was shed in twenty-six race riots. This heightened racial consciousness prompted the NAACP—which had long overlooked the contributions of women—to become aware of the tremendous efforts of Black clubwomen to combat racism. In May 1919, the NAACP held a national anti-lynching conference in New York City that drew 2,500 Blacks and Whites. Civil rights activist and suffragist Mary Talbert was instrumental in organizing Black clubwomen to take an active role in the nation's anti-lynching crusades, urging them to provide money, publicity, and solicitation of volunteers to promote the effort. As Dorothy Salem writes, one million women worked "with religious fervor" in their crusade against lynching. These efforts and the volunteer work of the women eventually led to the naming of women in key administrative roles in the NAACP, including the appointment of Talbert as one of six vice presidents of the group and Addie Hunton as a national field organizer.

By the early 1920s, Eunice had become deeply involved in the politics and cultural milieu of Harlem, and she felt she was part of a vibrant and thriving community. Not only did she and her family live in that part of New York City, but as a social worker, she was an integral part of the well-being of some of its residents, and she enjoyed the widely read *Survey* (later *Survey Graphic*), whose audience was primarily Black and was devoted to Harlem. The magazine published a series of essays, presumably by Harlem residents, that discuss the area's people and its strong sense of community. Eunice wrote one called "Breaking Through," in which she discusses the contradictory nature of the community and its residents. The area, she writes, had been called a "ghetto"—yet that reputation motivates many of its residents to succeed and make something of their lives, she writes. Within invisible barriers, "you will find a small city, self-sufficient, complete in itself—a riot of color and personality, a medley of song and tears, a canvas of browns and golds and flaming reds." Eunice echoed the sentiments of her mother when she wrote that ultimately "education is the way out of the ghetto." And in the thousand-word essay, she praises the activists and pioneers who attempt to improve the lives of others through "long dark years of dismal failure, of brave struggles to rise above mediocrity, of bitter fights for existence, a tale twisted with heartaches and heartbreaks, a tale drenched in sweat and blood, but still shot through with flashes of sunlight upon pure gold." Both Addie Hunton and her daughter by this time were prominent figures in the Black community, and both by this time had expanded their influence beyond New York; the nation's volatile racial climate fed the activism of Addie and others in the Black women's reform movement, and their anti-lynching efforts would ultimately set the stage for more activism both inside and outside the United States.

BY THE MID-1930s, several generations of Huntons had achieved many "firsts"; still, it would be hard to underestimate the magnitude of Eunice Hunton's accomplishments. She had not only thrived in the exclusively male, mostly White environment of law school but, after passing the bar exam, she entered a professional world that was overwhelmingly White and male. In 1920, there were 1,500 female lawyers in the United States; only four were Black; the number of Black women attorneys grew to only 25 by 1930. (As one of the era's Black female lawyers said, one's status as a minority in an all-White profession could be awkward—even a small error she made was met with disapproval or contempt from some of her White male colleagues.

A story about Black women lawyers published in 1947 in *Ebony* magazine featured photos and short interviews with ten Black women attorneys, including Eunice. These "colored Portias," as the story called them, said they faced more discrimination as women than as Blacks. Still, as several note, being a double minority in a profession required particular perseverance and hard work because they often did not have the same educational and professional opportunities as their White male counterparts, and chances to socialize or casually meet clients or other attorneys were nearly nonexistent. For that reason, most Black female attorneys did not enter private practice but worked instead for the government. And judges often passed over women jurists when naming commissioners and making other judicial appointments, usually naming women as legal guardians to children.

The *Ebony* story itself was unintentionally ironic by today's standards. In 1869, it stated, the first Black female attorney, identified as "Mrs. A. A. Mansfield of Iowa," did not yet have the right to vote and that "getting a man-sized job was harder than climbing a tree in hoop skirts." Yet, it continued, she "stood firm in her crinoline." (It should be noted that most historical accounts name Charlotte Ray, a Howard University law graduate, as the first Black female attorney.)

Even after Eunice had been practicing law for more than a decade, she was a member of a tiny "sorority" of Black female lawyers—a phenomenon that begs the question of why she decided to become an attorney in the first place. (Even finding a law school must have been a challenge; until 1935, Howard University's law school provided the main source of legal education for Blacks, and only after a series of lawsuits filed under the auspices of the NAACP, led by attorneys Charles H. Houston and Thurgood Marshall, did Blacks get the right to attend all law schools.) The *Ebony* story does offer a hint as to why the law would appeal to someone like Eunice whose background was in writing, social work, and, to a limited degree, activism. "Women lawyers are highly influential in their communities," the story says and were often leaders in organizations like the NAACP, the Urban League, and the National Council of Negro Women. Eunice came from a family whose members had been active in some of those and other powerful and prominent organizations, and upon passing the bar, she immediately became active in organizations including the National Association of Women Lawyers and the New York Women's Bar

Association. And Eunice Hunton Carter would show that as an attorney, her influence could be considered even more far-reaching than that of her parents.

WHILE EUNICE was raising her own family, working full-time and going to law school, her mother was further establishing herself as a serious activist. In the years since William died, Addie Hunton had proven that she was more than just the spouse of an influential and respected man. Her time in France during World War I would influence her worldview and her outlook forever, and that, combined with the turbulent times in which she lived, prompted her to take a more active role in social justice causes and reduce charity work. During the 1920s, Addie's activities took on a more international dimension and, as such, tilted toward organized efforts in the United States to promote peace—mainly through the Pan-African movement in the United States. Pan-Africanism emerged in the country in the late nineteenth century as a result of native Africans' resentment of colonial powers and economic exploitation; the Black media in the United States publicized attempts by native Africans to gain autonomy, and Black Americans linked this struggle to their fight for equality in the United States. Addie Hunton and other clubwomen were vocal in their beliefs that Americans could never coexist peacefully in the world until the country treated all nationalities, genders, and races equally within its borders. In an oft-quoted speech to delegates to the Second International Congress of Women in Zurich in 1919, Mary Church Terrell, the founder of the NACW, told a gathering, in German, "You may talk about permanent peace till doomsday. But the world will never have it till the darker races are given a square deal." These women felt it crucial to connect with Black people in other countries, particularly Africa, because they feared they would fall prey to colonialism by America and Western Europe. Addie had designed specific goals for her work after the war—all dealt with furthering and establishing new links to existing organizations. She proposed that primarily Black women's organizations build ties to create a deep international dimension in their work, and she wanted existing organizations to join their White counterparts in their peace efforts. Finally, she urged Black women to join the mostly male Pan-African movement. This last goal was one that was particularly problematic for Addie and her colleagues. In 1919, Addie had participated in the first Pan-African Congress in Paris that had been organized by her colleague and friend W. E. B. Du Bois and the NAACP. As one of only two women among fifty-seven delegates from fifteen countries, she tried to convey to the group a measure of female consciousness.

In a detailed review of the sessions in *The Crisis* magazine, Du Bois noted that Addie "spoke of the importance of women in the world's reconstruction and regeneration . . . and of the necessity of seeking their co-operation and counsel." Her participation in the conference made it clear how Addie's activities and her outlook had changed in a short time and become more politicized and international. In essence, Pan-Africanism was a global movement that concerned itself with the status of colonial people and the ramifications of colonialism worldwide. Addie did not attend similar Pan-African Congresses in the mid-1920s, but she did attend one in 1927 as a key advisor.

The women who worked with the NACW had gradually grown more sophisticated in their goals, their work, and their outlook; they had long realized the importance of forging alliances with other groups, and to some extent, their work was reaching fruition. By 1915, Addie and others in the NACW joined forces with the Women's International League for Peace and Freedom (WILPF). Formed in 1915 as an offshoot of the Women's Peace Party, the WILPF gave the NACW clout and influence, even though the road for acceptance in that group was a tough one. Initially, the Women's Peace Party was formed to oppose war and support women's suffrage, but during the war, one of its founding members, Jane Addams, reached out to suffragists overseas and held its first international women's peace conference at The Hague. During the conference, group leaders discussed the importance of forming global alliances and intensifying support for racial equality by aligning with groups like the NACW, the NAACP, and other prominent Black organizations. Renamed the Women's International League for Peace and Freedom, the group appointed Mary Church Terrell, Addie Hunton, and other prominent clubwomen to its first executive committee, and Hunton and Terrell, in particular, took an active role in WILPF efforts to create interracial peace communities worldwide. The group—spearheaded by Addie—stressed education and encouraged members to agitate for African-American studies in public schools. It had a particular interest in Haiti, which was occupied by the United States. In 1926, Addie and sociologist and pacifist Emily Greene Balch visited Haiti and coauthored an essay on race relations that was highly critical of US-Haiti relations. The essay stated that racism in Haiti was as rampant as it was in the South and that the occupying forces were corrupt and abusive.

But the road was a rough one—historians who have written about the WILPF's early years paint a picture of in-fighting and conflicts, some caused by the different life experiences and goals of the group's White and Black members. For instance, as Addie worked with the White members of the WILPF, she began to believe that they thought all women of color were the same—she wanted the group to recognize class differences among the Black members. Terrell left the group in 1921, telling Hunton that she believed it discriminated against some of its Black members. Nonetheless, Addie served as head of the group's Interracial Committee for several years, apparently believing that the WILPF was serious about its interracial efforts. Their work with the organization was a learning experience for Addie and others: their activity in it led them to recognize the need for another global peace group. In 1922, after a NACW meeting in Richmond, Virginia, the International Council of Women of the Darker Races was formed to fight racial and gender discrimination. As historian Michelle Rief writes, "After years of activism on the global scene, black women came to realize that no organization could represent them better than they could represent themselves." The organization named as its three top officers educator Margaret Murray Washington, widow of Booker T. Washington, as president; Addie Hunton as first vice president; and Terrell as second vice president. When Addie served as its president from 1925 to 1928, she traveled to Haiti and became instrumental in recruiting Black women into the group. The group held its first conference in 1922, and delegates from Africa, Haiti Ceylon, and the West Indies attended. By this time, Addie Hunton was a sophisticated and worldly activist who realized that the quest for equality and social change in the United States could not be separated from similar struggles taking place around the world. And she, like others, understood that women of all races and nationalities must be united in their quest for acceptance and equal treatment under laws. This realization about the increasing complexity of the postwar world prompted them to form another large organization for Blacks—the National Council of Negro Women, which was founded by former NACW president Mary McLeod Bethune in 1935. By this time, Addie had cut back on her activities with the NACW, and deepened her friendship with Bethune, to whom she introduced Eunice. The National Council of Negro Women would become the most influential and prominent organization for Black women since its founding, and Addie Hunton and her daughter, Eunice, would become key members and officers.

4

###

The Business of
Reaching New Heights

BY THE MID-1930S, Eunice Carter had established herself in the culture
and milieu of Harlem; she was an attorney in private practice in 1933 and
was recognized and respected in the Harlem community. And she had
her own family—a son, eight-year-old Lisle Jr., and a husband, Lisle, who
worked as a dentist in Harlem. A staunch Republican and a devout Episcopalian, she was solidly a member of the middle class and someone who
was dedicated to social justice causes, a sentiment ingrained in her by her
parents. By this time, Addie Hunton had introduced her daughter to many
of the women with whom she had long worked in organizations such as the
National Association of Colored Women (NACW) and later the National
Council of Negro Women, the YWCA, and some newer peace organizations, including the Women's International League for Peace and Freedom and the International Council of Women of the Darker Races. And
Eunice and her mother were both active in the Harlem YWCA. Addie's
increasing efforts to work on behalf of Black people overseas included
getting her son, Alphaeus, and daughter involved in the cause of Pan-
Africanism. (Alphaeus Hunton would eventually become far more active
in the Pan-African movement than his sister; four years younger than Eunice, Alphaeus earned a bachelor of arts degree from Howard University
in 1924 and a master's degree from Harvard University two years later.)
After earning a doctoral degree from New York University, he became a
professor of English at Howard. From 1932 to 1937, he was a member of
and later headed the Council of African Affairs.

As a prosperous and well-educated Black woman, Eunice Carter operated in a nearly all-White male power structure, so seeking influence and
authority required that she, like her mother, become particularly nimble in
navigating that specific environment. Over the decades, Addie had gained a
firsthand understanding of the great power of alliances and determination.
And while conditions for Black Americans had improved since the turn of
the century when Addie and William Hunton were at the height of their
careers, it is impossible to overlook the violence, racism, and degradation
Blacks felt sixty years after they were granted full citizenship under the
Fifteenth Amendment. And seasoned activists like Addie, Mary Church
Terrell, and Mary McLeod Bethune, who had been active in forming the
first Black women's clubs, found that their work alongside White women
who fought for women's suffrage also took on racist dimensions at times,
even though all the women were fighting for the same goal.

By the end of the nineteenth century, the nation's suffrage movement,
led by Susan B. Anthony and Elizabeth Cady Stanton, developed a state-
by-state approach to its goals, and at times these goals became exclusion-
ary. Black women were caught in the middle—they had to work within the
established organizations, but they also found they could achieve results
within their own groups. The NACW, for instance, maintained its own suffrage department and passed a resolution in 1916 in support of suffrage.
Terrell, however, was also a member of the National American Women
Suffrage Association, and she reminded women in speeches and writings
that excluding Black women from voting because of their race was similar
to excluding women from voting because of their gender. (Suffragists outside of the South rationalized that close affiliation with Black suffragists
would alienate voters in the Jim Crow South).

But the roadblocks erected to halt even the smallest move forward may
have motivated rather than discouraged women like Addie Hunton. Her
daughter, Eunice, apparently inherited this determination. Eunice also no
doubt experienced one of the dilemmas Addie and her colleagues faced
when they fought for racial and gender equality and suffrage: How much
should they work within accepted (White) parameters? And how much
should they defy conventional wisdom or established ways of doing things?

Eunice started her private law practice at a time of great social and economic upheaval. The country was in the throes of the Great Depression in
1934, with half of the nation's banks failing and unemployment at nearly 25
percent. But newly elected President Franklin D. Roosevelt had initiated
New Deal reforms in the mid-1930s aimed at providing federal relief for
the poor and creating federal agencies where educated middle-class Blacks

like Eunice could find jobs. In addition, First Lady Eleanor Roosevelt championed the work of Black women, and the president consulted with Black leaders and later appointed numerous Black people to his cabinet. But the federal government had still failed to pass anti-lynching legislation despite several attempts by lawmakers during the first three decades of the twentieth century and despite a push for several years by Eleanor Roosevelt.

As a result, Black writers and opinion leaders began pondering whether the Republican Party truly represented their interests. In 1928, W. E. B. Du Bois, in his regular column in *Crisis* magazine, "Postscript," indicates that to Blacks, the decision about whether to vote could in itself be a difficult one:

> If we keep out of politics, we give the whip hand to our enemies. They pass segregation laws; they curtail liberty of the press and of speech; they hinder the right to organize; they discriminate by law. . . . We have got to vote or be enslaved. . . . [But] can any man born south of the Mason and Dixon Line be for a moment considered as a man or must he always be put down as a raging beast, in alliance with lynching, disfranchisement [*sic*] 'Jim Crow' . . . and public insult?

Seven years later, shortly before a general election, activist and writer Oswald Villard, who was White, wrote a long essay in *Crisis* titled "Plight of the Negro Voter," in which he questioned whether either of the two major political parties represented Black citizens. Roosevelt's New Deal helped White workers, he said, but did little or nothing for their Black counterparts. But Republicans, also, offered very little: "I have no doubt that they will be willing to make all sorts of campaign and platform promises to the Negro, just as they have in the past, and then fail to live up to them," he wrote. He described the Socialist Party as "entirely friendly to the Negro . . . and without race prejudice," but it has too few followers, has not grown substantially, and is unlikely to attract high numbers of voters "under the name of Socialism."

It was in this schizophrenic moment in time—with Blacks still facing virulent racism in nearly all aspects of society, but seeing a glimmer of hope with the new Roosevelt Administration—that Eunice Carter decided to run for office.

NATURALLY, THE NATION's political landscape would change dramatically after women were given the vote in 1920. Both major political parties competed not just for the women's vote but also for the vote of Blacks. In northern states like New York, the Republican Party began to encourage Black men to run for office in primarily Black districts. In 1917, the party chose four Black women to serve as delegates and alternates in the New York Republican convention. And Warren Harding, in his 1920 campaign, made a special effort to seek Black votes in the North.

Both major parties knew it was necessary to get the votes of both women and Blacks during those first three decades of the twentieth century—and they did this by slightly altering their platforms and putting up minorities and women as candidates. The Socialist Party also made it a top priority to attract Black men and women by actively supporting women's suffrage and encouraging Blacks to run for office. In New York, attorney Edward A. Johnson, a Republican, won in his run for the Nineteenth Assembly District seat in the heart of Harlem in 1917, when he became the first Black person elected to the state legislature in New York. (In his bid for reelection, Johnson was defeated by Democrat Martin J. Healy.)

By the 1920s, however, the party of Lincoln could not take the Black vote for granted. Republican women began forming local clubs to raise awareness of civil rights and economic inequality, and two Black newspapers in New York—the *New York Amsterdam News* and the *New York Age*—urged women in Harlem to vote Republican. But women were beginning to observe racism in the Republican Party. At its 1920 convention, the NACW failed to pass a resolution endorsing Republican candidates after some speakers criticized the party platform because it did not take a bold enough stand against lynching. Some Black Republican women in New York left the party, while others tried to change it. Still, as historian Julie Gallagher notes, many Black Republicans felt they could not vote Democratic in national races as long as southern Democrats remained vocally racist and Democrats were seen as instituting racist practices. In a typical example, New York Democrats in 1924 hosted a dinner for six thousand New York City Democrats—all were White. Gallagher also relates an anecdote describing how, at the 1928 Democratic National Convention, Black delegates were led into a segregated area of the convention floor that had been cordoned off by chicken wire.

Interestingly, it appears as though it was gender and not race that marginalized many Black women when it came to politics. During the first part of the twentieth century, politics was nearly an exclusively male domain. Political leaders were men, and they were not inclined to cede their power to women: "Women were hammering away at one of the foundations of male privilege and power, and men were determined to give as little ground as possible," Gallagher writes. White women, as well, were content to preserve this domain of White political power, she adds. Finally, ideological discord among Black women also hindered their attempts at political office. Women of different classes, education, and income levels often had differing priorities, creating challenges to Black women seeking leadership positions.

Eunice Carter entered this splintered environment as a Republican candidate in 1934 for New York's Nineteenth Assembly District seat, campaigning on the reduction of the age limit for pensions, enforcement of legal standards for tenement housing, continuation of unemployment insurance, and opposition to racial discrimination in public works employment. It may have been no surprise to anyone who knew her that she would run for office in state government. When she was a senior in college at Smith, her thesis, "Reform of State Government with Special Attention to the State of Massachusetts," focused on ways to make state governments more efficient. (Eunice earned her bachelor's and master's degrees simultaneously.) At the beginning of her thesis, she writes that when state governments were first organized, they were designed to serve small populations that lived under relatively simple economic systems. Growing populations coupled with the increasing complexity of the industrial and social order had hindered the efficiency of state governments, she wrote. Eunice cited statistics that both the population of the United States and property values had more than doubled between 1906 and 1916. As an appendix, she includes a detailed hand-drawn chart of her proposals to increase efficiency in Massachusetts.

Eunice was very specific in the thesis, supporting her arguments with facts and data. When she ran for the state government slot in 1934, she ran in the first general election year since Franklin D. Roosevelt had become president, so it was theorized in advance that the results could be a referendum on his New Deal programs. Eunice was a political novice who had never run for public office, but she certainly knew the character and tenor of Harlem, the district in which she was running. Eunice's social-service work, combined with her experience as a local attorney and her links to the community, made her an appealing and qualified candidate to many.

The *New York Age* endorsed the Republican Eunice Carter, who ran against Democratic incumbent James Stephens, even though the district was heavily Democratic. Eunice received 45 percent of the vote on November 6, 1934, losing 6,005 to 7,582. To many, though, it was an impressive showing considering Democrats swept New York's local races that year, including the race for governor. The reason for the Democrats' success, the *New York Age* stated in the lead of the election-results story, was, indeed, the influence of President Roosevelt's New Deal. The *New York Times* proclaimed that the substantial Democratic victory in New York State was a "tidal wave that swept the state and . . . carried the party into control of both the Senate and Assembly for the first time since 1913." The next issue of the monthly *Crisis* ran a photo of Eunice with the headline "Runs Good Race": "Mrs. Carter ran a good race and on November 6 finished only 1,600 votes behind her veteran colored Democratic opponent, James E. Stephens." Carter, the story mentioned, was a member of "an old, well-known family."

Eunice may have lost the race, but her impressive showing as a Republican during a Democratic sweep caught the eye of Democratic New York Mayor Fiorello La Guardia. Ironically, it was once again a race riot—this time in Harlem—that triggered significant changes in Eunice's life, just as the race riot in Atlanta compelled her family to leave their home nearly thirty years earlier.

THE FIRST RACE RIOT in Harlem's history began in the late afternoon of March 19, 1935, when a sixteen-year-old Black Puerto Rican boy, Lino Rivera, stole a sixteen-dollar knife from Kress's, a Harlem five-and-dime store on 125th Street. But a series of misunderstandings and the misreading of simple events spurred violent demonstrations in the streets by more than three thousand people and, ultimately, led to the death of six and scores of injuries. But the investigation into the riot ultimately helped establish Eunice as a trusted and competent public figure; it was she who helped with the organization of an investigation into its causes.

The store owner had witnessed the theft, tackled Rivera, and called police. When asked if he wanted to press charges, though, he declined. Meanwhile, an ambulance had been called to treat wounds the store owner sustained when Rivera bit him after he was tackled. The police officer let Rivera go, leading him outside from the back of the store. When a spectator saw the boy being accompanied by an officer leaving through the back entrance—and when she noticed the ambulance—she became alarmed for the boy's safety. Adding to the confusion was the fact that the driver of a hearse was visiting somebody on the street and had parked his vehicle nearby. When passers-by saw the departing ambulance and the hearse, they concluded the boy had been beaten to death. Crowds began milling around, and rumors spread quickly that Rivera had been killed. Within several hours, three thousand people had rushed onto the streets in protest, smashing windows and looting. Fifty people had been arrested by early the next morning.

The next day, at the urging of the NAACP, LaGuardia appointed an eleven-person bi-racial panel called the Committee on the Conditions in Harlem to investigate the violence and hold hearings to determine its cause and recommend how similar disturbances could be avoided in the future. (Oddly, the day after the riot, New York District Attorney William C. Dodge said that the rioting may have been started by members of the Communist Party in New York or other radical groups, a theory that was proven unfounded, but one that may have been triggered by the presence of a radical Black group in Harlem called the Hamidic League that supported communism.) Eunice was named to the commission as its secretary, and as such, was the point person who would collect all tips, evidence, and other information about the event. And although the makeup of the commission—which consisted of six Black and seven White members—drew the ire of many Black citizens and organizations in Harlem, Eunice's appointment made it clear to the public that she was considered a hard worker and an honest broker. LaGuardia was initially attacked by many Black citizens for naming a committee whose composition did not accurately reflect the racial, economic, and cultural makeup of Harlem because it was too heavily weighted by people from a privileged class. One person quoted in a story in the *New York Amsterdam News* said that most people on the committee "are in no position to judge the condition of the man in the street, for they are not hard up themselves."

In addition to Eunice, the committee consisted of A. Philip Randolph, president of the Brotherhood of Sleeping-Car Porters; City Tax Commissioner Hubert Delaney; Municipal Court Judge Charles E. Toney; Countee Cullen, an author; Charles Roberts, a dentist; Arthur Garfield Hays and Morris Ernst, lawyers; William Jay Schieffelin, a trustee of Tuskegee University; the writer Oswald Villard; and John J. Grimely, a physician. Several community organizations, including the National Association of College Women, the Central Committee of the Harlem Parents Association, the Harlem Committee on Public Policy, and the Consolidated Tenants' League, suggested names for LaGuardia to add to the list, but none was added.

The group held its first meeting within a week of the disturbance and began to hold hearings immediately after that. Immediately after its formation, however, many in Harlem believed that the "cause" of the riot was no mystery: it was the inequality of a society that discriminated against its Black citizens. Roy Wilkins, then managing editor of *The Crisis*, wrote that economic discrimination "set up a tragic train of unemployment, undernourishment, bad housing, disease, vice, unrest and, last week, resentful disorder." The reaction by the Black community to the riot and the result-ing investigation marked one of the first times Blacks spoke out candidly and openly against what many believed was overt economic discrimination. Author Jeffrey Stewart, the author of a 2018 biography of writer and ed-ucator Alain Locke, mentioned that the riot was pivotal in changing the outlook and even the art and literature of Black artists; writers Langston Hughes and Zora Neale Hurston "built their literature on the working class but almost in an isolation from larger social and economic forces," Stewart believes. Still, later, writers such as Richard Wright, who rose to prominence during the Harlem Renaissance of the late 1920s "was basi-cally saying that humanity is being destroyed by poverty and segregation in the United States."

Overall, the commission in its findings blamed racial discrimination in employment as the major cause of the riot, but it also concluded that other factors created an environment that led to the riot, including poor housing and poor educational and medical facilities that were far inferior to those found in mostly White neighborhoods. The commission blamed the riots indirectly on inadequate educational facilities, in particular, noting "the disgraceful physical condition of the schools . . . as well as the lack of rec-reational facilities and the vicious environments that surround the schools [which] all indicate the presence of poverty-stricken and therefore helpless groups of people." The report noted that only $400,000 of $120.7 million earmarked for school improvements in New York went to Harlem.

IF PEOPLE OUTSIDE of Harlem didn't know Eunice before, her commis-sion work helped establish her as a critical player in the city's legal and law-enforcement world. As part of her role in the riot committee's investi-gation, Eunice went to the capital of Albany and persuaded the New York State legislature to consider seven bills, most of which dealt with long-overdue housing reforms. As one commission member wrote about her years later, "Mrs. Carter was a girl who knew her way around town, knew how to make things happen," he wrote. "She went around [the statehouse] quietly buttonholing the right people. . . . That is the kind of girl Eunice Carter is." Four of the seven bills she proposed passed the legislature.

It is unsurprising, then, that the work of Eunice Carter, an efficient, diligent, street-smart attorney, would catch the eye of New York's district attorney. In summer 1935, District Attorney Dodge named Eunice as an assistant prosecutor to work in Harlem in "women's day court." With her eye for detail and knowledge of the streets of Harlem, she was well suited for that job, which consisted mostly of prosecuting prostitutes and abuse cases in New York City's magistrate court. The job demanded hard, repetitive work and was decidedly not glamorous. And nationwide, it was a job that frequently went to women attorneys.

The previous month, New York Governor Herbert Lehman had named Thomas E. Dewey as New York's special prosecutor. Lehman sought an energetic, smart, and wily attorney who he knew could take on a special and important assignment: investigating and prosecuting organized crime in the gangland capital of New York City—rackets that were tied to the streets of Harlem under the mob leader known as Dutch Schultz. Shortly after Dewey's appointment, he learned of Eunice's reputation, and her work caught his eye, prompting him to ask her to work in his special prosecutor's office. Soon, Eunice Carter would become more than simply one of the dozens of assistant district attorneys in New York—she would take action that would set her apart and establish a working relationship with Dewey that would last for decades to come and help make Thomas Dewey a household name.

BY THE MID- and late 1920s, Addie Hunton continued her work with the National Association of Colored Women, the International Council for Women of the Darker Races, the Women's International League for Peace and Freedom, and other reform groups. But her perspective grew increasingly global in nature. For instance, she continued her involvement in the Pan-African movement even though her job as a field organizer for the NAACP was a strenuous one that took up much of her time. Her job duties included much travel, organizing, and communicating with individual branches of the organization, which, as she grew older, she found exhausting. Furthermore, she continued to emphasize the importance of women in the organization, a sentiment that was not always met with enthusiasm by the mostly-male NAACP staff. The trip she took to Haiti in 1926 to investigate race relations on behalf of the Women's International League for Peace and Freedom required much stamina and hard work, but Addie was able to link her Pan-Africanism beliefs and her peace work in this trip; and she and a few other women, including activist and educator Mary McLeod Bethune, helped establish an industrial school for Haitian children.

By this time, both Addie and Eunice had befriended Bethune, who was NACW president from 1924 to 1928 and who would become instrumental in planting the seeds for the formation of the National Council of Negro Women, which began operation in 1935. Based on talks she gave at NAACP conferences, Addie believed that after women achieved the right to vote, they gained a new status as citizens that required existing women's clubs to change their direction and become more international in nature. She and Eunice were early supporters of Bethune's efforts to form the National Council of Negro Women, an umbrella organization representing many national, state, and local organizations. Bethune also became a friend and confidante of Eleanor Roosevelt, who appointed her to a staff position in the newly created National Youth Administration, an agency created by President Roosevelt to promote employment for people aged sixteen to twenty-five who were not in school. Bethune had lobbied the organization for several years, seeking minority involvement in the agency, and she became a staff member in 1938. Within two years, she was promoted to director of the Division of Negro Affairs within the agency. Because of her friendship and working relationship with Bethune, Eunice had been invited to the White House several times during the Roosevelt Administration, generally as part of meetings sponsored by Bethune and hosted by the First Lady.

As Addie Hunton aged, she had intermittent health problems and at times was cared for by Eunice. After Addie quit her job with the NAACP in the mid-1920s, she suffered a bout of depression but soon pulled herself out of it. Writer and poet Alice Dunbar-Nelson, a key literary figure in the Harlem Renaissance, wrote in her diary on June 24, 1929, that she heard Addie speak at a New York gathering and "she is fighting . . . not for the WILPF [Women's International League for Peace and Freedom] and their programs, but for her life."

By the mid-1930s, Addie had begun working on the biography of her husband, William, which was published in 1938. Eunice, meanwhile, had become very active in the National Council of Negro Women, becoming its legal advisor shortly after its formation. Her deep involvement with that organization would become an important part of her life and last more than two decades, despite her demanding work schedule. Eunice Hunton had inherited her mother's dedication to social activism and her belief in its value to all citizens.

WHEN SHE JOINED the New York district attorney's office, Eunice Carter had achieved another "first"—she became the first Black woman to work in that office. The low-key Eunice had inherited her mother's easy-going personality and demeanor, and she rarely trumpeted her accomplishments. But she had contemplated the significance of her role as a trailblazer, or what it was like to be the "first" to accomplish something. In her 1925 essay "Breaking Through" in *Survey Graphic* magazine, in which she discusses the character of the thriving, lively community of Harlem, Eunice writes that "being first" is vital to racial minorities: "The pioneer in anything significant occupies, if only for a little while, an exalted position while a large portion of the race indulges in a mild form of hero worship. . . . These achievements are the pride of the race; this business of reaching new heights is taken very seriously . . . for each is a milestone on the road of progress which leads to the goal of unrestricted opportunity."

Eunice was twenty-six when she wrote those words, but she had already accomplished more than most of her peers—White or Black. Within ten years, she would have a law degree, a law practice of her own, and the respect of the community in which she lived and worked. She would also have a husband and a son—and, like her mother, begin to experience the challenges of combining work and family. And she would soon learn that "having it all" was nearly impossible.

EUNICE CARTER'S track record as a trailblazer—someone who achieved many "firsts" in her life—would cast her as a role model to many. Her comments in the *Survey* article make it clear that she saw the importance of role models to people who had been marginalized in society. But working among people who were different from her in race, background, and gender required a specific type of agility and the ability to navigate and assess her environment. So it is particularly impressive that she thrived in the setting of the New York district attorney's office, which consisted almost solely of White men. Yet, ironically, Dewey, who eventually selected her to work on his team of special prosecutors, was not as different from Carter as it might seem. They were three years apart in age—she was born in 1899 and he in 1902—but both viewed their paternal grandfathers as role models, both enjoyed writing and debating, and both were dedicated Republicans and devout Episcopalians. Even more important, both decided at an early age to devote their lives to public service.

Unlike Eunice, Thomas Dewey was raised in middle America—in the small town of Owosso, Michigan, located halfway between Chicago and Detroit. In his memoir, he describes a typical Midwestern upbringing—his mother was devoted to raising a family and keeping a home. His father worked as the editor of the hometown newspaper, the *Owosso Times*. Dewey's mother, the former Annie Thomas, enjoyed golfing and bridge and insisted that her son Tom take piano lessons throughout his boyhood.

By the time he was in high school, Tom Dewey had come to love theater, and, with his rich baritone, loved to sing. He seriously considered becoming an opera singer.

Politics and religion were important in the Dewey household. Tom Dewey was raised Episcopalian, and although he writes in his memoir that the family did not talk much about religion at home, they never missed a Sunday in church. What they did talk about, though, was Republican politics. Dewey, like his father and grandfather, was a devout Republican, and he, like Carter, viewed his paternal grandfather as a pioneer and driving force in his own life. George Dewey Sr. entered Harvard University at age sixteen, and before he graduated, he took part in an expedition to the upper Amazon. After teaching school for a year and becoming a deputy superintendent of public instruction for the state of Michigan, he, like his son, George Dewey Jr., became a newspaper editor and soon a staunch Republican and opponent of slavery. Dewey writes that after the "battle to end slavery was finally won," his grandfather bought the *Owosso Times*, promising in its first issue that under his ownership it would be an "outspoken Republican paper" that would "advance the prosperity of the party." (Dewey writes that by 1892, George Martin Dewey Sr. had become nationally known in Republican politics, and had traveled with William McKinley in his presidential campaign.) Dewey writes that he inherited his grandfather's determination, energy, personality, and, ultimately, interest in politics.

Dewey attended the University of Michigan, where he pondered the same career of his father and grandfather—journalism. He joined the staff of the *Michigan Daily* as a reporter, but it was during his final year there that his life took a fateful turn. He covered the university's law school and began taking classes there as an undergraduate. Unlike Eunice, Dewey was not an outstanding student—he had a B-minus grade-point average—but he worked hard at two majors; he could not give up singing, and his voice teachers praised his talent and encouraged him to make a career of music. During an uneventful internship with a Chicago law firm, Dewey met Texas native Frances Hutt, a grandniece of Jefferson Davis, who, like him, was studying voice at a New York–based studio that had been holding classes in Chicago. Hutt and Dewey fell in love, and he followed her to New York where they both could study voice, and where he would enroll in law school at Columbia University. Dewey had three loves at the time: singing, politics, and Frances Hutt. The two married, and he helped pay his law school tuition from singing gigs, most as the bass soloist at St. Matthew's and St. Timothy's Episcopal churches.

While at Columbia, Dewey was overshadowed by many of his class-mates, including William O. Douglas, the future Supreme Court Justice, but he worked hard and was seen as ambitious. Although the most promi-nent New York law firms did not court him after he passed the bar in 1925, it was his law degree from Columbia and his connections that allowed him to pursue politics. And it was his love of politics that ultimately linked him to Eunice Hunton Carter and earned him the enmity of New York's toughest and most brutal mobsters.

5

⁞⁞⁞

From Squash Racquet
to Racket Squasher

EUNICE CARTER'S UNSUCCESSFUL RUN for the New York State government was far from a setback for her. Despite her loss, the race raised her public profile and earned her the respect of many Harlem residents and other New Yorkers. Still, Eunice's reserved nature and her reluctance to promote herself and trumpet her achievements separated her from most other politicians, including the person who would, ultimately, propel her to public prominence.

Thomas E. Dewey, on the other hand, was a born politician and strategist. Of course, the man who would become a three-term governor of New York, a two-time candidate for the presidency, and one of the leaders of the Republican Party for years, would have to develop a keen sense of his environment and an intimate knowledge of the subtleties of politics. And once Dewey decided to become a lawyer in New York City and enter public service, he was usually a few steps ahead of his competitors.

New York City in the early 1930s was the perfect stage for Dewey, who set his sights on high office before he was thirty, and he no doubt knew that establishing a reputation as an energetic foe of organized crime was one way to achieve his goal. By the 1920s, organized crime had become a multilayered and highly sophisticated operation in New York and some other big cities, thanks in part to Prohibition but also to a tight and invisible structure that ensured maximum efficiency. It has been widely reported that legendary FBI director J. Edgar Hoover took little interest in prosecuting organized-crime figures and would not even acknowledge the existence of the Mafia until well into the second half of the twenti-eth century. Some historians believe Hoover socialized with Mafia figures during the era of Lucky Luciano and Al Capone. Others believe battling organized crime was a low priority for him because of his focus on com-munism and the protection of his own agency. Others think that he always felt the Treasury Department and not the FBI should handle bootleggers. Still others believe he did not want mobsters to blackmail him because of the rumors of his homosexuality.

Police and prosecutors in the 1920s were no match for the well-oiled machinery of the mob, so shrewd politicians in the 1930s—including Fiorello LaGuardia and Franklin D. Roosevelt—felt they could capitalize on the fear among citizens of an organization that many felt was unstop-pable. By the time Dewey became a lawyer and Eunice Carter had begun working in women's court in the New York prosecutor's office, government officials were beginning to establish a focused and systematic rhetorical attack against organized crime, saying that it did indeed affect the lives of all citizens through manipulation of government officials, hidden taxes, and fees generated by illegal payoffs and other often subtle means.

Dewey may have been a boy from small-town Michigan, but when he graduated from Columbia Law School, he knew that he was competing for jobs with some of the top legal minds in New York. (Interestingly, he and a friend spent a year touring Europe shortly after he graduated, and it was then that he grew his trademark mustache.) Disappointed that he was not hired immediately by one of the city's most prominent law firms (and after he was fired for being too argumentative after a brief stint with a small firm), he began work at the small firm of McNamara and Seymour. He quickly rose to the top of that firm, mostly through hard and meticulous work; but even more important, he established a relationship there with George Medalie, a former prosecutor who was widely respected in New York legal and political circles. He took the young Dewey under his wing, introducing him to the tumultuous world of New York politics.

As a law student, Dewey learned how to take advantage of a nascent and chaotic uprising against a long-established and deeply engrained New York political machine called Tammany Hall, which, by the early 1930s, had controlled New York politics for nearly five decades and created a Demo-cratic stronghold. Tammany Hall was a smooth-running operation adept at achieving its goals: getting its patrons elected to office, quashing those who threatened it, and handpicking district attorneys who never conducted serious investigations of the city's vice industry and rackets. The city's many immigrants were Tammany supporters because of the organization's pro-immigration policies. While there is little doubt that the city thrived to some degree under its control, it also had a reputation for corruption that was established since its early years of existence under the notorious leader William "Boss" Tweed. By the time Roosevelt entered office, however, its influence had begun to wane, and its approach to machine politics was successfully challenged by a group of reformers that included Roosevelt and Fiorello LaGuardia. Roosevelt took away some of Tammany's federal funding and also helped the Republican LaGuardia's successful mayoral run. LaGuardia was a popular mayor who had crossed party lines. By the time he assumed office in 1934, young New York Republican lawyers and law students saw openings to replace the engrained political status quo in the city. Even before he became a lawyer, Dewey had become active in the Young Republican Club, which not only resented the Tammany Hall machinery but also disdained the deals that Republicans made with Tammany government officials. Dewey served on several Young Republican committees, and he and other young attorneys and assistant prosecutors breathed new life into a group that had been dormant or impotent for many years since its founding in 1912. They hoped that, eventually, members of the Republican power structure would select candidates for office from the ranks of that organization.

Dewey's friendship with George Medalie would bear fruit. Medalie, a Republican power broker, became a US attorney for the Southern District of New York in 1930 and named his young protégé, Tom Dewey, as his chief assistant. And the job was a baptism by fire: Dewey oversaw an office of fifty-two attorneys, and he made it clear that all should expect to work long days—sixteen hours or more. It was in this job that Dewey put his perfectionism and workaholic tendencies to good use—both qualities were job requirements. And Medalie held all of the attorneys on his staff to high ethical standards.

To Dewey, though, the work was exhilarating. A relatively new group of city and state lawmakers knew that because of crimes borne out of Prohibition, the public desperately wanted someone to tackle organized crime, and law enforcement officials were particularly eager to prosecute mob kingpins Irving "Waxey Gordon" Wexler and Arthur Flegenheimer, also known as Dutch Schultz. The successful prosecution of Al Capone using the tools of the Internal Revenue Service meant an expanded role for the federal government in crime fighting. Dewey's hard work soon began to pay off. One of his most high-profile prosecutions was that of Waxey Gordon, a lifelong criminal, bootlegger, and bookmaker who through a vast underworld empire—and his refusal to pay taxes—became a millionaire. Medalie had encouraged Dewey and those in his office to employ the same tactics to prosecute Waxey Gordon for tax evasion that agents had used to get Capone. Gordon controlled a multimillion-dollar empire that included breweries, distilleries, and speakeasies, and he lived high: he owned four cars, including a Lincoln and a Pierce Arrow, lived in a ten-room apartment in midtown Manhattan, dressed in the finest suits, and took frequent vacations to Florida and Hot Spring, Arkansas. It was quite an elaborate lifestyle, officials thought, for someone whose self-proclaimed "income" was $8,100, for which he paid $10.76 in taxes. Dewey's office, with Treasury officials, worked painstakingly for more than two years to establish a detailed paper trail of bank accounts, loans, bills, and receipts that would lead back to Gordon. Investigators sifted through more than two hundred thousand paper records that Gordon and his associates had cleverly hidden, and they subpoenaed hundreds of people who had contact with Gordon and his associates and reviewed hundreds of files of brewing equipment and other business-related expenses. Dewey writes at length in his autobiography about the prosecution of Gordon, describing how charismatic and colorful the mobster was. He makes it clear that the capture of a worthy opponent like Gordon made his prosecution all the sweeter.

As the investigation began to wind down and the trial was scheduled to begin, Medalie announced his resignation—and the timing was not accidental. Nine federal judges immediately named Medalie's protégé, Tom Dewey, to replace him as interim US Attorney before anyone else could seek the job. On December 1, 1933—"after nine days, 131 witnesses and 939 exhibits," Dewey wrote much later—it took a jury less than an hour to convict Irving "Waxey Gordon" Wexler for tax evasion. He was sentenced to ten years in the federal prison in Atlanta and fined $80,000. A month later, Dewey left the US Attorney's office and returned to private practice. Medalie had retired, and Dewey, who was thirty-one, moved into the offices of his mentor at 120 Broadway.

IT WAS FATE—and an independent-minded grand jury—that ultimately ended Dewey's career as an attorney in private practice and brought him back into the public sphere. Within a year of Waxey Gordon's trial, a grand jury had been convened in New York City to investigate gambling in the city, but it sat for eleven months and prosecuted only a few people amid charges by jurors that politicians were routinely fixing gambling cases, and prospective witnesses were threatened if they agreed to testify. (A memo by Mayor LaGuardia's office showed that during eight months of 1934,

91 percent of gambling cases brought by police never came to trial, and of those that did, about one third resulted only in low fines.)

New York District Attorney William C. Dodge, a Democrat and Tammany affiliate, convened a grand jury to investigate gambling in the city in March 1935. Determined to make sure that their work did ultimately yield results without the outside "help" or influence and threats that characterized the previous grand jury, the twenty-three jurors told reporters that witnesses had complained about the extortion and terror to which they were subjected. Hoping to avoid action by New York Governor Herbert Lehman, Dodge agreed to appoint a special prosecutor whose sole job it would be to investigate organized crime; jurors, placated, gave Dodge a list of possible candidates. Dodge had hoped to avoid naming a Republican to the job, and selected H. H. Corbin as a compromise candidate proposed by former Republican Governor Nathan Miller. Grand jury members, however, still felt Dodge was injecting politics into the process, and, after a chaotic few weeks of negative publicity that triggered Corbin's change of heart about taking the job, the "grand jury," as it became to be known, issued a scathing report and disbanded.

Meanwhile, Democratic Governor Herbert Lehman felt he had to take matters in his own hands. Lehman originally handpicked four Republican lawyers as his candidates for special prosecutor, including George Medalie; another former US attorney, Charles Tuttle; Charles Evans Hughes Jr., the son of the United States Supreme Court chief justice; and Thomas Thacher, the former president of the Association of the Bar of New York City. The four veteran lawyers turned down the job offer in a public statement, noting the impossibility to "undertake the vast and continuous responsibility," and they jointly urged Lehman to give the post to Dewey, the only nominee proposed by the New York Bar Association. Bar Association President Clarence Shearn was particularly impressed by Dewey's success in convicting Waxey Gordon. Despite the refusals of Lehman's selections, the governor insisted on holding a meeting at his home, selling the job to them as "a call to the performance of most vital public service."

Despite Lehman's somewhat desperate invitation, all four nominees still refused, only more firmly this time. A "surprised and greatly disappointed" Lehman issued a statement the next day declaring his recommendation of Dewey as special prosecutor, stressing that the decision was made after his failure to persuade any one of his preferred candidates. In a three-hundred-word public announcement, Dewey's name came after the mentioning of four "especially well-fitted" nominees: "Under these circumstances, I am, therefore, recommending to District Attorney Dodge that he appoint as special prosecutor Thomas E. Dewey. While Mr. Dewey is less well known to the public than the four men I first designated, I am advised by those who know him best that he is well qualified by experience and ability to conduct a vigorous and independent investigation into racketeering and organized crime within the county of New York."

The statement was published on the front pages of the *New York Times* and the *New York Post* with coverage implying that Lehman had yielded to public pressure. The *Long Island Daily Press* said Dewey was chosen after four other lawyers "shrugged their shoulders at the task." It was also stated that Lehman had strong confidence in Dewey's acceptance, which made Dewey seem even more unwanted. Dewey himself was not too "flattered" by Lehman's "ungracious choice of words in the announcement," he later wrote in his autobiography.

Still, Dewey's credentials were nearly equal to Lehman's nominees. Why, then, was Lehman so reluctant in appointing him under the continuous pressure from the grand jury and several civic groups? When Lehman's list of nominees was first made public, the *Times* called Dewey's omission a surprise, considering that he was the only man recommended by the bar association. According to the *Times*, Lehman's reason was that Dewey's name was "not sufficiently well known to inspire public confidence." A *Times* editorial blamed Dewey's unpopularity on his obscurity and youth: "He has not long been in the public eye, and the atrocious crime of being a young man he will neither attempt to palliate nor deny." Although it's unclear why Dodge rejected Dewey specifically, his quotes in the *New York Times* might provide some insight—he said he'd go along with people "who are of mature age and judgment, and are free from political motives, who are not looking for political advancement, or to satisfy political ambition."

On July 1, 1935, Dewey took the job amid the awkwardness, claiming modestly that he had been very happy in private practice, and commenting that he was very surprised at his selection as special prosecutor. Still, he could not have been surprised, though, with his connections and his insider's knowledge of the workings of Manhattan politics. As time would tell, it is unlikely Dodge could have selected someone who would have more success in fulfilling the assigned task.

AT THIRTY-THREE, Dewey had his work cut out for him when he took over as New York City's special prosecutor in summer 1935. "I found myself appointed Special Prosecutor to clean up New York," he wrote in his autobiography decades later. "With no staff, no office, no police, no budget appropriation, and as I look back on it afterward, no sense whatsoever."

When the appointment was announced by the news media, he was quoted as saying that he would take the position under several conditions: that he would have adequate funding and full cooperation from the city, that he could work independently, and that he would have at least a year to produce results. The appointment immediately launched the unknown Dewey from obscurity to fame. His reputation as the fearless crime fighter who outmaneuvered Waxey Gordon, his youth, and, apparently, his good looks made him the darling of reporters, who considered him good copy. In the editorial published shortly after his appointment, the *New York Times* noted that "lawyers [who recommended him] knew of his outstanding record as a federal attorney in this district" and "the city will get the industry, the intelligence, and the zeal for justice which the situation requires." *Time* magazine referred to Dewey's "handsome face" and noted that the "athletic" Dewey's "favorite indoor sport is squash racquets," but he found himself "in a position to become the biggest racket-squasher in the US." (The term "rackets" itself was just starting to emerge in the public lexicon. In the 1800s, it was used in England to define a type of fraud and in the United States to describe a public commotion. By the first few decades of the twentieth century, however, American crime fighters saw "rackets" as sinister, organized, and pervasive crime networks that victimized businesses and demanded of them part of their profits.) A reporter who covered Dewey's office and the mob prosecution wrote many years later that, indeed, Dewey's life as an attorney in private practice seemed ideal. "He had an office in the Equitable Building, a reasonable number of paying clients," wrote Hickman Powell in his book about Lucky Luciano. "Summer Sundays he sailed in the races at fashionable Tuxedo Lake. In winter evenings he played indoor tennis two or three times a week."

Dewey knew from the start that his success as a prosecutor of the mob would not stem only from his investigatory efforts. He knew that the cultivation of the media—and consequently the public—was vital to his success, and he had a sense of what is known in the twenty-first century as "branding." He had to cultivate a carefully crafted public image as a fearless crime fighter who protected witnesses, and never deviated from that image. Dewey also knew that he would be only as effective as the team he would build. He complained immediately that his government-paid staff would never get rich. He would make $16,695 a year as special prosecutor (about $375,000 in 2020 dollars), and his attorneys could make half of that. But the fanfare associated with Dewey's appointment indicated that those with whom he worked would take the jobs not for the money, but the prestige. He boasted publicly that he would appoint the

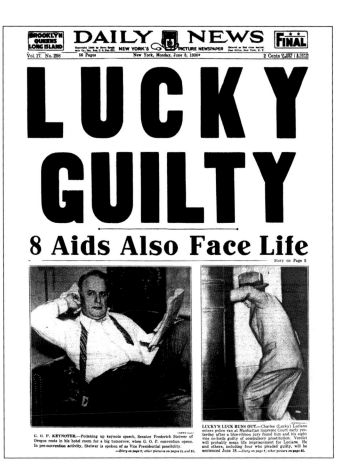

Daily News front page on June 8, 1936, announcing the verdict in the sensational New York mob trial. Courtesy of Getty Images.

A triumphant President Harry Truman proves the *Chicago Daily Tribune* wrong in the 1948 presidential race. Courtesy of the Everett Collection.

Top: This *Washington Star* editorial cartoon shows that challenger Thomas Dewey was the favorite in the 1948 presidential race. Courtesy of Abbie Rowe, National Park Service, Harry S. Truman Library.

Left: Thomas Dewey's 1948 presidential campaign poster. Courtesy of Harry S. Truman Library.

Defendants in the mob trial of 1936: (*from left*) Meyer Bergman, Benjamin Spiller, Joseph "JoJo" Weintraub, Al Weiner, and Jack Eller. Courtesy of Municipal Archives of the City of New York.

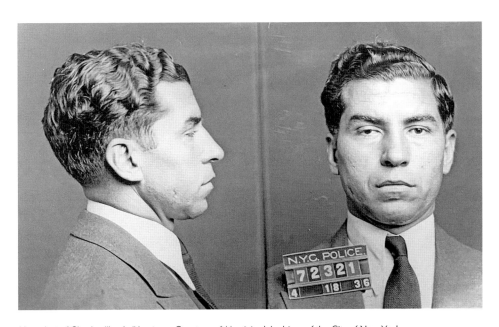

Mug shot of Charles "Lucky" Luciano. Courtesy of Municipal Archives of the City of New York.

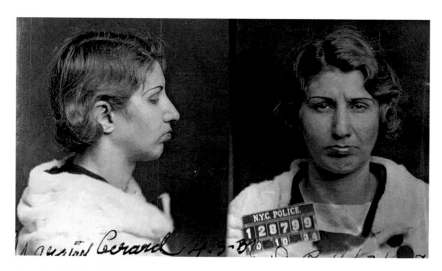

Mug shot of "Cokey Flo" Brown, one of the prostitutes who provided important evidence against Lucky Luciano. Courtesy of Municipal Archives of the City of New York.

William Hunton, Eunice Carter's father. Courtesy of Kautz Family YMCA Archives, University of Minnesota Libraries.

Top: Addie Hunton, Eunice Carter's mother, in France during World War I. Courtesy of Kautz Family YMCA Archives, University of Minnesota Libraries.

Right: Image of the plaque dedicated to ADA Eunice Carter at the Louis J. Lefkowitz State Office Building in Manhattan. Photo Courtesy of the Manhattan District Attorney's Office.

EUNICE ROBERTA HUNTON CARTER
1899-1970

Eunice Carter, a graduate of Fordham Law School, was the first African-American woman to serve as a prosecutor in New York State. In 1935, Special Prosecutor Thomas Dewey appointed her to be a member of his "Twenty Against the Underworld" legal team. Assistant Special Prosecutor Carter's analysis of the prostitution racket led to the most significant organized crime conviction of the era. After joining the New York County District Attorney's Office, ADA Carter headed the Abandonment and Special Sessions Bureaus and was liaison to the Women's Day Court. Ms. Carter later served as a national leader of the YWCA, a member of the U.S. National Council of Negro Women, secretary of the Mayor's Commission on Conditions in Harlem, and a consultant to the newly-formed United Nations.

Assistant District Attorney
New York County District Attorney's Office
1935, 1938-1945

Stanton Hunton, Eunice Carter's grandfather. Courtesy of Chatham-Kent Black Historical Society and Black Mecca Museum.

Eunice Hunton's Smith College yearbook photo, 1921. Courtesy of Neilson Library, Smith College.

Eunice Carter in her thirties. Courtesy of Schomburg Center for Research in Black Culture.

Eunice Carter driving to her job in the New York prosecutor's office. Courtesy of Schomburg Center for Research in Black Culture.

Eunice Carter at home in 1942, near the photo of her son, Lisle Jr. Courtesy of Schomburg Center for Research in Black Culture.

city's most brilliant attorneys and office workers to his staff, and it was reported that three thousand lawyers applied for the twenty jobs on his legal team; seven hundred applied for the ten accountancy openings, and five hundred secretaries and stenographers sought one of the twenty positions in those areas. (Other employees included investigators, process servers, clerks, telephone operators, and messengers.) Like anyone in his position, Dewey made some of his selections from a pool of people with whom he already worked. Three attorneys on his team—Barent Ten Eyck, William Herlands, and Murray Gurfein—worked with him in the US Attorney's office and were named as chief assistants. Other picks were attorneys who worked with well-respected attorneys and judges in New York. But nearly all the people on Dewey's team were young, with the oldest forty and the youngest twenty-five. And Dewey knew that his selection of a chief accountant was pivotal—smart and cagey accountants were able to painstakingly and thoroughly review bank records and company books and make sense of them. He selected Goody Goodrich and allowed him to pick his own staff.

Interestingly, Dewey believed diversity among his staff was a must, and that a homogenous team of White Anglo-Saxon Protestant (and Republican) men might not get the job done. Seven of the twenty attorneys were Republicans, six were Democrats, and the rest independents, some of whom were known at the time as Fusionists, an amalgam of Republican, Democrat and populists. Half were Jewish.

And one was Black—and female.

DEWEY HIMSELF suspected he'd be underestimated in his new job as special prosecutor. Even when he first appointed him, Governor Lehman made it clear that the young Columbia University law graduate was not his first choice for the job, a sentiment that embarrassed Dewey, but one that ultimately propelled him to work particularly hard to prove Lehman wrong. In his biography of Dewey, Richard Norton Smith writes that a day after his appointment, Dewey asked a crime reporter what underworld criminals thought of him. Dewey, the reporter said, was considered a "Boy Scout" who would soon be outmatched by the crafty and experienced mob that controlled so much of New York at the time. "In a few months, they won't be calling me that," Dewey responded.

Part of the special prosecutor's ultimate success may have stemmed from his willingness to think and act in new ways. For instance, it is unlikely that most public officials at the time would have picked Eunice Carter for a spot in the special prosecutor's office. After all, her race and gender separated her from the others on the team, and it would be easy and safe for members of a boy's club to fill slots with others like themselves. In a newspaper interview four years after the appointment, Dewey said that he hired Eunice at the recommendation of a judge who knew that he was seeking a "woman assistant." He hired her after their first meeting, he said in the story. But Dewey was smart enough to realize that Eunice's experience in the magistrates' court and her deep knowledge of the streets of Harlem instilled in her a perhaps unmatched understanding of the breeding ground of crime. And her experience as a social worker, political candidate, and assistant prosecutor indicated that she was a hard worker. Dewey respected that combination and hired her away from the prosecutor's office on August 6, 1935.

The appointment made a big splash: "Dewey Gives Post to Harlem Lawyer," the *New York Times* headline read, with the subhead, "Naming of Mrs. Carter, Negro, as Aide Viewed as Move to Break Policy Racket." The story announced the appointment and then provided some background about Eunice, including that "her mother and father were active in YMCA and YWCA work among Negroes." The weekly *Pittsburgh Courier*, a Black newspaper, announced, "Eunice Carter on Important Staff," under a two-paragraph story that noted she was the only woman on the special prosecutor's staff. Her literary alma mater, *Opportunity*, noted her appointment in a brief item in its Appointments section. The item listed her appointment, her education, and the names of her parents. The *New York Amsterdam News* reported that there was no question that Eunice would be the only woman and the only Black person on Dewey's legal staff—that had been stated at Dewey's press conference, the story said.

THOMAS E. DEWEY believed that public opinion of his work and the dispelling of prevailing ideas about law-enforcement impotence were pivotal to his success as a special prosecutor. So he had two priorities upon his appointment—one was immediate and the other long-term. He had to let the public and potential witnesses know that those who testified were safe and would be protected from harm. (He had boasted that he "never lost" a witness, even in the high-profile prosecution of Waxey Gordon.) And he wanted to capture one of the most colorful crime figures of the era: the elusive Arthur Flegenheimer, also known as Dutch Schultz. Schultz had great success in eluding lawmakers in the past despite some close calls, but the mobster would quickly learn that the mustachioed dark-haired young prosecutor was a worthier opponent than the others.

Still, the public relations were tricky to deal with during the investigation: publicity could mean investigators were showing their hand, yet it wasn't prudent to disappear from the scene completely. One of Dewey's aides, Harris Steinberg, remembered: "You don't want to get completely out of the public eye because then you lose the impetus of the public indignation which is helping you." For an investigation that was plodding and arduous, working from the bottom up required a good deal of time, which the public didn't realize. "It became necessary to work around the clock because every day that went by represented another day of anxiety and tenseness on the part of the public waiting to see what would come forth," Dewey's chief assistant, William B. Herlands, stated. He added, "There was a tremendous amount of pressure on everybody, and in the midst of all this we met with the obstruction on the part of witnesses, the delay occasioned by instituting contempt proceedings, the delay in persuading people to talk, the delays necessarily involved in order to permit the accounting staff to go through books, examine them carefully—all this required time." Herlands and Sol Gelb, another member of Dewey's team, believed that at the beginning of the investigation, the public was skeptical that Dewey and his team could, in Herlands's words, "crack the nut"—that is, succeed at prosecuting any key mob figures.

THE FOURTEENTH FLOOR of the Woolworth Building in lower Manhattan came to life in August 1935 as Dewey and his team established their headquarters there. The ten thousand square feet of floor space was broken up into corridors and twenty-three offices on a plan designed by Dewey. Absolute protection was guaranteed to the witnesses of the investigation who would come to the office and be examined and interviewed. The entire building was heavily protected with police patrolling and guarding every entrance and exit at all times. The quarters had a private elevator, soundproof frosted-glass offices, and tamper-proof telephones. As Dewey and his assistants knew, the security measures were in part for show: to assuage the fear of any prospective witnesses.

Every morning before dawn, Dewey would walk through a narrow corridor to his office, passing all the cubicles, anterooms, and small offices of his lawyers who would already be hustling, answering the previous night's telephone messages, decoding anonymous letters, and writing notes. Dewey's own office was barely larger than the small rooms assigned to the lawyers. The arrangements were modeled after those used in Dewey's investigation of Waxey Gordon when he was US Attorney. The fourteenth floor also housed a railway office and several small businesses, making it clear to bystanders that a person exiting one of the elevators there was not necessarily headed to Dewey's offices. Ultimately, Dewey and his team questioned about one thousand witnesses, and not a name leaked until the successful trial.

FOUR WEEKS into the investigation, a day after Supreme Court Justice Philip J. McCook swore in a grand jury, Dewey decided to deliver a radio speech on his fight against the underworld over New York City's three largest stations—WOR, WMCA, and WABC—claiming that this would be his first and last public address throughout the inquiry. The public had been doubtful about this grand investigation and many people were cynical that any kind of racket investigation could yield results.

At 8:30 PM on July 30, 1935, Dewey—who never underestimated the power of public relations—delivered to an impatient and cynical public an impassioned speech that summarized his goals in the investigation, defined what and whom he was after, and emphasized the widespread and pervasive effect of racketeering on the public. At the same time, he said early in the speech, "a talking prosecutor is not a working prosecutor," warning that the public would hear little more from him in the coming months.

Dewey began his half-hour speech on a strong note, stressing that organized crime undermines every citizen's pocketbook, safety, and daily life. Further, he said, he and his team had their eyes on large-scale wrongdoing and had no interest in prosecuting small-time gambling or petty crimes. Instead, their efforts "will deal with vice only where it exists in an organized form," and on a large scale "for profit of the criminal underworld. . . . We are concerned with those predatory vultures who traffic on a wholesale scale." He went on to explain in explicit detail the far-reaching—and very organized—nature of the rackets, whose leaders not only dealt in blackmail, extortion, and threats to workers and ordinary citizens but also in payoffs and the bribing of public officials. Racketeers, he said, were "organized gangs of low-grade outlaws who lack either the courage or the intelligence to earn an honest living. They succeed only so long as they can prey on the fear or weakness of disorganized or timid victims."

Like all competent public relations practitioners, Dewey also stressed the widespread effect of organized crime on society in general, using stark imagery and persuasive rhetoric. "There is today scarcely a business in New York which does not somehow pay its tribute to the underworld—a tribute levied by force and collected by fear. There is certainly not a family . . . which does not pay its share of tribute to the underworld every day it lives with every meal it eats," he said, explaining that the mob exacts an "unofficial sales tax" on everything from flour, which affects the price of bread, to chicken, vegetables, meat, and fish.

Even worse, he said, racket operations work in disguise and may first appear to be legitimate businesses, perhaps in the form of newly formed corporations or trade associations. But racketeers soon reveal their true selves, Dewey said, explaining criminal actions in vivid and stark terms: "It is always a case of pay up or take the consequences," he said. "Truck tires are slashed in the night, fresh vegetables and fish are soaked in gasoline, plate glass windows are broken, and often whole stores are completely wrecked." In his speech, Dewey did not avoid mentioning politics, even alluding to the fact that the process of picking a special prosecutor had been steeped in it: "I happen to be a Republican. I was appointed by a Democratic District Attorney and have received the magnificent support of Mayor LaGuardia . . . I am choosing my staff among Republicans, Democrats, [third-party] Fusionists. . . . They owe no allegiance to any political party or leader," he said. Although he gave listeners every reason to expect that he would be successful in his quest, Dewey also warned that a victory against the New York underworld would not happen overnight, and that it took as much as three years to nab Waxey Gordon, Al Capone, and other top underworld figures. He predicted it would not take his team that much time—but he also warned that their work would not be done in mere months.

At the end of his speech, Dewey explicitly sought cooperation from the media. "Crime cannot be investigated under a spotlight," Dewey said. "Publicity does not stamp out crime. It is my sincere hope that the work we are doing will vanish from the newspapers until it produces criminal cases to be tried in court." He said he wouldn't deny or confirm any rumors, and publicity would only encourage the "already over-confident underworld."

HUNDREDS OF LETTERS started to show up on the fourteenth floor of the Woolworth Building—letters from citizens reporting any suspicious activity in the city. Most were anonymous complaints about gambling and prostitution. Also arriving at Dewey's desk were letters from various newspaper editors. Marty Berg, the editor of the *Police Gazette*, wrote to Dewey the day after the radio address, saying the newspaper was "fully cognizant" of his policy of secrecy and willing to cooperate with Dewey "to the fullest extent possible," adding, "Be assured that the pages of this publication are yours for the asking at any time." In a letter from William M. Hewitt, a representative of the consortium known as the American Association of

Foreign Language Newspapers, Dewey was invited to a luncheon to discuss the newspapers' editorial direction. "I do want to be all of the help that I possibly can to you," Hewitt wrote. Hearst publisher Arthur Brisbane wrote to Dewey the same day, congratulating him on the excellent radio address and informing him that he had printed some excerpts from the speech in his column in the *New York American* and two hundred other Hearst dailies. Dewey wrote back, "Your repetition of portions of it [the radio address] should be of immense value to the investigation." Determined to work quietly, Dewey hoped to conduct his investigation without daily scrutiny, but, at first, he knew that he would be in a fishbowl as far as the press was concerned. In his autobiography, Dewey acknowledges that he understood the role of the city's newspaper reporters, who initially were under pressure from their city editors to get stories about the investigation. He writes that because they knew they would get no information from members of Dewey's team, they were forced to focus on innuendo and gossip if they wanted stories. Dewey believed that it was newspapers that indirectly triggered the mob investigation, and holding them at bay would be nearly impossible. Yet he believed it was necessary for the team to work in relative obscurity, especially at the beginning. So he took advantage of news executives' initial willingness to help.

Arthur Hays Sulzberger, the publisher of the *New York Times*, invited Dewey to have lunch with editors and tell them "some of the problems which are confronting you." The president of the North American Newspaper Alliance, Ira Wolfert, in a letter to Dewey, enclosed some clippings and indicated that Dewey had been helpful to reporters for the wire service: "Here are two clippings on that story you were good enough to give me last week," he wrote. "You've been kind and helpful and I have a feeling that I shall ask you to be so again in another few months." (The story he enclosed noted that the investigation was a "rollercoaster" and could take up to two years to complete.) The North American Newspaper Alliance was a key wire service whose members included many large newspapers in Boston, Los Angeles, Chicago, Detroit, Cleveland, and other major cities.

The correspondence between Dewey and the newspaper executives showed that he started building relationships with the media at an early stage. The press seemed very open to having the prosecutor dictate their coverage and direct their editorials, which might be seen as a conflict of interest today. As Dewey's assistant Harris B. Steinberg recalled, "seeing editors about editorials" was an essential part of Dewey's job during the investigation. As Dewey notes in his autobiography, his campaign to "guide" press coverage by currying favor with newspaper executives was ultimately successful: he quotes a *Washington Post* story from September 9, 1935, that notes that there were few stories in the New York papers about the investigation that fall. A widespread investigation into the rackets was underway, the paper wrote, but very little about it appeared in the newspapers. And the stories that did focus on it were relegated to inside pages.

Dewey's dramatic radio address grabbed attention outside New York and all over the country. A Newspaper Enterprise Association wire story featuring Dewey's fight against organized crime in New York City ran in newspapers as distant as the *Burlington Daily Times News* in North Carolina, *Daily Globe* in Michigan, *Jefferson City Post-Tribune* in Missouri, *Cumberland Evening Times* in Maryland, *Manitowoc Herald Times* in Wisconsin, *Lowell Sun* in Massachusetts, *Anniston Star* in Alabama, *Piqua Daily Call* in Ohio, and *Berkeley Daily Gazette* in California. The wire story spoke overwhelmingly highly of Dewey, saying the racketeers in New York were faced with the "admirable Dewey," who was known for building "airtight cases."

Gaining cooperation from the press was essential to Dewey. On the one hand, the less that was leaked and reported by the newspapers, the less the underworld could play defense. On the other hand, Dewey didn't want to get entirely out of the public eye because then he would lose the impetus of the public indignation that could help him. It was important for Dewey to have high-level and positive coverage to remind people of what he was working on.

WHEN EUNICE LEFT her job prosecuting prostitutes in New York City's magistrates' court, she recalled something she had found curious: many of the prostitutes brought into her office had the same attorney and bail bondsman, and many told similar stories while trying to proclaim their innocence. And, indeed, with able legal representation, many were acquitted. Many times, there also seemed to be a crucial fact left out of the arresting officer's testimony. Eunice suspected that these prostitutes might have had links to the mob—which, officials had long thought, was not involved in prostitution. It was a theory that Eunice was hesitant to bring to Dewey. She knew she needed ample evidence to change Dewey's mind about the link between the mob and prostitution.

There was never a dull moment for Eunice since the day she joined the special prosecutor's office. And her experience working and living in Harlem served her well. She remembered that thirty years ago, members of the New York Anti-Saloon League formed a committee to crack down on prostitution. Back then, the laws that banned alcoholic activities on

Sundays for religious reasons had just been loosened, and prostitution had become so pervasive that saloon owners started to build bedrooms in the back. The "Committee of Fourteen" was founded to allow law enforcement officials to demand premise inspections to distinguish between legitimate hotels and saloons. Within a few months, a law was passed requiring saloon licenses to be contingent upon a city inspection; by 1911, most saloons operating as hotels were closed. The committee remained active until it ran out of money in 1932 when it was disbanded. Eunice thought its work could provide useful clues about former prostitution operations, so she spent countless days and nights at the New York Public Library going through the voluminous records that contained the names of prostitutes and descriptive data concerning tenement houses and other places where prostitution was practiced. Eunice also contacted the Alcohol Control Administration in Washington, DC, for the records of the Committee of Fourteen, even though she suspected that the years-old material would probably yield nothing more than historical value.

In the meantime, she decided to go back to the magistrates' court, where she used to work. She had determined that prostitution would be the key to crack the nut, and now all she needed was enough evidence to connect the dots. She started to sort out all the prostitution cases on the docket. Going through the court records, she found that the majority of prostitutes were represented by a lawyer named Max Rachlin. Rachlin handled all cases arising from arrests in brothels and "disorderly houses"—places where illegal activity took place. Other lawyers came into the picture only when the volume of business became too great for him to handle alone. And to Eunice's surprise, in most of those cases, the applications for bail were signed by someone named Jesse Jacobs and people who appeared to be his relatives—Donald Jacobs, Max Jacobs, Morris Jacobowitz, Shirley Klingsberg (Mrs. Shirley Jacobs), Harry Klingsberg, Leo Klingsberg, and Rose Klingsberg. Eunice thought there was something strange about the signatures—it seemed as though the same person signed them. She knew she was onto something.

Eunice couldn't help but let Murray Gurfein, one of her colleagues, know about her discovery. Soon enough, Dewey heard it through the grapevine, but he was skeptical. As he wrote in his autobiography years later, he doubted that the mob controlled prostitution when the idea was first presented to him. He did not want the investigation to turn into a morals crusade: "I had no enthusiasm [to investigate prostitutes]. I thought it was our job to attack organized crime, and specifically not to go after prostitutes who were social problems in what still was called the oldest profession." Although disappointed by Dewey's reaction, her instinct was too strong to let it go entirely.

EVEN THOUGH he urged patience by the public in his radio address, Dewey knew that he had to nab a big fish relatively quickly. So within a few months after taking over as special prosecutor, he hooked his "fish"—only he might have considered it a white whale: Dutch Schultz. Schultz was one of only a few organized crime figures who was known by name to the public. While citizens knew he was a criminal, some viewed his skirmishes with seasoned law enforcement officials as almost a David-and-Goliath battle. Some respected his ability to outmaneuver everyone who sought to capture him. Schultz (or "the Dutchman" as some in the underworld referred to him) made vast amounts of money through bootlegging and racketeering. By 1933, he was indicted in a case prepared by then US Attorney Dewey. Still, the slippery Dutch Schultz had managed to avoid capture until 1934, when the newly elected Mayor LaGuardia exerted added pressure for his prosecution. Schultz turned himself in for the crime of tax evasion, but, because of extensive pretrial publicity, the trial was moved upstate to Syracuse and ended in a hung jury in April 1935. In the second trial, in Malone, New York, he was acquitted. As Dewey wrote in his autobiography, the small-town jury felt the mobster was the victim of "government persecution." (Dewey also wrote that the flamboyant Dutch Schultz spent large amounts of money while in Malone, gave to local charities, entertained its residents, and, in general, ingratiated himself to the citizens of the tiny town.)

Still, New York law enforcement officials were determined to get Dutch Schultz. LaGuardia was furious that he was acquitted. Dewey wrote much later that a high-profile cat-and-mouse game between Dewey and Schultz eventually grew dangerous—and, by fall 1935, it wasn't exactly clear who was the cat and who was the mouse. Frances Dewey, who was pregnant with the couple's second child at the time and who usually stayed home with their infant son, began receiving threatening telephone calls, including one that suggested she come to the morgue to identify her husband's body. FBI Director J. Edgar Hoover warned Dewey in October 1935 that Schultz had put a $25,000 price on the prosecutor's head. Dewey, of course, had traveled with bodyguards since the day he was named special prosecutor, but his team took these threats very seriously.

In the end, Dutch Schultz may have been hoisted on his own petard. He had indeed hatched a plot to kill Dewey, but other key New York mobsters felt Schultz was growing paranoid, and they believed assassinating Dewey would cause far more problems than it would solve. Charles

"Lucky" Luciano was one of a handful racket leaders who concluded that it was not Dewey but Schultz who had to go. On October 23, 1935, the Dutchman was shot in a restaurant in Newark, New Jersey, two days before the planned assassination of Dewey. And, as if in a movie, Schultz didn't go easily. After he was shot in the men's room, Schultz staggered out and had the bartender call an ambulance; after being taken to Newark City Hospital, he lingered for three days, surrounded by his mother, his sister, and his wife. America's Public Enemy No. 1 died on October 26, 1935.

Thomas Dewey may not have put Dutch Schultz behind bars, but the special prosecutor had been successful in ensuring that he no longer headed the New York rackets. Dewey and his team now had their eye on another big—and more sophisticated—target: Luciano. "Charlie Lucky," as he was known, did not earn that nickname for nothing. And the wily native of Sicily was smart enough to pay attention and learn from the mistakes of others.

6

###

"I Must Save My Sister"

IN HIS RADIO ADDRESS and his communication with editors, Thomas E. Dewey stressed that the successful prosecution of organized crime figures could take time. He wanted the public to know that the painstaking process of presenting airtight cases could not be done overnight—or even throughout many months. Moreover, Dutch Schultz was killed by mobsters and out of the way by the fall 1935, so he was not considered a notch on Dewey's belt. Dewey was well aware of the fact that if his team did not come up with results soon, the public would turn against them. He needed to buy some time.

For that reason, in October 1935, about three months after he was named special prosecutor, Dewey and his team went after what turned out to be a relatively easy target: the city's loan sharks. With his intimate knowledge of the workings of the New York court system, he managed to work around the city's cumbersome and often plodding judicial system to obtain quick prosecutions.

From a public relations point of view, loan sharks were the perfect prey. They victimized nearly everyone from small-business people to union leaders to blue-collar workers such as beauticians and transit workers, demanding interest rates as high as 1,000 percent and threatening violence and murder to those who didn't pay up. Witnesses could testify directly without the need for complex records or paperwork searches. By October, Dewey's staff had interviewed more than one thousand witnesses in usury cases because Dewey wanted more than one witness in each case. And it was during this investigation of the loan rackets that Dewey would employ an investigatory method that would become pivotal in his prosecution of key mob figures: the use of silent but deadly group arrests executed with no advance notice. On the morning of October 29, Dewey sent out fifteen squads of investigators to arrest two dozen of the most notorious loan sharks in the city. None of the suspects was picked up at home for fear their families would tip off the others of the raid. Instead, they were found outside on the streets, in public locations such as restaurants or on public transportation. By nightfall, seventy-four had been marched into the Woolworth Building, where victims could identify them behind Venetian blinds.

The secrecy of the raids and the unorthodox nature of the booking process was characteristically Dewey: he realized that under normal circumstances, once the raid began, other prospective suspects would get wind of it immediately and disappear. Dewey understood the efficiency of the underworld's grapevine, and he knew the value of the element of surprise. Rounding up the loan sharks, however, was just the beginning. Dewey used his imagination to manipulate the New York judicial system to ensure speed and protect witnesses. He turned the grand jury that was convened in July into an impromptu magistrates' court, with Judge McCook presiding for nearly twelve hours. (At the time, New York City had two courts for misdemeanor cases. In the magistrates' court, one magistrate heard minor cases handed up by the grand jury, and names of witnesses were given to magistrates, who filed them publicly, making it easy for suspects to find them and to intimidate witnesses. In the special sessions courts, three-judge panels were able to hear cases based only on evidence from a city prosecutor.) Dewey was able to use grand jury secrecy by presenting information before the grand jury, with McCook sitting as magistrate. McCook signed warrants, and the defendants were all charged with usury, with some charged with assault and kidnapping. And Dewey could hold the trials in the Court of Special Sessions rather than the regular magistrates' courts, so the process was speeded up considerably.

The suspects, of course, protested what they considered their lack of due process—and their protests may have been valid—but this creative system worked: Dewey succeeded in prosecuting all but one of the loan sharks, who was acquitted because of a procedural error. The city's newspapers either overlooked or were not aware of Dewey's creative use of the judicial system. The trials went on until January, buying time for Dewey's team and indicating that he was doing the job he was hired to do. Eventually, Governor Lehman granted a request from grand jurors for some time off, and he lavishly praised jurors and Dewey for their work. "I am very well satisfied and pleased with the progress that has been made in both the investigation and the prosecution that has been carried out by the special prosecutor," he told the *New York Times* six months later. He joined grand jurors in praising Dewey for his "excellent record." Because the current grand jury worked six hours a day for six months, he said he was relieving them of their duties and impaneling two new grand juries concurrently to sit for three-month terms for the next two years, he said. (Interestingly, both the grand jury and the governor were so hyperbolic in their praise of Dewey that some officials wondered if Dewey himself was behind the grand jury's report and its recommendations to Lehman.) Many years later, Dewey's assistant Emmanuel L. Robbins acknowledged how vital the usury convictions were for the image of Dewey's team:

> It did give us some way of showing the public we were on the ball. We were then operating for some time and were without a lot of arrests. The public, I guess, thought that we would swoop down in about two months and the whole investigation would be over. Meanwhile we didn't realize how lengthy the investigation would have to be and how much time it would consume and how much time breaking witnesses involved. . . . The usury cases were a stop gap in many ways because we were showing the public that we were starting, that we were doing something.

ULTIMATELY, IT WAS prostitution and not loan sharking that played a key role in the prosecution of the New York mob in the 1930s. Eunice Carter first deduced that the links she uncovered between the attorneys, bail bondsmen, underworld figures, and prostitutes in New York were probably not coincidental. Yet Dewey knew he had to tread very lightly if he decided to take Eunice's theory seriously and move on it. Dewey had taken great pains to persuade the public that organized crime affected nearly every aspect of their lives directly or indirectly. He certainly did not want the public to think that he was on a moral crusade aimed at taking on poor "working girls" trying to make a living. So when Eunice floated her theory about the link between prostitution and the mob to fellow team member Murray Gurfein, he took notice and persuaded Dewey to give them the green light to do some initial investigating. As history has shown, it was this connection between organized crime and prostitution that ultimately clinched Dewey's case—with the jury and with the public. Eventually,

Dewey framed the prostitutes' role as one of victimhood: the crimes of Luciano and his henchmen also included the degradation of innocent women, the prosecution maintained.

MANY QUESTIONS were left unanswered when Eunice stepped out of the magistrates' court to peruse the dockets and the court files—chief among them was the role of attorney Max Rachlin, who, it appeared, represented many of the prostitutes who were arrested. Who is Rachlin, she wanted to know, and why were all the women's bail applications signed by Jesse Jacobs and by others with similar surnames? Were Donald Jacobs, Max Jacobs, Morris Jacobowitz, Shirley Klingsberg, Harry Klingsberg, Leo Klingsberg, and Rose Klingsberg his relatives? Did Jacobs forge the signatures? What was the link between Rachlin and Jacobs? Meanwhile, one of her primary tasks was reading the large volume of letters from the public that flooded the office—these were letters with tips, complaints, and other information related to the special prosecutor's investigation. Every letter— along with every telephone call—was logged and got a response.

Among the large pile, one letter piqued Eunice's interest.

"Writing this letter [is] more for the benefit of the unfortunate women. I have a sister whom I saved and is now married happily. I have some information and address of disorderly houses also an agent of these women who sends them out to work also the lieutenant and helper." This came from an anonymous letter describing a booker who had been on Eunice's radar for quite a while. (Bookers were men who arranged to send women from brothel to brothel to meet clients.)

At one point, Eunice had interviewed Morris Wachs, who was seeking a position as an investigator on Dewey's team. He had information about a ring for the procuring of prostitutes operated by a man and woman whose names he didn't know, he said. It was conducted in Manhattan on Delancey Street between Norfolk and Essex streets, and sometimes this group was to be found in front of Paramount Cafeteria on the same block. The ring's operators leased small apartments and installed one or two women in them throughout the East Side of Manhattan and in Williamsburg in Brooklyn. The letter writer described the leaders of this group as a stout, red-haired woman, and a slim man who was using a car with license number 2L4237.

A few weeks later, the office received an anonymous letter from a woman who stated that someone named Sadie Kaplan, whom the writer described as a stout red-haired woman, about thirty-five years old, along with two men—one short and stocky and blonde and the other tall, slim, and red-haired—operated a ring for the procuring of prostitutes. They also ran fifteen different houses of prostitution where drugs were sold. The letter writer said these people had cars, including one bearing the license number 2L4237. The headquarters for this group was at 159 Rivington Street and 157 Rivington Street. They also frequent the Paramount Cafeteria on Delancey Street, the writer said.

Eunice concluded that the persons referred to in the complaint by Morris Wachs and the anonymous letter were undoubtedly the same. She forwarded the information to the police department for further investigation, and, to her surprise, a folder of an old case soon landed on her desk. It turned out that about three years ago, John P. Lutkins, then the Brooklyn district attorney, had prepared considerable evidence to prosecute a booker named Louis Weiner, who went by the name Cockeyed Louis because his left eye was partly shut. The file said "Sadie" was a madam who ran fifteen brothels in Manhattan and Brooklyn. She booked with Cockeyed Louis and "JoJo," paying them 10 percent commission. The magistrates' court eventually dismissed the case.

For the past three months, Eunice had been interviewing people who complained about disorderly houses and prostitution activities, trying to will her suspicion into substantial evidence. She had interviewed women at the Girls' Service League, an organization designed to provide help to needy women but one that had gradually become the bookers' target to recruit women. She had talked to many timid girls and women who told her they had girlfriends and acquaintances who seemed to have an unlimited source of money. She had also talked to people who submitted information on matters that had been adjudicated by the New York City's magistrates' court, but they were always dismissed, and the prostitutes involved were all bailed out. Eunice struggled to come across a witness who was directly connected to a prominent booker like Louis Weiner.

Eunice's eyes lit up because she had seen the name Louis Weiner in another letter she just received. The pieces were starting to come together: "I don't have his exact home address, but I know how you can get him. He keeps himself in a restaurant owned by a woman Yedis Porgamin on 2925 West 22nd Street on Coney Island," the letter writer said, adding that the man's name was Louis Weiner. "He sends the women to the disorderly houses and receives their pay every Saturday night or Sunday." The letter writer had large amounts of detailed information, including the names of the men who tended to the details of obtaining women for prostitution. The letter said Weiner's lieutenant, "Looky, or Al Lucks or Albert Letz buys and sells his women. . . . White slave girls from out of town 16 or 17 years old. Sells them off to Bethlehem, Easton or Lancaster, Pa. The owner of the restaurant, Yedis Porgamin, bonds and fixes the girls' cases when arrested." The letter listed a telephone number and the writer suggested law enforcement tap the phone. "They are very suspicious of strangers. The addresses I'm going to give you are disorderly houses and I will give you the house [where] they work. I hope you make a good job of it."

The writer of that letter knew that he or she had valuable information and urged investigators to move quickly. Also, the person revealed at the end a personal stake in the matter: "Please work on these right away and I hope you don't send men that you can bribe. Once you can land Cockeyed Louis and Al Lucks and Yidis Porgamin, you break the biggest white slave ring in the country. . . . I remain respectfully. A good citizen. I'm sorry I cannot let you know who I am. I must save my sister."

By this time, Dewey deemed the evidence compelling enough to make prostitution a priority of his investigation. He authorized a full-scale investigation and ordered wiretaps and the tailing of Louis Weiner. The record of the wiretaps on Louis Weiner was made by Patrolman William Mack in 1934 and was kept in the Brooklyn District Attorney's office. Also, by now, the puzzle pieces came together: Jesse Jacobs was Louis Weiner's attorney. Rachlin was the mob's lawyer. Rachlin's office was located at 117 West 10th Street. He worked in that office as a subordinate of Jesse Jacobs, by whom he was paid.

By the end of 1935, Dewey's team would find that the mob was indeed involved in prostitution in New York, and in a big way: it was involved in two hundred houses that employed up to two thousand prostitutes. The team, spearheaded by Eunice, found that most of the women worked twelve hours, six days a week, and went through one of four major bookers. It was run like "a sort of Orpheum circuit in the business of women," Dewey wrote years later.

MOST HISTORIES of organized crime in this country recount the pivotal role prostitution played in the successful prosecution of organized crime figures in New York after Prohibition. It is in some ways surprising that it took law enforcement as long as it did to link the two, considering that under the mob, prostitution grew quickly into a booming and organized business. But Dewey's initial reluctance to believe that prostitution was mob controlled made sense. He did not want to turn a rackets investigation into a morality issue, nor did he feel inclined to portray prostitutes—most of whom were poor and addicted to drugs—as criminals in the same vein as bootleggers, gamblers, and murderers. In hindsight, however, it seems natural that the mob would control prostitution in New York. It was an illegal activity, and most of its workers were defenseless, poorly educated, and easy targets of exploitation. Even clever mobsters like Luciano did not believe that lowly prostitutes would ever be taken seriously as witnesses in court cases, even if they happened to be privy to sensitive discussions. (In his history of the mob in the United States, Ernest Volkman quotes Luciano doubting both the credibility and intelligence of prostitutes, saying they would never be called as witnesses "even if they had the brains to understand what they were hearing.")

In popular culture even today, call girls of that era are bestowed with a certain world-weary glamor, perhaps because of their flashy clothes and wisecracking demeanor. The most prominent of these women, like their gangster counterparts, frequently went by imaginative and colorful nicknames: Gashouse Lil, Jennie the Factory, Frisco Jean Erwin and others joined the world of Crazy Moe, Tommy Bull, Cockeyed Louis Weiner, and Little Davie Betillo (who was in charge of the prostitution racket). Dewey's eventual focus on them shed light on their lives and the lives of the bookers, madams, johns, and other assorted (or sordid) characters who inhabited their world.

In his biography of Luciano, journalist Hickman Powell, who covered the mob trials of the 1930s and who later became an aide to Dewey, tells the stories of several of the prostitutes who ultimately testified in Dewey's mob case. Some, like Nancy Pesser, were naive teenagers who came from small-town America—in her case, Albany, New York—to Manhattan, in search of excitement and romance. Nancy's first job in the big city was as an artist's model, but her fresh-faced appearance and eagerness to please ultimately led her into organized crime circles and drug addiction; other young women were forced into prostitution to support families. Still others, many of whom had little education, saw it as an easy way to earn a living. But Powell writes that only those call girls who were considered the best mingled with top underworld figures and had access to their conversations or plans. Nearly all, however, were encouraged, or even forced, to use alcohol and narcotics—especially opium and morphine, which was readily available to them, frequently through "parties" or gatherings with underworld figures.

The well-known madams of the era were Pearl "Polly" Adler and Florence "Cokey Flo" Brown; Brown, whose real name was Florence Newman, provided pivotal testimony against Luciano after she supposedly heard him say once that he wanted control of the houses of prostitution in New York to run them "on a large scale, same as a chain store system." The Russian-born Adler, considered one of the most famous madams in New

York history, ran a string of high-class brothels on and near Fifth Avenue for more than twenty years. Adler began work in her profession shortly after World War I—and despite an arrest during Dewey's crackdown and the serving of twenty-four days of a thirty-day prison sentence—she continued until the early 1940s.

CONSIDERED THE FATHER of modern organized crime in this country, Charles "Lucky" Luciano was born Salvatore Lucania on November 24, 1897, in Sicily. He moved to New York with his parents and three siblings when he was nine, but he and his family soon learned that the slums of the Lower East Side were far from the land of opportunity that they had envisioned. Disillusioned by the terrible living conditions and poverty, Luciano was drawn to criminal activity at an early age. He quit school at fourteen and joined teenage street gangs. He first landed in prison when he was nineteen, having been convicted for selling heroin on the city's East Side. By that time, though, Luciano's criminal record included armed robbery and assault.

On the streets of New York, Luciano was known primarily as Charlie Lucky. Historical accounts differ as to how he earned his nickname. Some state it was because of the frequent mispronunciation of his surname, and others maintain it was because of his luck as a gambler or his ability to survive several violent crimes, including knifings and shootings. (In 1929, he was beaten and strung up from a beam in a Staten Island warehouse. It was here where he acquired a noticeable scar on his chin and an injury that led to a lifelong droop in one eye, according to mob legend.)

But Luciano did not become a billionaire and one of the most feared—and respected—mobsters in the country because of pure luck and happenstance. He was a brilliant tactician and shrewd judge of human nature who was willing to abandon old customs and methods if they weren't working, and he learned from the mistakes of others. Luciano also ingratiated himself to some of the top underworld figures of the era: Meyer Lansky, Benjamin "Bugsy" Siegel, and, most important, Arnold Rothstein. Rothstein, as one historian noted, provided the advice and capital that turned Luciano "from a small-time hood into a well-heeled bootlegger." Rothstein also taught him that he needed to unify New York's disparate criminal enterprises if he wanted to succeed. In the mid-1800s, the thousands of gang members in the city were loyal to Irish gang leaders on the Lower East Side. As the city grew after the Civil War, the gangs' reach extended throughout the city. After a wave of immigrants entered the city in the late nineteenth and early twentieth centuries, Italian and Jewish gangs gained control of portions of the city—the Irish led the West Side, and Jewish and Italian gangsters controlled the East Side. Although there were nearly as many Jewish bootleggers as Italians, the Italians were viewed as better disciplined and more vicious. Yet, the Italians did not have the political influence of the Irish, who could pay off members of a largely Irish New York police force.

During Prohibition, only the well-financed and best organized of New York's gangs could survive, and two Sicilians—Salvatore Maranzano and Giuseppe "Joe the Boss" Masseria—fought for control. Luciano had been recruited by Massaria and served as one of his bodyguards, but that didn't stop Charlie Lucky from selling out his boss. Luciano was growing frustrated with Massaria and his refusal to modernize his business dealings, and the rivalry between the two bosses served as a way for Luciano to kill two mob bosses with one stone. So he told Maranzano he would set up his boss and arrange for his murder—which he did in April 1931. But the wily Luciano did not trust Maranzano either and arranged for his murder five months later.

Interestingly, despite his high profile in the underworld by the mid-1930s, Luciano was unknown to the general public and certainly did not have the name recognition of Dutch Schultz, Waxey Gordon, or Rothstein. But he wanted it that way—Luciano knew that to succeed, he could not be placed in the spotlight. And he did manage to stay "underground" for a time, despite his tremendous wealth, a penchant for handmade European suits and shoes, expensive cars, a private plane, and a lavish $7,600-a-year three-room suite in the Waldorf Astoria (about $100,000 in 2020). A bachelor, Luciano cultivated a debonair and savvy image as a man about town, rubbing elbows with such luminaries as George Raft and Frank Sinatra. As Hickman Powell described him, "He was . . . calm and firm in times of danger, never emotional or flighty. . . . He always thought before he spoke. . . . He was never stingy with his money but cultivated the free and easy generosity of the gambler. That made him popular."

As he rose to the top, Luciano was finally able to modernize and organize the rackets as he saw fit, and as he had suggested to his former boss Masseria. Luciano recognized that organized crime had to become an equal-opportunity enterprise of sorts. He believed the then disparate groups of criminals—Italians, Irish, and Jews—needed to band together if they wanted to succeed.

In 1931, he summoned the top mob leaders to a meeting in Chicago, where a new "corporate" structure was proposed. Luciano insisted on an end to the turf wars that he believed were bad for business and only sowed discontent among the workers. Instead, he proposed a detailed and elaborate organizational structure of the five leading New York crime families to prevent turf wars and heighten profits. Each family would have a "consigliere" or chief advisor, and there would be no "boss of all bosses." The newly restructured organization, called the Commission, was labeled by historian Selwyn Raab as "the mirror image of American capitalism." It even had a seven-person board of directors: five board members represented New York, one represented Chicago, and one Buffalo. And the new structure worked perfectly. Luciano, writes historian Raab, "was like a [Microsoft founder] Bill Gates or [Berkshire Hathaway chairman] Warren Buffett."

With his street smarts and practical intelligence, Luciano bore an amazing resemblance to a man who also operated in Manhattan crime circles in the mid-1930s—someone he would come to know well: Thomas E. Dewey. Both Dewey and his nemesis, Luciano, brought novel ways of thinking to their jobs, and both were pragmatic men who wouldn't be distracted by existing stereotypes or bias. Dewey's team consisted of several Jewish lawyers in an era when many law firms would not hire Jews. Luciano knew that the coalition he formed had to be blind to ethnic and religious differences. Dewey and Luciano also knew they had to work in relative obscurity to be successful. Dewey managed to achieve this by manipulating media executives. Luciano was a known name to underworld figures by the mid-1930s, but he was unknown to the public at large and worked in relative obscurity, which is how he wanted it.

But to achieve his goals, Dewey knew he needed a fall guy, and he knew that the public needed an individual on whom to place blame for the uncontrolled growth of crime in New York City. Charlie Lucky, with his miles-long criminal record, his lavish lifestyle, and his weathered, handsome face, would become that man.

DEWEY'S TEAM estimated that about two thousand prostitutes were employed in two hundred houses in the five boroughs of New York City. If they were to sporadically raid some houses and arrest the "girls" as the prostitutes were known, and their madams, the gangsters higher up would catch wind of it and vanish. Dewey had asked his trustworthy detectives to keep some big bookers under surveillance. They would need to gather enough information to arrest as many people as possible all at once, and they would need to cover everyone on the prostitution ladder. There had to be a seamless master plan.

Every day and night, Dewey sat down to brainstorm with his team, along with the police commissioner Lewis Valentine and deputy chief inspector David J. McAuliffe. "214 Riverside Drive Apt 24—madam is Little Jennie, large place," Dewey wrote on the board as he started to map out a plan. Large houses would need three police officers for a successful raid, he said. To ensure they act as quickly as possible, it would be better if the policemen grouped together did not know each other so that there would be no distraction. For a long time, the mobsters relied on tips from police bribery whenever there was a planned raid, so if Dewey revealed the raid details beforehand, it would have been leaked. Considering that the operation would be such a grand scale, they would have to inform the police at the very last minute, right before they hit the houses.

At 9 PM on February 1, 1936, it was go time. Dewey assembled 160 plainclothes police officers to raid eighty houses of prostitution simultaneously under secret orders. The undercover policemen gathered in the West 68th Street station and were divided into groups of two and three who had not worked together before. Each little squad was given a sealed envelope that they were warned not to open until they had reached the assigned locations. Each envelope directed a raid on a designated address.

"I understand that the above place is a house of prostitution and I have set forth above all of the information which I have which will be useful to you. Hit this house at 9pm, tonight on a jump raid. Make proper effort to make a complete case which will stand up in court," the instruction read.

The policemen were told to act quickly enough to catch some of the men breaking the law. The officers were instructed to search the house for all records, memoranda, diaries, and phone numbers and question each man regarding payment of money, the names of those who introduced him to the place, and how he got the password if there was one. Dewey instructed them to have each man identify himself with name and address as well as their excuse for being in the house. Most importantly, the police needed to hold all of the prostitutes, madams, managers, maids, and doorkeepers.

"Do not leave the house until you have reached me on the telephone and received my instructions. Keep strictly to yourself all instructions I give you. Do not discuss this matter with any person regardless of who he is. Permit no one to make or receive any telephone calls to anyone under any pretext whatsoever. This applies until you have received direct personal instructions from me to the contrary. Keep this paper and return it to me," the instruction stated.

By the end of the night, ten men and one hundred women were caught in Dewey's net; they were taken first to the Greenwich Street police station and later to the special prosecutor's offices in the Woolworth Building. The women were all questioned by Dewey's team, one by one, all night and into the next afternoon. But the initial results were far from satisfactory. The madams said they were innocent housewives, and the "girls" claimed they were just art students, models, telephone operators, and the like. Most taken into custody were between the ages of seventeen and twenty-seven, and virtually none of them were New Yorkers. Many had been lured to New York and into prostitution in the belief they would be given jobs in nightclubs or shows. Not surprisingly, they all believed the mob would bail them out, as had happened before.

Although the number of prostitute arrests was unprecedented, extracting information from them that could help the mob prosecution proved difficult and time-consuming at first. Dewey decided to call Supreme Court Justice Philip McCook for help. It took some persuasion, but McCook came to Dewey's office to fix bail. At 3 AM, McCook held a unique court session in which eighty-seven of those arrested were ordered to pay a whopping $10,000 bail each. Dewey also managed to jail the prisoners in the New York House of Detention in Greenwich Village as material witnesses until the stories of the women could be obtained.

The vice syndicate recruited its women mainly from small towns. The women reported to designated managers each day and were assigned to houses, seldom the same one twice in succession. They collected $150 to $350 a week each, working twelve hours a night, six nights a week. But they had to pay extortionate prices for meals at the houses as well as for maid services and other services. With these charges and the split with the managers, the women seldom had more than $30 or $40 profit at the end of the week (about $575 to $760 in 2020 dollars).

As Dewey's team continued to question the suspects, they scored an unexpected win—one of the big four bookers in the prostitution ring, David Miller, in exchange for his wife's freedom and his children's safety, turned himself in. Miller started as a regional police officer in a small town near Pittsburgh, where he cracked down on speakeasies and houses of prostitution. His wife became involved in prostitution, serving as a madam connecting women with house owners. The two were eventually caught, and Miller was fired from his job. The family moved to New York, and with his knowledge about the business, he began testing the waters of the big city. Soon he joined the ring and became a prominent booker under Luciano. When Dewey pressed him about who his bosses were, Miller uttered the name "Charlie Luciano." It was the first time Dewey secured actual testimony that Luciano was indeed the mob boss of the vice ring.

Meanwhile, Dewey's detectives successfully located and arrested Luciano in Hot Springs, Arkansas. A resort in Hot Springs that was owned by bootlegger Owen "Owney" Madden had long been known as a refuge for some crime figures, and the city was known for its compliant attitude toward crime. But things did not go as planned. Justice McCook, on the back of an extradition warrant, had asked that a minimum of $200,000 bail be set, but an Arkansas judge ignored the request and freed Luciano on $5,000 bond within eight hours of his arrest. "I cannot understand how any judge could make such an order unless he was ignorant of the facts," Dewey told the *New York Herald Tribune*. He focused his comments on Luciano as a leading crime figure: "Luciano is generally and correctly regarded as the most dangerous and important racketeer in New York City, if not in the country. This case involves one of the largest rackets in New York and one of the most loathsome types of crime."

Although Luciano's team of six lawyers initially prevented his extradition from Arkansas, Dewey knew he had the law on his side. He urgently telegraphed Governor Herbert Lehman: "Desire call to your attention. Shocking situation Hot Springs where Charles Luciano, most dangerous New York gangster, is held by Sheriff Garland County in defiance [of] extradition warrant issued by Little Rock Court pursuant compulsory prostitution indictments here and extradition warrants by Governor New York. Extradition this prisoner matter major importance. I earnestly urge your intervention and action to terminate defiance courts and state officials and prevent possibility of release of prisoner and avoidance extradition and punishment."

Luciano was rearrested quickly and held in the Garland County jail while waiting for a hearing. The judge, Sam Garrett, who initially freed Luciano on $5,000 bail, ordered him held without bail until Little Rock authorities could handle his extradition. Garrett, in ordering Luciano rearrested, explained to reporters, "When the matter was first brought to my attention, the seriousness of the charge was not fully revealed to me. I fixed what I considered to be a sufficient bond, but after learning the facts in the case, I immediately ordered the bond revoked and Luciano remanded into the custody of the sheriff."

When Dewey's assistant Edward McLean and Arkansas attorney general Carl Bailey arrived at Hot Springs to take Luciano to Little Rock, a deputy sheriff defied the order and refused to surrender Luciano, claiming that Luciano's attorney had obtained a writ of *habeas corpus* from a federal district judge. It was only when twenty state troopers arrived—armed with machine guns, rifles, and pistols and acting under the direct orders of Arkansas Governor J. M. Futrell—that Luciano left the Garland County jail.

The next day, at a *habeas corpus* proceeding, a judge granted Luciano ten days to show the Circuit Court of Appeals in Kansas City and St. Louis why an appeal should be heard. Lehman had requested that Futrell extradite Luciano. (Back in New York, Dewey had been ready to invoke a federal law making a flight from one state to another a federal offense to bring Luciano back to New York.) Luciano's attorneys eventually missed the twenty-four-hour notice to file an appeal for an extension before the ten-day stay was up. Finally, $350,000 bail was fixed by Judge McCook, the highest bail in the history of the state.

Unable to raise the bail, Luciano languished in the Brooklyn city prison, pending his trial with eleven other defendants on four indictments charging him with compulsory prostitution. But, ironically, his return from Hot Springs after the series of legal skirmishes shows how his lawyers were outwitted by Dewey and members of his team, who had taken advantage of one of those legal technicalities that had served Luciano so well in his many encounters with the law.

ONE THING Dewey excelled at during his vice crackdown was leveraging the media to work to his advantage and raise his profile. On the evening of the Dewey raid, Luciano was far from a household name. He had been known only by gangsters, politicians, and some members of New York's Italian community. "Luciano had never gotten any publicity to speak of before," said Dewey's aide Sol Gelb. "After he was convicted, the newspapers began to write about his position in the underworld, and frankly for the first time I realized how big he was in the underworld." After agents successfully arrested Luciano in Hot Springs, Dewey, who had been silent about the investigation, sought newspaper interviews and claimed in them that Luciano was the leader of the most extensive racket organization in New York City's history, exerting complete control of organized prostitution, horse-race betting establishments, and three industrial rackets. Dewey drove home the idea that Luciano oversaw a vice ring doing a gross business of $12 million a year in Manhattan and Brooklyn. Dewey burnished Luciano's image as a brutal mob boss, while newspaper reporters described his extravagant lifestyle and decades-long mob career. To Dewey, Luciano was the perfect villain, with his scarred face and oily demeanor. In his memoir, Dewey quotes an unnamed crime magazine that described the mob boss as "wily, rapacious," and "savagely cruel. . . . For years, like some deadly King Cobra, this droopy-eyed thug coiled himself about the eastern underworld and squeezed it implacably of its tainted gold. . . . He was the bookmakers' joy, the torch singer's delight, a Dracula masquerading as Good-time Charlie."

Before the trial began, Dewey had labeled Luciano as "New York's Public Enemy No. 1," an appellation that first appeared in the *New York Times*, *Long Island Daily Press*, and *New York Daily News* and soon caught on with the public. Newspapers also came up with creative ways to describe Luciano: "scar-faced vice overlord," "Charles 'one-time Lucky' Luciano," "super-ruler of the underworld," "the head man of the unholy three," and "czar of city's vice realm." Through his nickname for Luciano and the newspapers' creative portrayal of him, Dewey had turned the public against the mob boss before his trial began. Charlie Lucky, like his crime-fighting *doppelgänger* Tom Dewey, worked hard to keep a low profile while he was conducting business. Dewey methodically launched a major publicity campaign to turn the obscure Luciano into the nation's most notorious mobster.

Dewey knew that the public couldn't wait for the trial of New York's Public Enemy No. 1, so the pressure was on. He knew he had to get a conviction.

7

Getting Lucky:
The People v. Charles Luciano

THE LONG-AWAITED TRIAL of Charles "Lucky" Luciano began on May 11, 1936, and the court setting looked like an armed camp. A heavy police guard surrounded the defendants as they emerged from a prison van and made their way through a crowd of several hundred spectators in front of the court building. Each of the ten defendants had an armed guard as they entered the courtroom and sat in chairs that lined the side of the room.

Outside, detectives and uniformed cops formed a human barricade that extended into the street. Luciano, dark and heavy-jowled, wore a blue suit, white shirt, and black tie. He appeared in good spirits, chatting and laughing with his fellow prisoners as the trial got underway. Prospective jurors, batteries of lawyers, and the defendants and guards jammed the courtroom, leaving no room for visitors.

At 10 AM, in the New York Supreme Court in Manhattan, Thomas E. Dewey officially started the proceedings against Luciano and nine other men on trial for compulsory prostitution. They were held on an aggregate bail of $1.175 million, Luciano's being the highest at $350,000 ($1 million in 1936 would be worth about $18.6 million in 2020). All had past records of indictments, but this time they were indicted by an extraordinary grand jury, which filed a sixty-page document accusing the ten defendants on ninety counts. If convicted on every count, they would face a maximum sentence of 1,950 years.

News of the trial filled the front pages of New York newspapers before it began, the stories hyping it and claiming it was a "departure" in America's fight on crime—it would mark the first time an underworld vice lord was charged with the crime of which he was actually suspected. Previously, wily and well-known mobsters like Al Capone and Waxey Gordon had been convicted only of the crime of tax evasion.

Before the trial, all 110 witnesses had been kept in jail—for their own protection and to make sure they would not flee. Eighty of the witnesses were women, fifty-five of them residents, and twenty operators of houses of prostitution, which were known as "disorderly houses." Dewey's team carefully selected the ninety proposed cases in an attempt to prove that Luciano maintained complete control over the vice syndicate. Based on Eunice's work at the magistrates' court, she made sure all the prostitutes who were material witnesses had an immediate connection to Luciano's ring. They were all tried in the magistrates' court and represented by the mob boss's attorney Max Rachlin or someone in his office—usually bail bondsman Jesse Jacobs and attorney Abe Karp. None of them had any prior jail time. Eunice had also set forth the old records from magistrates' court in detail from docket book entries and court files, to serve as the immediate foundation of evidence in the trial.

In the courtroom, all eyes were on Eunice, who, being sworn in, said:

> I'm a Deputy Assistant District Attorney of the County of New York, associated with Thomas E. Dewey, Deputy Assistant District Attorney of said County.
>
> Charles H. Farrell, Esq., Clerk of the Women's Day Courts, located at 425 Sixth Avenue, Borough of Manhattan, County of New York, is in the possession, in his official capacity, of certain papers and records more particularly described in the order hereunto annexed. Said papers and records are necessary and material evidence in the People's case in the Criminal Action now pending in the Extraordinary Special and Trial Term of the Supreme Court of the State of New York, held in and for the County of New York, entitled The People of the State of New York v. Charles Luciano, etc., et al., defendants.

The papers and records she referred to related to the arrests of people charged with acts of prostitution, she said, and were "a part of the criminal enterprise conducted by the defendants in said criminal action." Eunice continued that this was the first time such evidence had been introduced in a vice trial: "I have been orally advised by Charles H. Farrell Esq. that neither he nor the court of which he is clerk will be seriously inconvenienced by the production of said papers and records at the trials of said criminal action above referred to. No previous application has been made for this or any similar order to any court or judge."

Eunice not only played a crucial role in laying the groundwork for the trial but as the solo woman on Dewey's team, she was also instrumental in extracting evidence from the prostitutes. It wasn't smooth sailing for the investigators on Dewey's team to question the prostitutes jailed at the New York House of Detention in Greenwich Village before the trial. Most of them approached the women with a tough and threatening attitude, while some wouldn't come close to them without wearing gloves. The prostitutes were so intimidated that they wouldn't speak up or only told lies at first.

It was not until Eunice decided to talk to them in a warm and soft manner that the team was able to obtain their stories one at a time. Eunice knew it was essential to gain their trust and make sure they were treated well in prison, so she bought clothes for them and let them see family members if possible. Many of the prostitutes who worked indirectly for the vice syndicate were also drug addicts, and most were poor; Dewey's team knew they could not be under the influence of drugs when they testified, so some were undergoing withdrawal. Eunice realized it was necessary to treat those vulnerable with extra care and sensitivity.

Over the weeks of detention, those prostitutes had gone through a change in attitude and manner, a matron at the jail told *New York World Telegraph*. "They were generally hard and tough when they came in and most have changed. Some were college girls and quite a number were high school graduates. Contact with the young lawyers and investigators who questioned them brought back something of their home culture. They spoke better, acted better, and forgot the manners of the places they had been in, for the time being at least," the matron said.

To Dewey, getting a conviction against top members of the mob's governing council, known as the Commission, began with the process of jury selection. He believed it was vital to put together a panel consisting of middle- and upper-class New Yorkers whom he thought were inherently offended by prostitution and suspicious of immigrant defendants. And, as it turned out, he didn't have too much trouble getting what he wanted. He managed to handpick jurors who were mostly bankers, executives, and businessmen. The trial impaneled a so-called "blue-ribbon" jury, where the prerequisite for serving was previous jury service—at the time, it was mostly those who were self-employed or employed in managerial positions who had the flexibility to serve. The jury pool was weighted heavily with professional men, stockbrokers, and business owners. The jury selection would be made from a pool of two hundred, "made up of bankers, brokers, business executives and a sprinkling of clerks, teamsters and tradesmen," the *New York Daily News* claimed. As the writers of a lengthy *New Yorker* profile of Dewey wrote, members of blue-ribbon juries usually felt naturally predisposed to believe that they were part of the prosecution and that they have been "divinely appointed to convict."

When it was time to winnow down the pool of candidates, only the most elite made the cut. Dewey had his eye on the president of Goldman Sachs, only to be informed that the company was about to launch a new bond issue, and the man had planned a trip around the country in May and June to arrange it. "Any interruption of his plans will, no doubt, cause considerable irritation," Dewey's assistant wrote in a memo to the team. The team, headed by the detail-oriented and perfectionist Dewey, wanted to leave nothing to chance. Ultimately, the final jury with alternates was composed of fourteen successful White business people with prior jury experience, all of whom had read about the case in the newspapers.

Dewey spared no expense with these blue-ribbon jurors, and he made sure they had luxurious accommodations at a five-star hotel. He booked them large rooms at the Grosvenor Hotel and instructed hotel personnel to give them an unlimited supply of free breakfast food each day. Dewey made sure that jurors ate without charge at the hotel restaurant, and they were not expected to pay gratuities of any kind while at the hotel. On the days when the court was in session, lunch would be provided at a restaurant near the courthouse. In contrast, the women who testified were paid about $3 a day, earning a total of $150 to $200 for their participation. But Dewey's team did treat them in the weeks before the trial to perks such as shopping trips and movies.

The last obstacle to the trial was removed by presiding Judge Philip McCook, who denied three last-minute motions for separate trials on each of twenty-eight crimes alleged in the ninety-count indictment and said that all charges would be combined against the vice mob. Defense counsel argued that the jury would be prejudiced by having the twenty-eight women connected with each of the offenses take the stand and repeat their stories. It would, they said, "create a general atmosphere of guilt and the lay mind will be utterly confounded and confused."

So it was clear that by 1935, part of the vice syndicate's job controlling the sex industry included getting the prostitutes it employed out of trouble. Records introduced by Dewey showed that not one of the 144 women arrested for prostitution and working for the ring went to jail. Those who ran the syndicate did indeed live up to their promise that no prostitute who paid them $10 a week would be imprisoned. In fifty-five cases, the prostitutes had been found not guilty; in fifty-six cases, they were discharged without needing to put up a defense; in eighteen cases, the women jumped bail; and in the other cases, they received suspended sentences or were put on probation. Eunice prepared for the jury a chart summarizing those 144 cases—if jury members weren't paying attention to Dewey's words, they had the graphics of the situation in front of them.

Indeed, Dewey and his team believed a picture—or chart—was worth a thousand words. On the first day of the trial, Dewey also prepared for reporters a "family tree" showing the complex web that comprised the organization of the vice commission. Heading the list was, of course, Luciano, followed by his eight major associates and bookers. Dewey gave each of Luciano's men a descriptive nickname: "chief lieutenant," "one-time strong-arm man," "handy man and money man," "stick-up man," and "general manager." This chart did more than just help reporters and newspaper readers comprehend Luciano's great power in the underworld—it also contributed to the public's image of the mobsters' glamorous lives. This image was cemented in newspaper coverage of the first day of the long-awaited trial. Several of New York's daily newspapers ran a photo of Luciano raising his handcuffed hands to pull his hat over his eye as he left the courtroom—the stereotypical villain. Newspaper stories quoted at length Dewey's opening address, which focused on the ubiquitous nature of the vice rackets: "The vice industry, now highly organized and operated with business-like precision, thrived into an enterprise running to $12 million a year, embracing more than 200 houses in Manhattan, the Bronx, Brooklyn and Queens," he said. The *New York Daily News* published two side-by-side headshots of Dewey and Luciano on page one, with Dewey's face turning upward and Luciano's sullen and crooked—the perfect portrayal of the duality of right and wrong and crime and justice: "Their battle really begins now," the caption read.

The climax of the trial's first day came when three of Luciano's underlings unexpectedly pleaded guilty minutes into the court proceedings. Peter Balitzer (alias Pete Harris), Al Weiner, and David Marcus (alias Dave Miller) were minor players in the vice ring's "family tree" and announced that they wished to change their pleas from not guilty, proclaiming that they all previously had clean criminal records. Dewey accepted their surrender without a word, and the three were remanded for sentencing at the end of the trial. (In fact, the three turned themselves in hoping for a lower sentence.) Luciano's counsel Samuel Siegel then moved for the dismissal of the entire blue-ribbon panel on the grounds that it had been influenced by the guilty pleas. "My client has been grossly prejudiced by the fact that the talesmen [jurors] heard the guilty pleas," he declared. Judge McCook overruled his motion.

DEWEY, IN HIS OPENING statement, had tried to emphasize that Luciano sought to maintain a monopoly of vice in New York City. "We will prove that upon one occasion, Luciano boasted, 'We are going much further than this. We are going to put every madam in New York on a salary and then we will raise the prices. A $2-house will become a $4-house and a $4-house will become a $6-house, and so on,'" Dewey said in his two-hour opening statement. Step by step, he detailed how prostitution progressed from a small business to a million-dollar-a-month racket. Before 1933, he said, vice was mostly in the hands of four men, one of whom was Nick Montana. (At the time of the trial, Montana was serving a fifty-year sentence in Sing Sing Prison.) Once, women could earn as much as $400 a week. When Luciano and his men took over, they either forced bookers to work with them or drove them out of business. As one magazine article noted, Luciano was to the prostitution industry as John D. Rockefeller was to petroleum.

"Now, if a girl made $300 a week, she had to pay half to the madam," Dewey told the jury. "Also, she had to pay 10 percent of what remained to the booker and $5 a week to a doctor. Of the remaining $130, she had to pay $10 for a 'bond.' Often the bond and her board to the madam were combined. Then she paid, all told, $30 to $35 a week. Thus, of her gross earnings of $300, she had left to herself, $100." The bond was a key fee levied by the Commission, he explained, because it guaranteed that no prostitute would ever go to jail. The bond fees provided the main revenue for Luciano and his men, and Dewey hoped to show that the men on trial with Luciano made the actual collections but were merely the agents of Luciano.

Dewey had purposely transformed Luciano from a relatively unknown mob boss—known primarily in the underworld—to a celebrity of sorts; he became the human symbol of the wealth and power organized crime generated for those who control it. And while the public was anxious to see him on the stand, there was equal interest in hearing the stories of the women who served as the state's chief witnesses against him.

The first female witness Dewey called to the stand was Rose Cohen, twenty-five, who told her story candidly. She started working in a house operated by Molly Leonard after breaking up with her boyfriend, she said. She met Pete Harris in summer 1933, just before Luciano and his mob organized their vice ring. At first, Cohen earned more than $200 a week, but half of that went to the madam. Harris quickly became her booker, connecting her with various houses, charging her 10 percent of each transaction, and a general weekly expense, which varied from $2 to $4. Also, Cohen had to pay a weekly $10 "premium" for a type of jail insurance if she were arrested. Not surprisingly, Cohen did get arrested in 1935. She described how the lawyers in the bond office coached her what to say in court—that she was visiting from Philadelphia and worked in the sewing room of a large department store. It was a narrative Eunice Carter had heard often in magistrates' court and knew by heart.

Dewey's second witness was twenty-year-old Muriel Ryan, who had auburn hair and ivory skin. Ryan said she booked two years with Nick Montana, but changed bookers in 1934 to Pete Harris because she could make more money. She testified that she paid Harris a weekly commission, and each month worked two weeks and rested two weeks. She testified that she didn't pay Montana a bond until one day when he told her that she would have to begin to pay him one because "there was a new combination and all girls will have to pay from now on."

More witnesses gave testimony about their earnings in disorderly houses as the trial progressed. By the end of the first week, however, the most devastating testimony against Luciano and his henchmen came from a bespectacled madam named Jean Martin. To "persuade" individual madams to join the "combine," they were threatened with violence, she said. One of Luciano's men hit her with a lead pipe, knocking her out, and another jammed a pistol in her back and robbed her and another woman of their night's earnings. Finally, Martin joined the ring.

Another witness, Thelma Jordan, testified that women caught up with the vice mob were subject to torture that included the burning of body parts and slashing of tongues if it was determined that they talked too much. Jordan acknowledged that she was afraid to talk to Dewey's team and gave them information only after repeated interview requests. "I know what the combination does to girls who talk. Plenty of girls who talked too much have had their feet burned, and their stomach burned with cigarettes and the tongues cut," she said.

One key—and well-known—witness for the prosecution was Florence "Cokey Flo" Brown, a veteran of the New York streets and brothels and a known drug addict. Brown testified that she was the mistress of Luciano's second in command, codefendant Jimmy Fredericks. Brown's career in vice had started with her seduction by a businessman, who made her his mistress when she was fifteen years old. At eighteen, she became a prostitute and moved to Chicago, where she was "kept" by three men—each unaware of his rivals.

Her testimony reached its climax when she nonchalantly singled out Luciano as the driving force behind New York's vice ring. She had become the second witness to directly accuse Luciano. The first was Joe Bendix, who was serving a fifteen-year sentence in Sing Sing for theft at the time of the trial. Bendix said he had known Luciano when the crime boss offered him a job as "collector" for his syndicate. The prostitution business had been the subject of sixteen or eighteen conversations he had with Luciano over the last eight years, Bendix testified. Defense attorneys tried unsuccessfully to confuse him by having Luciano stand up, unidentified, but Bendix acknowledged that "this is the man I have been talking about. He said, 'when you are around collecting, and you'll get wise, you can make some extra money from the madams if you know a few tricks.'"

Brown testified that she had been a narcotics addict for six or seven years, and she had been either a prostitute or a brothel keeper for almost half of her twenty-nine years. She said she lived for more than one year with Luciano associate Fredericks, and as his girlfriend sat in on syndicate business meetings. What she heard at those meetings formed the basis of her testimony, she said. On cross-examination, defense attorneys tried a dramatic maneuver, demanding Judge McCook order that physicians examine her to determine whether she was under the influence of narcotics during her testimony. McCook granted the motion and called an abrupt recess—but not before Dewey requested that the prosecution be permitted to have its own physician present at the examination. That request was granted as well. Physicians for both defense and prosecution performed the examination and reported that she was not under the influence of drugs.

This was a crucial moment for Dewey. Although the dozens of witnesses before Brown helped paint a picture of the soul-robbing business of prostitution and detailed the nuts and bolts of its revenue structure, many of them were reluctant to admit they were prostitutes, and none said they ever met Luciano. Brown was able to recount meetings in which Luciano was present.

In addition to prostitutes and madams, Dewey had other weapons in his arsenal during the trial. Three soft-spoken employees of the Waldorf Astoria Hotel appeared in court and identified Luciano as "Mr. Charlie Ross" who had frequented the hotel's opulent tower apartment on the thirty-ninth floor; they linked him to three codefendants. A hotel maid, a

waiter, and the hotel manager testified that they had seen Jimmy Fredericks and "Little Abie" Wahrman, Luciano's right-hand man, visit Luciano's
lavish suite. They said hotel employees were horrified when they discovered the true identity of "Mr. Ross" and evicted him as soon as they saw his
photo in the newspapers in connection with the murder of Dutch Schultz.
The maid testified that she saw Wahrman, Fredericks, and a third defendant, bondsman Meyer Berkman, leaving Luciano's room. Overall, with
so much firsthand testimony that mobsters visited Luciano's suite, it was
becoming increasingly evident that Luciano was running a business from
his residence.

DEWEY'S TEAM was well aware that bringing in star witnesses like Brown
could be a gamble. On the one hand, their close contact with the defendants could bolster the prosecution's case immensely. On the other, under
the pressure of the witness stand, and in front of a jury, it was possible that
they would blurt out something unexpected or become tongue-tied. Prosecution witness Nancy Presser was an example of that gamble. She said she
had known Luciano for eight years and was his lover for six months, during
which he told her about his plans for the vice ring. And, indeed, Presser's
story about their intimacy waivered during hours of cross-examination by
Luciano's counsel. The attorneys got her to admit that she didn't know
much about the Waldorf suite's furnishings—including such details as to
whether there was a piano in Luciano's suite, what kind of beds were there,
and whether there was a refrigerator in the kitchen. "Come, Miss Presser,"
said defense attorney Samuel Siegel. "Just describe, as any woman would,
this bedroom you visited so often." To Dewey's disappointment, Presser
said, "Oh, I'm sure I can't." Then she said she felt ill. Judge McCook re-
cessed the trial for five minutes so she could gather herself. But Presser
didn't rally. She failed to describe Luciano's apartment at the Waldorf-
Astoria, but she insisted that she had intimate relations with him "a third
of the number of times" she saw him. In his memoir, Dewey writes that
he felt Presser did a good job on the stand and that she was frail from
drug withdrawal. She gave her testimony "bravely and without tremor," he
recalled decades later.

The last prominent witness Dewey brought out was Mildred Harris, the
red-haired wife of Pete Harris, who already pleaded guilty. She testified
how she pleaded with Luciano to let her husband leave the syndicate. "You
know he can't get out unless he pays the money he owes us," she said
Luciano told her. Mrs. Harris first sought to extricate her husband from

Luciano in 1935, but the mob boss refused, telling her, "You know the racket. Let him alone!" She also calmly informed the jury that she received death threats warning her not to testify. "I was on my way to Mr. Dewey's office with a policeman when I saw [Luciano assistant] Gus Franco coming," she said. "I asked the policeman to step aside so Gus wouldn't know I was in custody. Gus stepped up to me and told me that if I testified against these people, I would not live." Mrs. Harris once had an extramarital affair with Franco, she testified.

The appearance of Mrs. Harris signaled the close of the prosecution's case. Her testimony made up for some weak testimony by other prosecution witnesses, who claimed they could not remember some important details. Still, for two-and-one-half weeks, Dewey and his assistants—through the testimony of prostitutes, madams, bookers, and others—had been able to disclose the inner workings of a metropolitan vice syndicate whose income was about $1 million a month. Some of the female witnesses wore their "scarlet letters" proudly; some exhibited great shame on the witness stand; some were hardened madams with a lifetime's experience in the business. Some were barely out of their teens. Dewey managed to produce evidence connecting the defendants with administrative and executive activities of the vice ring and to show that Luciano was its supreme boss.

The defense would open its case the next day, and Dewey expected it to finish in two days. Meanwhile, Luciano announced his eagerness to take the stand and deny everything so he could get back to his everyday life. "All I'm thinking about is liberty. I always concentrate on one thing at a time, and now it's liberty," he told reporters, adding, "I don't even have time to play the ponies these days, or do a round of golf. I have more important things on my mind."

Counsel for Luciano spent the first day paving the way for his time on the stand in his own defense. Their first task was to introduce testimony designed to cast doubt on the credibility of two witnesses whom Dewey relied on to implicate Luciano as the vice syndicate chief. One was Joe Bendix, the first witness to identify Luciano as the boss who offered him a job collecting money from houses of prostitution; the other was Nancy Presser, who claimed she was Luciano's lover and as such had access to his residence and his secrets.

The defense counsel came back strongly by providing a letter Bendix wrote to his wife when in jail earlier in the year, asking her to "think up some real clever story to tell" that might be of interest to Dewey's assistant Raymond Ariola. Reading from the letters, the defense attorney said

Bendix had offered to give him some information concerning a robbery in exchange for reducing his latest alleged crime to a misdemeanor. In another letter to his wife, he told her to come up with ways to show his willingness to help Dewey's team. "The chances are he may not need it, but it will help nevertheless. . . . My implicit faith lies with him, and his promises are worth far more than coming from the other District Attorney's offices," he wrote. The defense was making the point that Bendix was willing to say anything to get a plea deal or to please Dewey's team.

Later, an assistant manager of the Waldorf Astoria Hotel gave brief but precise testimony that Nancy Presser could not have reached Luciano's suite on the thirty-ninth floor by taking the "ordinary elevators," as Presser testified. He said it was doubtful that Presser would have been able to go to the tower level of the hotel at 2 AM unless she announced herself to hotel personnel.

Defense lawyers also introduced the testimony of nearly a dozen professional gamblers who tried to build Luciano's reputation as a long-time gambler who had time for little else. They testified that during the last three years, when Dewey said Luciano was organizing the rackets, Luciano bet at racetracks nearly every afternoon and operated dice games at night. The gamblers, who acknowledged Luciano with smiles, testified that he was accustomed to laying bets of $200 to $500 on horse races and ran dice-game concessions. The defense claimed that Luciano had money because he knew how to pick the right ponies, not because he ran a prostitution ring.

Before any defendant took the stand, Jack Eller (also known as Jack Ellenstein), a minor booker of women, pleaded guilty. Eller's attorney declared that his client, who he said had a clean record, entered the plea because he wanted to pay the penalty for his crime. The most damaging evidence against Eller was that a prostitute said he booked her in a house even though he knew she was suffering from a social disease at the time.

Ralph Liguori, an alleged strong-arm man for the $12 million vice syndicate, was the first of eight defendants, along with Luciano, to testify on his own behalf. His attorney asked him if he knew Betty Anderson, one of the prostitutes he was supposed to have booked. "I did not," Liguori replied. "Did you ever place her in a house of prostitution?" the attorney asked. "I did not," Liguori said. "Did you ever receive money from the proceeds of her prostitution?" "I did not." The attorney asked the same questions about a dozen prostitutes who had testified that Liguori acted as their booker, but his reply was always the same: "I did not." He also denied knowing Luciano and the other defendants prior to the trial, except for Jimmy Fredericks, whom he knew "only by sight."

THERE WAS A RUSTLE of excitement through the courtroom when the clerk called out the name "Charles Luciano." The slim figure in the conservative gray business suit rose from the counsel table and walked up to the stand to be sworn in. Luciano, who was thirty-eight, wore a white shirt and a plain black tie. His wavy hair was shiny and neatly parted on the side. His jaw tightened as he placed his hand on the Bible, and he swore to tell the truth in the case against him for compulsory prostitution. In a low voice, he said his name was Charles Lucania, and he lived in the Waldorf Astoria. He said his mother died last August, and he had two brothers, one a hairdresser, the other a garment presser. He said he was convicted on narcotics charges when he was nineteen and got a six-month jail sentence. Luciano had insisted on taking the stand in the trial against the advice of his legal team. And, by the end of his four hours of testimony, he may have wished he had listened to his counsel.

On direct examination by his own counsel, George Levy, Luciano even made a joke. "Did you ever receive the earnings of a prostitute?" Levy asked. "I gave to them. I never took," Luciano responded. There was no laughter in the courtroom at this supposed gag line, and he didn't try again to be funny. He denied any knowledge of witnesses who had linked him closely to the vice racket—Nancy Presser, who described herself as his ex-lover; Cokey Flo Brown, in whom Luciano supposedly confided; Mildred Harris, wife of Pete Harris, who already pleaded guilty; and Joe Bendix, who claimed Luciano offered him a job with the syndicate.

"Before this trial started, how many of these defendants did you know or ever see?" Levy asked. "Only one—Davie Betillo." Luciano said he had known Betillo for eight or ten years. "What's your business?" Levy asked. "Gambling houses and booking horses," Luciano said. "Did you ever see any of these prostitutes and madams and others who took the stand and said they saw you?" Levy continued. "There hasn't been a witness that got on the stand except the Waldorf employees I never saw before," Luciano answered. "Did Davie Betillo ever visit you at the Waldorf in 1935?" Levy asked. "Yes, he wanted me to go into business with him running a gambling boat off Asbury Park or down there somewhere," Luciano answered. "Did you go into business with him?" "No." During his direct examination, Luciano denied all evidence indicating he was the ruthless czar of a massive vice ring. Levy also made much of the fact that his client had a record of only two previous convictions recorded against him. One of them, Luciano said, took place when he was only eighteen. At that time, he sold narcotics for three weeks and was caught and sentenced to eight months in a reformatory. In 1930, Luciano acknowledged he was arrested in Florida on a gambling charge and paid a $1,000 fine.

"Gentlemen, there is prostitution in New York and the evidence here is overwhelming that women were booked into houses and bonded," Levy concluded. "Whether the bonding was legal or illegal we are not concerned with. Luciano had nothing to do with prostitution, booking or bonding. That's where we stand."

Predictably, proceedings took a dramatic turn when Dewey began his cross-examination of Luciano. His cross-examination was something Dewey had been long planning—he knew he had to give the public the drama that they craved when it came to a match between the nation's leading gang buster and the underworld's evil genius. Dewey's main goal was to make Luciano reveal himself as the brutal underworld criminal he was rather than the suave, well-dressed businessman he pretended to be. And Dewey was extremely well-prepared. Small in stature—Dewey was five-feet-eight and of average weight—with his bland visage, thin dark moustache, and bushy eyebrows, he became a human dynamo during cross-examination. The former professional singer raised and lowered his voice several octaves, depending on the emotion he wished to convey. According to one magazine story, "he has a habit of rotating [his eyes] furiously to punctuate and emphasize his speech, expressing horror and surprise, but shooting them upward, cunning by sliding them from side to side. . . . At climactic moments he can pop them, almost audibly." And if he didn't like a ruling by the judge, he was an expert in expressing moral outrage, rising in his chair and questioning the judge in an irate tone: "You mean to say that . . . ?"

Dewey questioned Luciano carefully at first about his background selling narcotics but quickly caught him in several lies when Luciano said his drug arrests had been limited. Then Dewey pounced: "On June 2, 1923, do you remember selling a two-ounce box of morphine to John Lyons, an informant for the United States Secret Service?" Shocked that Dewey managed to dig up his past, Luciano lowered his voice and said, "I was arrested but I never sold any." Dewey didn't stop there. "On June 5, 1923, didn't you again sell some heroin to Lyons? Your apartment was searched at that time, and two one-half-ounce of morphine, two ounces of heroin and some opium was found," Dewey persisted. Luciano remained silent and shook his head. He was equally at a loss when Dewey brought up the subject of income tax. Luciano admitted that his first federal tax return was filed a year and a half ago because he had "suddenly decided to be honest." He said he didn't know why he had failed to pay state income tax, though Dewey suggested it was because he didn't fear the state much as he feared the federal government. At this point, Luciano began stuttering, admitting that he had lied frequently under oath about narcotics peddling and tax evasion. The existence of records and documents also seemed to trip up Luciano. When he denied knowing leaders of New York's different rackets, Dewey flashed telephone slips from the Waldorf Astoria, showing that calls had been made to them.

James Murray, one of the defense lawyers, tried to indicate that it was the bookers who had already pleaded guilty—and not the defendants in the trial—who took advantage of the prostitutes who testified. Murray, speaking for the bondsmen defendants, commended Dewey for bringing to justice the four bookers of women who had pleaded guilty. Murray contended the bookers were the ones responsible for the vice ring. He resorted to a unique and odd analogy to show that his clients had a legal right to accept bond payments from women:

> Suppose a fallen woman went to a large department store and said, "I am a prostitute and I want to buy a bed, a good strong bed, on which to practice my profession. I want to give you a down payment from the fruits of my earnings as a prostitute and I shall pay the remainder from what I earn with this bed." If a prostitute went to a store with such a story, the salesman would have every legal right to take her money. The bed would be a legal consideration. When [bondsman] Jesse Jacobs put up his own money to bail out these women he gave a legal consideration and is no more guilty of compulsory prostitution than would be the department store I have cited.

By the time it rested its case, the defense had called forty-eight witnesses, including two policemen who testified they wouldn't believe anyone connected with the vice racket, even under oath.

In Dewey's six-hour closing, he acknowledged the hard work his team put into the investigation. "This case has not been pleasant for me or my fine young assistants. It has not been pleasant to deal for four-and-a-half months with gangsters, pimps, madams, and prostitutes and to hold their hands and try to keep them from repudiating their testimony once they were in court," Dewey said. He wanted to convey to the jury that the prosecutors had extremely stressful and dangerous jobs: "I wonder if any one of you has ever dealt with sheer, stark terror? Have you ever been faced by complete and paralyzing terror? Have you ever had to sit down to attempt to alleviate terror? We had to," he said.

Dewey told the jury that Luciano was "a monster fattening on the profits of the bodies of women." He painstakingly reviewed the evidence presented during the four-week trial before yielding to Judge McCook, who read instructions to the jurors for two hours and forty-one minutes. In his charge, Judge McCook analyzed the testimony of the month-long trial in detail. "The State has put on the stand pimps, bookers, madams, prostitutes and convicts. The majority were women taken in adultery. A prostitute is at once a victim, and one who entices and her life is full of lies. I will not tell you these women are beyond belief, but their testimony must be corroborated," he said.

Now Luciano's fate was placed in the hands of the jurors. The blue-ribbon jury deliberated all night, and at 5:30 AM, after six-and-one-half hours, they announced their verdict to Judge McCook. It turned out jurors had disagreed at one point about the innocence of Luciano himself. They were unanimous in their conviction of his nine codefendants but at first voted nine to three for the conviction of Luciano. In their second ballot, only one juror held out in Luciano's favor; but the third ballot brought the unanimous decision of guilty for all defendants on all sixty-two counts. Luciano and nine codefendants were found guilty of compulsory prostitution, facing penalties of twenty-five years on each count. Predictably, it was Luciano's guilt that dominated the front pages of New York newspapers that day: "Lucky's luck runs out," the *New York Daily News* screamed. "Luciano and Lieutenants in Vice Ring, Each of Whom Faces 1,865 Years in Prison," read the *New York World-Telegram*'s headline.

Dewey, ever the public relations man (and future political candidate), issued a statement immediately after Luciano's conviction, which ran in the New York City newspapers:

> This, of course, was not a vice trial. It was a racket prosecution. The control of all organized prostitution in New York by the convicted defendants was one of their lesser rackets. The four bookers of women who pleaded guilty were underlings. The prostitution racket was merely the vehicle by which these men were convicted. It is my understanding that certain of the top-ranking defendants in this case, together with the other criminals under Lucania [*sic*], have gradually absorbed control of the narcotic, policy, loan shark and Italian lottery syndicates, the receipt of stolen goods and certain industrial rackets.

In the public statement, Dewey also praised his assistants for their months of hard work. In an editorial, the *New York Daily News* expressed admiration for Dewey, reminding readers that the Luciano conviction represented the first time racketeers had actually been convicted for crimes involving racketeering. It said that the usual method had been for the government to go after them on charges of evading their income taxes—"a wrong and hypocritical procedure," it said. "Altogether, a racket-ridden city owes Mr. Dewey the well-known debt of gratitude," the editorial said.

Judge McCook sentenced Luciano to serve thirty to fifty years in state prison for his leadership of a vice syndicate that preyed upon the proceeds of compulsory prostitution. His sentence was more severe than that of the others, and some believed it was excessive, due in part to the publicity the trial generated.

The *Daily News* editorial symbolized in many ways the love affair between Dewey and the press. In addition to cultivating editors to make sure they did not publish too much information during the investigation, Dewey appeared to have persuaded reporters to take at face value some of the legal procedures he employed before and during the trial. Some of these would be considered shaky or are illegal today. For instance, the concept of the blue-ribbon jury consisting primarily of the same type of persons—in this case, professional or upper-class White males—cannot be used today in criminal trials because it denies defendants their right to a jury of their peers. But perhaps more important was the way that Dewey treated most of the witnesses for the prosecution. Most were prostitutes he arrested in secret round-ups, and his strategy to make them talk was to keep them isolated from their families and lawyers for days and jail them indefinitely until they agreed to link Luciano to the vice ring. This controversial technique was never revealed in newspaper coverage, but it was brought up multiple times during the trial. On cross-examination, some of Dewey's witnesses admitted that they were threatened with prison time if they didn't agree to name Luciano, and Dewey's men questioned the witnesses so many times that they lost track of what they had told them. These factors, if brought to light, might have generated controversy around Dewey and the trial. Surprisingly, it seemed as though reporters made a conscious decision to omit the vital elements of the trial, only fixating on the witnesses' sensational accounts of Luciano's threat to "cut tongues and burn feet."

One of the explanations of the uncritical coverage of the trial could be Dewey's relationship with the reporters. The *New York Herald Tribune's* beat reporter Hickman Powell, who followed Luciano's trial from its inception to the jury verdict, was a good friend of Dewey's. He wrote in his book *Ninety Times Guilty*—the most complete account of the Luciano trial—that Dewey gave him a front seat at the trial. Powell later worked for Dewey for years as a volunteer speechwriter and researcher, and in 1943 he was rewarded with a paid position on Dewey's staff, probably in preparation for Dewey's 1944 presidential run. In 1950, Dewey appointed him to the New York State Power Authority, which compensated him on a per diem basis. In 1951, Dewey created a six-member committee on water and land resources and named Hickman to it.

TO SAY THAT the Luciano prosecution rocketed Dewey to fame would not be hyperbole. He was voted second only to Walt Disney as *Time's* "Man of the Year" for 1936, and he immediately became an overnight sensation, starring in newsreels of the era, fueling the public's fascination with underworld figures and dashing crime fighters and inspiring Hollywood movies. In 1937, studios hastened the release of *Marked Woman*, which starred Humphrey Bogart as a fearless district attorney who fought the mob and Bette Davis as the woman who bravely testified against a brutal mob boss. When Dewey's investigation began, a radio drama called *G-Men* debuted on NBC radio. It was renamed *Gang Busters* after the trial. A year after Luciano's prosecution, New Yorkers recognized Dewey as the man who made the most outstanding contribution to the welfare of the city.

Naturally, Dewey touted his record as a heroic crime fighter to further his political ambitions, and Republicans in New York were happy to feed the narrative. One magazine article noted that his gang-busting persona was now present in all his interactions: "His private and public conversation always mentioned the menace of the underworld, omnipresent, almost omnipotent, crouched for a leap."

As it would turn out, though, the verdict in the Lucky Luciano vice case did not signal the end of the relationship between the crafty and brilliant criminal and the wily hard-working prosecutor. Their paths would cross again, and their fates would once again be linked.

8

"Making History for the Race"

AFTER THE LUCIANO TRIAL, Eunice's hard work—and dedication to Thomas E. Dewey—would pay off. By spring 1937, Luciano was safely behind bars, and Dewey indicated to friends and associates that his work as a public servant was finished. He said he was ready to leave the public sphere to earn a better living to support his wife and, now, two small sons. But most people who knew him were well aware that the crafty Dewey had other plans. He was considering entering politics, perhaps on a grand scale, considering the public's grateful response to his prosecution of Lucky Luciano. And when he made the final decision that year to remain in the public sphere, Eunice was there with him.

District attorney William C. Dodge had announced in early 1937 that he would not seek reelection, and by this time, Tammany Hall control of the city had dissipated somewhat. Still, Dewey was characteristically coy about his decision to stay in public office, although he was well aware that he now had a high profile and that New Yorkers viewed him as a heroic crime fighter.

As Dewey biographer Richard Norton Smith tells it, after the Luciano trial, Dewey adopted the posture of a weary public servant anxious to return to private practice and his family after a strenuous tenure as special prosecutor. (And that was believable—as special prosecutor, he rarely worked less than a twelve- or fourteen-hour day, and he and his family were continually surrounded by bodyguards. His wife, Frances, began having a series of minor health problems at the time, indicating her unhappiness with their life.) The reality, however, was different. Dewey was at first reluctant to run for New York prosecutor. Still, he made it clear he could be persuaded if city officials, the newspapers, and Republican leaders indicated that he was their top choice and would give him unqualified support. It was true that many Republicans wanted Dewey to run, believing that he might be one of the few Republicans to have a chance at winning the district attorney's job in heavily Democratic New York. It had been twenty-five years since a Republican—Charles Whitman—was elected district attorney in New York City, and party registration records showed 563,000 registered Democrats and only 122,000 registered Republicans in New York City. Dewey was adamant that he would have to have a clear path to victory—otherwise, he feared he would be branded a loser, a label that could taint any future political runs. His friend and mentor George Medalie advised him against it.

When Dewey did decide to run for New York district attorney, he launched his campaign with characteristic zeal, energy, and single-mindedness. And some of what he did ran counter to accepted Republican orthodoxy. He began by courting the city's myriad ethnic voters—including the city's Jewish population—and dispatched some of his assistants, including Eunice, to host rallies and urge people to register to vote. (His efforts to court the ethnic vote were more characteristic of Democrats than Republicans of the era.) No detail was too small, including the installation of phone banks operated day and night by campaign callers and endless rallies by the candidate himself, who honed his image as a friend of the working person. In another move uncharacteristic of Republicans, he attended union rallies and the signing of new contracts by union workers. All of this paid off—Dewey's campaign chest rose to $130,000 (about $2.5 million today), and his biggest contributors were, interestingly, the Rockefellers and the International Ladies Garment Workers Union.

Dewey was a natural public relations man who knew exactly how to hone his crowd-pleasing image. In rallies, he framed himself as the tireless mob buster who defeated Lucky Luciano and Dutch Schultz and kept the streets of New York safe. As special prosecutor, he learned that radio addresses got results, so, with this smooth and melodious voice, he used the radio to court prospective voters. In the end, Dewey was elected as one of New York County's five district attorneys, and on December 31, 1937, in the Criminal Courts Building in Manhattan, he was sworn in. His wife and mother attended the small ceremony.

NOT SURPRISINGLY, the newly elected district attorney immediately instituted changes to the offices at 137 Centre Street, a building across the street from the Criminal Courts Building and down the street from the prison known as The Tombs. When it came to hiring, he indicated that loyalty was a two-way street for him—those who served him well in his previous job were first in line for jobs in his new office. Of Dodge's sixty-four assistant prosecutors, he kept only three; one man because he was very near retirement and pension eligibility; John McDonnell because he had a steel plate in his head due to his distinguished service in France in World War I; and Felix Benvenga, because, in Dewey's opinion, he was a fine attorney (who would go on to become a judge).

He also rearranged the structure of the office to mimic the organization of his special prosecutor's office, a structure that would remain in place for decades. He moved what was the rackets investigation office in the special prosecutor's office into a permanent part of the district attorney's office. Fellow Luciano racket buster Murray Gurfein was put in charge. Because Dewey had long believed that illegal complex business transactions and stock fraud had never received the attention they deserved in the prosecutor's office, he put seven assistant district attorneys in a new Frauds Bureau, and he named another of his mob busters, Barent Ten Eyck, to head it.

He also wanted more emphasis on three existing offices. One he labeled the "workhouse" bureau, the General Sessions Bureau, which handled more than three thousand felony cases a year; the Homicide Bureau, which was open twenty-four hours a day; and the Special Sessions Bureau, which handled fourteen thousand misdemeanor cases a year. Running that last bureau were two more mob busters who had previously worked with Dewey: Sol Gelb and Eunice Carter. With the appointment, the latter would become the first Black female assistant prosecutor in New York. Within a month of taking office, Dewey named another woman to the office—Florence Kelley, who assumed the title of "law assistant" and whose job would be to assist "the only other woman appointee on Mr. Dewey's staff . . . Mrs. Eunice H. Carter, a Negro, of 103 West 141st St.," according to the *New York Herald Tribune*. Kelley, a Smith College graduate like Eunice, would earn $1,500 a year (about $27,000 in 2020 dollars). The story notes that she is the daughter of Nicholas Kelley, who was assistant secretary of the Treasury under Woodrow Wilson and the granddaughter of Florence Kelley, founder of the Consumers' League of New York and a social worker who was a colleague of Jane Addams at Hull House in Chicago.

Eunice's appointment to Dewey's staff made her a minor celebrity almost instantly. As was the case in the special prosecutor's office, she was the only Black attorney in the prosecutor's office. Within about two months of Dewey's election, she was labeled by the media as one of the highest-paid—and one of the most respected—attorneys in the city. "I Earn $5,500 Per Year," ran a headline in the (Baltimore) *Afro-American* in March 1938, quoting Eunice. (The amount would equal about $103,000 in 2020 dollars.) The story goes into great detail about Eunice's daily life as an assistant prosecutor, as well as a bit about her personal life, focusing on her long hours and dedication to her job. It begins: "Eunice Hunton Carter, the first woman appointed to the staff of New York's racket-busting district attorney, Thomas E. Dewey, and for a time the only woman member of his staff, draws a salary of $5,500 a year but admits that it takes training, much of which she acquired after becoming a housewife, indefatigable energy and twelve hours a day on the job, to do it." The story notes that the thirty-seven-year-old Eunice begins her twelve-hour days at 8:30 AM when she drives to work and her third-floor office. She immediately consults with her assistants—"all of whom are white"—about that day's work and then walks to the Special Sessions Court, where she works until 1 PM. She occasionally goes out for lunch at that time, the story said, but usually has it sent up to her while she works at her desk. At 2 PM, she is back in court, where she stays until 5 PM and then returns to her office, where she talks to witnesses, interviews police officers, and dictates to her secretary until about 7 PM. At least three nights a week, she works until about 11 PM and eats her dinner downtown, the story said.

The story also discusses her life as a "housewife" and mother of a young son. Her mother (who was mistakenly called "Annie") is a "prominent clubwoman" who wanted her daughter to be a teacher, but she instead took after her father, who was "the first paid colored YMCA secretary" in Norfolk. The story goes on to describe her college years at Smith, and later at Fordham Law School, and to outline the steps that led to her appointment by Dewey to his special prosecutor's office—including the pivotal link she detected between prostitution and the mob. Interestingly, it describes Eunice's legal philosophy and what led to her success as a prosecutor in Dewey's special prosecutor's office: "A good prosecutor must be absolutely honest. . . . He must win the respect of witnesses if he would gain their confidence. He must make few promises, but those promises he does make, he must back them up with his honor." The story says that it is this straightforward attitude that gained her the trust and confidence of witnesses who ultimately testified against Lucky Luciano. "This woman, who allows no feminine frills and sentimentalities to sway her from an objective handling of the cases that come before her, could not be bought off."

Little had been written in detail in newspapers about Eunice's private life, other than she was married to a dentist from Barbados and had one child. This story quotes her as saying that son Lisle Jr., who was then twelve, spent much of his time in his father's native Barbados, ostensibly because the climate was beneficial to his health. (It had been speculated that because of her job, she felt he would be safer if he did not live with her.) The story also mentioned Eunice's brother, Alphaeus, who was then an English instructor at Howard University. Her dedication to her job keeps her from indulging in most hobbies, the story said, although she enjoys playing bridge, reading, "and goes in for horseback riding to keep her figure under control." Stephen Carter notes in his biography that Eunice had a passion for sports that was not mentioned in the story. She particularly enjoyed baseball and boxing.

The story did not explicitly mention—but it certainly implied—that Eunice's long workdays did not leave much room for a personal life. In reality, her relationship with her husband had long been strained, and her son indicated decades later that he believed they had been separated when he returned from Barbados as a teenager. Stephen Carter writes that she may have had a longtime affair with jazz musician Fletcher Henderson, who was also married. He writes that it would be unlikely that Addie would have known about the affair, and that she would be mortified if she did. Interestingly, at least one acquaintance of Eunice's indicated in her diary that she believed Eunice might have been gay, although there appears to be nothing else to support this. In a passage from her published diaries, writer and activist Alice Dunbar-Nelson, who was active in the Harlem Renaissance, wrote that at a social gathering in Harlem in 1928, Eunice and someone named Anne Dingle "were very much together." (Dunbar-Nelson wondered in the entry if they were a lesbian couple). Addie may have been mortified had she known, but years earlier, she herself had been the object of gossip columns in the Black press. In 1924, she was sued for divorce after a year of marriage to Captain James Floyd of Jacksonville, Florida, who sued her for desertion. "On account of the high social standing of the couple, the reported suit elicited much comment," the *Pittsburgh Courier* reported. It also said that the marriage apparently failed because Addie was not willing to relocate to Florida because of its "rabid race prejudice." The story also included a tidbit that "it is said that the 'wealth' of the captain was not what it was reported to be."

The last tantalizing item about the supposed wealth of Floyd was intriguing; on and off during her adulthood, Addie had worried about money. By this time, concern about money was not a problem for Eunice. And it was a good thing—she had a taste for expensive clothes, jewelry, and elaborate vacations, according to Stephen Carter. And she—and her son—always flew in first class.

If Eunice was preoccupied with her job, her husband, Lisle, also spent much of his time with his dentistry practice and work with civic causes. In addition to work with the National Urban League, YMCA, and NAACP, Dr. Carter was also in many professional dentistry groups, including the American Dental Association, International Dental Association, and others. According to his obituary, he devoted much of his time helping to improve dental services to Harlem residents and worked with young dentists there, sometimes helping them financially with their education. He had been president of the North Harlem Dental Society. Stephen Carter writes that based on information from Lisle Jr., his father, there is little doubt that his marriage to Eunice was not a happy one, but that the two apparently agreed to stay together in part to avoid upsetting him and Addie. When Lisle was a child, the couple began to take separate vacations and stopped appearing together at social events. He also writes that neither Eunice nor Lisle Sr. was anxious to raise their son on a day-to-day basis, which is why Lisle Jr. spent much of his youth in Barbados. Stephen Carter attributes this to the fact that she too had spent much of her youth living not with her parents but with relatives. Stephen Carter also quotes his father as saying that as a child, Lisle Jr. always felt that his parents wanted him to be seen and not heard.

Eunice's career soared after the trial and the public plaudits for her kept coming. She and two other Smith College alumni were given honorary degrees during a ceremony at that college in Northampton, Massachusetts. Eunice received the Doctor of Laws degree during the 1938 commencement ceremony, becoming the first Black woman to receive that honor. Eunice, class of 1921, had a "distinguished record as an undergraduate [that] has been followed by seventeen years of public service, by which her brilliant abilities have been devoted to the welfare of her city and have brought high credit to her college and to her race," according to the college. Other women receiving honorary degrees were a former director of religion and social work at Smith and head of a seminary; a Chicago surgeon; and a professor of history at Mount Holyoke College.

The prestige of this honorary degree, combined with her pioneering appointment by Dewey and her high profile as a crime buster, earned Eunice even more publicity in 1938. *Opportunity*, the magazine that had published her reviews and short stories when she was in her twenties, published two long stories about her in the 1930s—one in August 1936, when she worked in the special prosecutor's office, and one a few months after she received the honorary degree. Both took up an entire page of the magazine, and both were glowing. The first praised her lavishly for her work with Dewey prosecuting the mob: "There is a gifted young woman . . . who is playing an important role in the fight that is being waged by the organized forces of law and order in New York City to crush racketeering," the story begins. "This young woman, Mrs. Eunice Hunton Carter, has been in the practice of law only a little over four years but in the brief period she has maintained the brilliant record which she made as a student at Smith College and in later years in the field of social work." The story goes into great detail about her parents' work and her studies at Smith and Fordham: "She had begun the study of law while engaged in a full-time social work job, an indication of her exceptional ability which had been apparent in her college career and in social work." The article also mentions her work with Dewey, her unsuccessful political run, and her dedication to the betterment of Harlem. It ends: "A persuasive speaker, a trenchant writer, a profound student of political and social conditions, [she] has the courage but not the foolhardiness of youth. There can be no question that she will go far. She is on her way."

Two years later, the magazine again was lavish in its praise, announcing in an editorial the honorary degree she received, and calling it "one of the most significant events that has occurred in the history of Negro women in America." It also praises Smith College, which it said had "courage" to give the degree to a Black person—and one who had an ancestor who was a slave: "By this act it reaffirms its position of leadership in the education of women in America without regard to racial theories, which have all but destroyed intellectual freedom in Europe; with fine disdain for the absence of precedence; with high courage which in the precedent day is all too rare among those who administer our university and colleges, Smith dared to bestow its greatest gift to a young colored woman whose ancestors less than a century ago were held in bondage." The writer elaborates on what he or she believed were the profound ramifications of the honor given to Eunice: "No one can measure the far-reaching effect of this act on the education of colored women. No one can estimate how much it will do to elevate the status of those among all women who have been called up to suffer and to sacrifice most." It ends by saying that nothing taught at Smith could contribute to "the advancement of womanhood" as much as giving this honorary degree to someone like Eunice.

Black publications of the era made it a practice to write lavishly about the accomplishments of people like Eunice in part to publicize their work, but partly because editors felt that the subjects served as role models for others. Shortly after the *Afro-American* story about Eunice was published ("I Earn $5,500"), the *Chicago Defender* published a three-paragraph item proclaiming that Eunice "is making history for the Race" as a top official in Dewey's prosecutor's office. "This is the first time a Race attorney has ever been given the spot of trial attorney in this court in behalf of the people of the state of New York," the story said. "Being placed in the spot by a Republican administration, it is now believed that the next Democratic administration in the city will be forced to give the Race such a place." Within a short time, Dewey appointed two more Black attorneys to his office: James Yergen and Francis "Frank" Rivers.

Eunice's national stature as an attorney and public official rose dramatically in 1938 to the point that she was featured in a special section of *Life* magazine in October titled, "Negroes: The U.S. Also Has a Minority Problem." The magazine offered a listing of twenty of the nation's "Distinguished Negroes," which included public officials, poets, composers, writers, and others. Included in the group is Eunice: "Dewey's smartest, most effective attorney," it says. Others included on the list are writer Langston Hughes, scientist George Washington Carver, musician Duke Ellington, writer-editor W. E. B. Du Bois, actor Paul Robeson, and labor leader-activist Asa Philip Randolph. The only other woman on the list was opera singer Marion Anderson.

The special section seems condescending by today's standards. However, its tone and content indicate that Black people in the United States still had far to go to achieve anything resembling equality with their White counterparts. The story noted that seventy-five years had passed since Abraham Lincoln signed the Emancipation Proclamation, a time when there were four million Black people in the United States; in 1938, that number had grown to fourteen million. The status of those fourteen million, the story states, refutes the idea that all men are created free and equal: "The Negro may be free but in no way—economically, politically, socially—is he the white man's equal." In American society at the time, Black people had two stark choices, the story said. They could be assimilated and "merge into the life and ways of the white man," or they can "boldly build, within the white civilization, a black civilization of his own. Either solution seems unattainable in the time of any living generation."

The story describes the way Black people of the era were viewed by many Whites. "Few [White people] know the Negro. He is recognized as the bale-heaving stevedore chanting the unhappy songs of a happy-go-lucky race," the story says. "Or as the crapshooter who has given America a picturesque jargon; or as the hysteric convert, or as the old 'darky' who has borrowed trappings, bearing and beard of the Southern colonel and thus created a caricature of his old massa."

For reasons that may seem ironic today, *Life* editors said they published the series to help dispel these stereotypes and to illustrate the lifestyles and many accomplishments of Black people of the era: "The white man will, however, be surprised at the achievements of the Negro in America, some of which are set forth on the following pages." In addition to its twenty most distinguished Negros listing, it provided small photos and biographical information about such leading Black figures as Frederick Douglass, Booker T. Washington, Phyllis Wheatley, and others. It provided photos and information about primarily Black higher-education institutions like Howard, Hampton, and Talladega. It also published information and photos of Black persons' participation in the arts, athletics, labor, the armed forces, journalism, and societal events.

But the series is far from upbeat and instead offers a graphic and chilling history lesson. It explains in detail and with diagrams how Black people were brought to America through the slave trade, noting the horrific and inhumane conditions on the ships, where one in five people died. And, primarily through photos, it illustrated the lives of slaves in the United States, showing how abysmal living conditions were commonplace.

Another part of the series notes that the political landscape for Blacks of the era had started to shift in the early 1930s—many Black people left the party of Lincoln for the party of Roosevelt: "Today . . . the Negro is forgetting the party of the man who released him from bondage and is going over to the party of the forgotten man and the New Deal." This switch away from the Republican Party would represent a pivotal philosophical turn for many Black people in the United States. Four months earlier, the magazine had published an extensive series, complete with charts and photos, about the overwhelming appeal of the New Deal for poor Americans and Blacks. "Negroes Like Roosevelt and the New Deal Best," the headline read. The series used results of a *Fortune* magazine poll about the popularity of Roosevelt's government program among Blacks and poor and middle-class Whites. "The American's vote has always been affected by the amount of money in his pockets, but never before has this factor counted for so much as under the New Deal. . . . There have always been more poor than well-to-do people. It remained for Roosevelt to unite the less prosperous, waken them to their political strength."

Many Black people had indeed begun questioning their allegiance to the Republican Party—or any organized political group, for that matter— as early as the 1920s. In 1920, at its annual convention, the National Association of Colored Women declined to pass a resolution endorsing Republican candidates, in part because some speakers labeled the party racist, while others criticized the party platform because it did not take a tough stand against lynching. In 1928, W. E. B. Du Bois summed up the attitudes of many Black people in an editorial in *The Crisis* when he questioned whether either party truly represented them, particularly in the South. Activist and writer Oswald Villard echoed those thoughts seven years later, writing that Roosevelt's New Deal initiatives helped White people far more than they helped Blacks. Villard said that the Socialist Party was the political party that was without racial prejudice—although he acknowledged it was unlikely the party would gain any real traction with voters, Black or White.

Still, under Roosevelt, race and inequality became national issues and ones in which the federal government would become involved. In 1935, two years into his term, Roosevelt had established several federal agencies and programs, including the Works Progress Administration that employed hundreds of thousands of Black workers. The National Youth Administration hired more Black administrators than any other New Deal agency, and in 1934 the Public Works Administration required all government construction contracts to establish a quota for the hiring of Black laborers based on the 1930 US Census. For women like Addie Hunton, her daughter Eunice, and the thousands of Black clubwomen in the United States, the most notable achievement of President Roosevelt—and First Lady Eleanor Roosevelt—was to acknowledge racism publicly and make it a national issue. It marked the first time since Reconstruction that grievances by Blacks were taken seriously with "sympathetic understanding and interpretation," according to educator and activist Mary McLeod Bethune, who had led the National Association of Colored Women. Bethune's appointment by the president as head of the National Youth Administration's Division of Negro Affairs and the appointment of others in what Bethune labeled his "black Cabinet"—consisting of about a dozen high-ranking Black administrators—symbolized a major move toward racial equality.

Bethune became a close friend of the Roosevelts, a status that gave her a critical voice in shaping the administration's efforts toward racial equality. The hard-working Bethune was also a talented and astute judge of people, and, through diplomacy and persuasion, she became an active government administrator and social activist—and someone who vocally encouraged Blacks of the era to switch their political allegiance to the Democratic Party. Bethune, with twenty other Black women, founded the National Council of Negro Women (NCNW), a coalition of twenty-nine organizations, including fourteen Black women's groups. The formation of the NCNW was the culmination of five years of efforts by leaders of the clubwomen's movement to unify the diverse Black organizations that had many of the same goals. Bethune believed that a strong umbrella organization like the NCNW was needed to provide leadership and help set goals for Black women. Her relationship with Eleanor Roosevelt gave the newly formed organization legitimacy and power. At the Southern Conference on Human Welfare in 1938, held in Birmingham, Alabama, Eleanor Roosevelt requested a seat next to Bethune despite state segregation laws—a symbolic act that many viewed as a testament to the close bond between the two women. Mrs. Roosevelt referred to Bethune as "her closest friend in her age group."

With Bethune as its president and with the help of many of her friends and devoted activists, including Addie Hunton, the NCNW became a well-organized, smooth-running, and influential group. It dealt with many political, cultural, and social issues but emphasized education, child care, child welfare, and labor issues. It was concerned primarily with employment issues during its first few years of existence, and it spent much effort starting a way to document and archive its activities.

The culmination of the group's early efforts came in April 4, 1938, at its national meeting in the North Interior building of the White House. The group was received by Eleanor Roosevelt. The main topic was the improvement of welfare programs for women and children, but the women also discussed federal aid programs for the elderly and handicapped, housing, and unemployment. "The purpose of the session was to discuss the extent to which women and children may share in various federal social welfare programs with a view to promoting larger participation and closer integration of the Race into the entire federal program," the *Chicago Defender* wrote. Both Addie and Eunice attended.

Correspondence between Bethune and Mrs. Roosevelt indicates that theirs was a close and, to some degree, informal relationship. It also shows the influence of Bethune on Mrs. Roosevelt's thoughts and actions. In one letter, Bethune thanks Mrs. Roosevelt for her birthday wishes and tells her that she is "happy" that the president appointed Earl Dickerson "to a post so many of us desired for him." (Dickerson was an attorney and civil rights activist who was appointed by Roosevelt to the Fair Employment Practices Committee.) In the same letter, she invites the First Lady to an NCNW conference about national defense in Washington: "Now, listen, Mrs. Roosevelt," she writes, the attendees will include "our sororities; our college and professional women, national nurses, our church women; our fraternal women; women in business and industry, all classes of women. . . . We need you again this year." She went on to say that it would be Mrs.

Roosevelt's "one opportunity to stimulate and encourage the Negro Womanhood of America. We would like for you to have them at the White House as you did last year and we want you to be their guest speaker at their dinner."

Bethune's correspondence offers a glimpse into the intricate organizational structure and specific goals of the NCNW—a structure that would be impressive for any government entity or private business but is even more so considering the group was an organization made up primarily of volunteers. The organization also took seriously its publication, the *Aframerican Women's Journal*, a slick and sophisticated magazine that carried news and photos about past events of the group, profiles, and information about current members, and articles about current issues. (The journal was renamed *Women United* in 1949.) It also periodically devoted entire issues to specific topics, such as "defense," "women face the post–world war," "reveille for humanity, justice, freedom" and others. Interestingly, the group also worked hard for admission of Black women into the Women's Air Corps (WAC) and Women Accepted for Voluntary Emergency Service (WAVES). Stories after NCNW conferences offered detailed information on those conferences, including information about complex legal matters. Eunice, a longtime board member of the group, often handled the group's legal work. The magazine also published details of conference proceedings, goals, and future activities. For instance, its primary goals for the year were outlined in a special conference issue in January 1941. They included immediate passage of an anti-lynching bill; extension of the Social Security Act to include domestic and agricultural workers; extension of the federal Wages and Hours law to include domestic workers; and "putting teeth" into a law that prohibited discrimination in hiring at plants receiving defense contracts. Three years later, in 1944, the world had changed dramatically, as had the goals of the NCNW. The advent of World War II brought with it the growing problem of child labor: "Two and one half million children are now employed in America," according to an account of the conference in the magazine. "There is a need for an urging back to school campaign for boys and girls in their teens." The story also mentioned that Eunice had chaired a panel discussing "The Negro in the Armed Forces," a group that included activist Roy Wilkins and her brother, Alphaeus. Various issues of the *Aframerican Women's Journal* list Eunice as a "life member" of the group, chair of multiple committees, and chair of its committee of laws. Indeed, she did much of the group's legal work during her tenure as a member. In fact, despite its large membership, the organization apparently relied on only a handful of women to conduct most of its business and ensure its longevity. Historical accounts of the group indicate that it was often the same group of women who did the "heavy lifting" of the group—planning and administration. Bethune was the group's president from 1935 to 1949, and a handful of others shared administrative duties. Dorothy Height, who would become NCNW president and who was a longtime board member, said in an oral history interview that many of the women who joined the organization at its founding and shortly thereafter worked for the group until they became successful and no longer needed it for contacts or to pad their resumes. But, she added, Eunice was not one of those women: "[Some] women saw the Council as a kind of launching pad, and when they could no longer use it just for that, then it didn't have any place for them," she said. "They liked to be there when Mrs. Bethune could have all the glamor around . . . but they don't like to be there when you just have to get in and dig." Height said she established a longtime friendship with Eunice: "Eunice Carter had a very good mind. Eunice Carter was one of the few who remained with the Council for a number of years."

Based on stories in the *Aframerican Women's Journal* and Bethune's correspondence, the group did take care of its own—especially if they provided service to it. For instance, in its Summer and Fall 1940 edition, the magazine published a four-hundred-word profile of Addie, complimenting her service to groups such as the NAACP, YWCA, and NCNW: "[Addie] would be the choice of younger women over the country who were called upon to exercise selective judgment in choosing their ideal of perfect balance in wife-mother and career woman." The article noted that she had been the perfect "helpmate" for her husband as he traveled across the country with his YMCA job. "Traveling with Mr. Hunton, which took her practically everywhere, or remaining at home, during his frequent absences, she became the tower of strength, filling his place at home and sending him bright, heart-warming messages." The story notes that Addie successfully combined a professional career with a family life—implying that such a balance is important—and it goes into detail about the careers of Eunice and Alphaeus. "Laurels go to Mrs. Hunton, who must look back upon her years with quiet satisfaction." And papers of the NCNW indicate that it honored Eunice for her work at least once—a 1955 letter from NCNW Region One Director Daisy George to Bethune noted that at a twenty-fifth anniversary celebration of the group, Eunice would be honored at a special breakfast for the group's past presidents.

Eunice's life was full as she began working for her friend and boss, Thomas E. Dewey, in the prosecutor's office. In addition to having a job that took up most of her time, she also maintained a home, continued her activism, and remained close to her mother, who in 1936 likely turned seventy (her exact birth date is uncertain), and was becoming increasingly frail. Eunice's job as assistant prosecutor meant not only working in the office but helping to further Dewey's political ambitions, a task she was happy to undertake. Still, while many of her friends in Harlem and the NCNW were turning away from the party of Lincoln, Eunice remained a committed Republican.

9

"A Prelude to Greater Tasks"

EUNICE CARTER WAS accustomed to working hard, but for the first time in her life after the mob trial, her efforts drew praise from an influential person—Thomas E. Dewey—and, in turn, from the public. Her work with Roosevelt confidante Mary McLeod Bethune and the National Council of Negro Women was intensifying at a time when that group's priorities appeared to be at odds with the Republican-led prosecutor's office in which Eunice worked. She continued to be active in Republican politics, though at a time when many Black people had switched their political allegiance to the Democratic Party. When Eunice joined the prosecutor's office, she did more than just legal work for Dewey—she helped further his political career.

Not surprisingly, within a year of Dewey's election to the district attorney's office, he was eyeing a much higher office: the governorship of New York. Buoyed by his ongoing public image as a fearless gang buster and his recent and relatively easy victory in the prosecutor's race, he decided to take on incumbent Governor Herbert Lehman. Of course, given the Byzantine nature of New York politics in the 1930s, he knew he could not do it alone. Ultimately, he earned the support of influential state Republican Party chairman Edwin Jaeckle, and even though the two were opposites in temperament, their alliance would help further Dewey's political career. (Jaeckle wielded considerable political power but preferred to remain unknown and work from the sidelines. The charismatic Dewey was just the opposite when it came to currying favor with the public and achieving his political goals.)

Predictably, Dewey planned to shake up the status quo when it came to campaigning for the state's highest office. History had shown that his radio addresses had yielded positive results, and he chose to convey his campaign message through weekly radio speeches rather than focusing on traveling by car to outlying areas, the traditional method of campaigning during that era. Dewey preferred to travel by train during his campaign. He routinely drew crowds that ranged from six hundred to fifteen hundred people, and he always tailored his speeches to each region. Many in the group wanted to shake hands with the famous crime buster, but Dewey knew that his crime-busting image would take him only so far. He also focused on his youth, his enthusiasm, and what he said was the incompetence of the current state government and the dominance of Democratic Party bosses. Dewey also perfected the art of personal appeal. For instance, when attacking Governor Lehman for chaos in the system that provides unemployment insurance, he trotted out a cabinet maker who was told his claim was "lost" in Albany; and a machinist who waited nine months to receive benefits. To illustrate the state's housing crisis, he described the plight of residents who lived in poverty yet paid high amounts of rent. As he had done during his campaign for prosecutor, Dewey was well aware of the importance of the Black vote. He told a Harlem audience, for instance, that federal officials should take a tour of one of the area's burned-out houses, as he had done as prosecutor. He also endorsed the reapportionment of the state legislature because Harlem residents "haven't got a colored man in the Senate, and we propose to get one." Still, as Dewey biographer Richard Smith noted, the energetic Dewey faced a tough battle when it came to the 1938 governor's race: he opposed a popular incumbent with a record for integrity, so he needed to tread lightly when responding to personal criticism of him. Although the polls near the end of the campaign indicated a tight race, most of the state's big unions endorsed Lehman. *New York Times* publisher Arthur H. Sulzberger, who liked Dewey and who had been compliant when the special prosecutor asked him to lay off coverage of the mob investigation until it was complete, told him five weeks before election day that the *Times* would endorse Lehman. In a short, handwritten note to Dewey, he wrote, "it will seem queer indeed not to be on your bandwagon." Indeed, Sulzberger apologizes for this lack of support, and he is quick to point out that he is happy to "cheer for a fellow in whom I have the utmost confidence." Sulzberger's cheerful and mildly obsequious note indicates that he suspected that even if the thirty-six-year-old prosecutor lost this time, he would no doubt have a long and successful political career ahead of him. And that's what happened. Incumbent Governor Herbert Lehman squeaked by and was reelected governor of New York by slightly more than 1 percent of the vote. The challenger, however, won every county outside New York City but one. As Dewey's biographer notes, "he had lost an election but won a national audience." It was now clear that Thomas E. Dewey was one of the Republican Party's rising stars.

DEWEY HAD MADE it clear that as a prosecutor he highly valued loyalty. He frequently appointed staff attorneys with whom he had already worked, and those attorneys usually had three qualifications in common: they were smart, they worked long hours, and they considered loyalty from Dewey a two-way street. Eunice fit these criteria, as evidenced by her natural intelligence, her self-described long workdays, and her years in Dewey's special prosecutor and prosecutor offices. Accounts of Eunice's home life during this period indicate that she and her husband did not have a close relationship, and that her only child, Lisle, spent much of his years growing up in his father's native Barbados. Eunice did remain close, however, to her mother, Addie. And the two of them had a distant and at times rocky relationship with Eunice's brother and Addie's son, Alphaeus.

IN HER MEMOIR about her husband, *William Alphaeus Hunton: A Pioneer Prophet*, Addie Hunton writes about her two young children and their relationship with their father. Because of the frequent travel associated with his job, William Hunton was away for much of the childhood of Alphaeus and Eunice. As Addie describes it, while William greatly admired his daughter's intellect and sense of humor, he was much closer to his second child, Alphaeus. During the last few years of William's life, when he, Addie, and Alphaeus spent much of their time in Lake Saranac, New York, Eunice, who was four years older than her brother, was finishing high school in Brooklyn and staying with relatives. It was during these last few years of his life that the teenaged Alphaeus and his father grew close. William died when his son was thirteen and his daughter seventeen. The two siblings did grow up in the same household for much of their youth. But as they became adults, Eunice and Alphaeus did not maintain a par-ticularly close bond, and as the two entered young adulthood, their paths diverged to the point where they were nearly estranged.

Like his father, William Alphaeus Hunton Jr. was an idealist and ac-tivist, and, like his sister and mother, he was devoted to social justice and civil rights. William Sr. long held a worldview that the struggles of Black people around the world were linked. He was particularly interested in extending YMCA services to Africa. So Alphaeus had been exposed to this international view since he was a child. After graduating from Howard University in 1924 with a bachelor's degree, he earned a master's degree at Harvard two years later. Alphaeus Hunton began teaching in the Romance Languages and English Department at Howard shortly after completing a PhD in English literature from New York University in 1938, where his dissertation focused on Tennyson. Alphaeus Hunton's activism can be traced to his work with the National Negro Congress (NNC), which he joined while still at Howard. He became interested in Marxism while a student at NYU and had helped launch the Washington, DC, branch of the NNC, an organization of civic and religious organizations dedicated to racial equality and labor issues—but one that the federal government believed was tied to communism. The group organized anti–Jim Crow campaigns and fought racial discrimination in the federal government. Hunton soon became one of its key players, helping to organize boycotts, strikes, and petition drives. By 1943, and after taking a leave of absence, he left Howard to focus on his activism.

Overall, Alphaeus Hunton's beliefs about how to achieve racial equality were far more radical than those of his sister and mother. But the paths of the three would cross, and their work would be linked through the efforts by the three on the subject of anti-colonialism and Pan-African Black identity. The National Council of Negro Women (NCNW), a group in which Eunice and Addie were active, stressed globalism and advanced the idea of shared Black identity around the world; in this way, their beliefs matched those of Alphaeus. At its conferences, the NCNW hosted speakers from around the world. The group's magazine, the *Aframerican Women's Journal*, featured stories by women in Cuba, Haiti, and Mexico. But the end of World War II brought about significant changes in the world order that would result in a rethinking about the best ways to achieve racial equality in the United States and the relationship between Blacks in the United States and around the world.

By the beginning of World War II, Alphaeus's activism had taken a radical turn. Like many Black leaders and intellectuals, he believed that White oppression indirectly was furthered by an American foreign policy that supported European colonialism. In that way, the fate of Blacks in the United States could not be separated from that of Blacks around the world, they believed. In the preface to a biography of Alphaeus written by his widow, Dorothy, she explains the major appeal of Marxism among

Blacks. Believers in Marxism thought that it opposed racial oppression, she writes. Alphaeus became an acolyte of W. E. B. Du Bois, who was a major proponent of the international Black identity that formed the backbone of Pan-Africanism. As chairman of the NNC's labor committee, Alphaeus called for the integration of Washington labor unions, organized the city's domestic workers, and led a campaign for pay raises for Black laundry workers. He also pushed for the hiring of Blacks in the city's transit system and an aircraft factory in Baltimore. By 1943, at the urging of some of his Communist Party colleagues, he took a job as educational director with the Council on African Affairs (CAA), a leading anti-colonialism organization that advocated some of the tenants of communism, and moved with his third wife, Dorothy, to New York City.

Like his father, who traveled and worked tirelessly to create YMCAs for Black citizens, Alphaeus Hunton spent long days promoting a cause about which he was passionate. Actor Paul Robeson was head of the CAA at the time, and Du Bois was a key player. As educational director, Alphaeus had vital responsibilities. He produced brochures and newsletters, served as lobbyist, and organized picket lines and rallies. His particular talent was rallying working-class Blacks to support the causes of Africans and linking the interests of the American labor movement with those of African work-ers. Later he would assist anti-Apartheid efforts in South Africa and aid famine relief in West and South Africa. (Although he is known primarily as an entertainer, Robeson had long been a civil rights activist and was somewhat of a lightning rod in the movement. His comments during the early Cold War period that much of the wealth in the United States was ac-quired on the backs of poor Blacks in Europe drew criticism among some Whites and Blacks, as did testimony he gave to the House Committee on Unamerican Activity opposing a bill requiring communists to register as foreign agents.)

Despite their mutual devotion to social causes, Eunice and Alphaeus had little reason to socialize or even get together during this time. Eunice's son said that as a child and young man, he occasionally saw his uncle, but he indicates he remembers little about him. Addie, Eunice, and Alphaeus attended the Fiftieth Annual Conference of the Negro YMCA in 1938 and were introduced together, but it was a rare meeting of the three. Stephen Carter writes that his grandmother Eunice and great-uncle Alphaeus's differing political views forced them, for the most part, to be estranged as adults. However, they occasionally met at professional meetings and events. Also, elements of Aphaeus's personal life alienated both Eunice and Addie. For instance, Alphaeus was openly seeing his soon-to-be third wife, Dorothy, when he was still married to his second wife. And he abandoned the religion that he grew up with, and that was always a part of the lives of his mother and sister. Stephen Carter writes that it is likely the last time the three were together was on Christmas in 1942; Eunice and her brother would meet again in April 1944, after Addie's death, at the Pan-African conference in New York.

DURING THE EARLY years of World War II, the CAA's anti-colonial efforts intensified, and, in March 1946, it organized two highly successful events calling for aid and famine relief in South Africa. Some celebrities, including Paul Robeson, Judy Holliday, and Lena Horne attended. Later that summer, a fundraiser at Madison Square Garden drew fifteen thousand people and featured singer Pete Seeger, Du Bois, officials of the United Auto Workers union, and a representative of the Communist Party. Lutz writes that the efforts of the CAA in the immediate aftermath of World War II were considered highly successful, and officials of the organization communicated frequently with officials of the State Department and the US Treasury. Within three years of the war's end, however, it was a different story. Alphaeus and the CAA began to focus on apartheid in South Africa, and the group grew increasingly vocal in its campaign against White supremacy and fascism. But the dawning of the Cold War brought seismic shifts in the politics and beliefs of many Americans—Black and White. President Harry Truman had become convinced that the newly formed Soviet Union was behind anti-colonial efforts, and communism had suddenly replaced imperialism as the common enemy of the United States. As historian James Roark writes, a strong wave of anticommunist sentiment overtook the nation in 1948, and protests on behalf of colonial people and expressions of international racial solidarity declined sharply. And it was a wave that had racial and anti-Semitic overtones. Robeson had been performing a benefit concert on August 27, 1949, in Peekskill, New York, when locals who opposed civil rights suddenly attacked audience members, causing the first of what became to be known as the Peekskill Riots. The incident resulted in hundreds of injuries—some serious—and much destruction of property. A week later, Robeson was invited back, and up to twenty-five-thousand supporters showed up to hear him, protected by scores of union members. But violence erupted again, and police were called. As audience members attempted to leave, the officers attacked them, apparently believing that they caused the uproar. Dewey, now New York's governor who had long campaigned on his belief in racial equality, blamed Robeson and his supporters, claiming that communist groups provoked the incident.

By the late 1940s, Alphaeus Hunton, Robeson, Du Bois, and a handful of other high-profile civil rights activists promoted ideas and actions that suddenly became antithetical to prevailing American sentiment. (Major Black publications of the era, including the NAACP's *Crisis*, the *Chicago Defender* and the *Courier* in Pittsburgh, had taken strong anti-colonial stands in the past, but stories in those publications now had begun focusing less on anti-colonialism and more on the threat of communism.) Ultimately, the NAACP decided to downplay its anti-colonial stand and agreed that anticommunism was the proper American strategy in the Third World because Russian imperialism was considered at least as dangerous as European imperialism. Du Bois, a founder of the NAACP and, by this time, an advisor to it, remained adamant in his anti-colonial beliefs. He was dismissed by the group in 1948.

As Stephen Carter writes, the federal government had long been suspicious of his great-uncle Alphaeus and his fellow activists and had them under surveillance for years. By the late 1940s, the federal government had indicted and jailed hundreds of left-wing and civil rights activists and forced the resignation of scores of government and private-sector workers believed to be "subversive" and in violation of US interests. Bail bondsmen, out of fear, were often reluctant to offer bail to people accused of being Communist sympathizers, so a newly formed organization called the Civil Rights Congress began its own bail fund. Alphaeus Hunton served as a trustee of the group, along with a few other prominent citizens, including writer Dashiell Hammett. In 1951, the government demanded that Hammett and Alphaeus provide it with names of contributors to that bail fund. Both were sentenced to six months in jail when they refused. Lisle Carter Jr., Eunice's son, recalled in an interview decades later that Eunice distanced herself from her brother while he was imprisoned, refusing to speak with him. Lisle Jr. did visit him, however, when he was released, much to his mother's dismay.

Although many prominent Black citizens maintained their support of Alphaeus Hunton after he was released from prison, donations to the CAA gradually decreased, and in 1953 it was deemed by the US attorney general as "subversive." The Internal Revenue Service audited it in 1954, and FBI agents kept a close watch on Alphaeus, at times calling his wife, Dorothy, and harassing her. The CAA disbanded in 1955.

Alphaeus continued his volunteer efforts, but because of his prison record, he now had trouble finding work. However, friends he had in the labor movement were able to find him jobs as a semi-skilled laborer using the name "Bill Hunton." Alphaeus moved to Ghana in 1962 to work with Du Bois compiling the *Encyclopedia Africana*, which was meant to be a chronicle of the accomplishments and culture of Black people. Alphaeus took over that work after Du Bois's death. He was forced to leave Ghana after the ouster of that nation's president, and he moved to Zambia in 1966 to continue work on the encyclopedia and research the history of Zambia's nationalist movement at the request of Zambia president Kenneth D. Kaunda. Alphaeus was living in Zambia when he died of pancreatic cancer on January 13, 1970.

Dorothy Hunton's love for her husband and the grief she felt about what she believed was the mistreatment and harassment of a devoted and peaceful activist prompted her to write a biography of him fifteen years after his death. She writes: "He was disturbed wherever injustices occurred [and] wherever man was denied his rights, and he went to prison in defense of his principles. . . . A tireless worker, sympathetic and just, who gave little thought to his meager personal needs. He was one of the unsung heroes of our time."

EUNICE AND OTHERS in the NCNW maintained a deep interest in anti-colonialism and other international issues, but the group treaded lightly with the advent of the Cold War. Still, issues of the NCNW's *Aframerican Women's Journal* indicate that internationalism, in general, remained high on that group's agenda. President Truman's foreign policy had drawn criticism from some Blacks, but he positioned himself as a strong advocate of civil rights, making an appearance at the 1947 NAACP convention and, the following year, advocating for strengthening the Civil Rights Division of the Justice Department and the enactment of federal anti-lynching legislation. Many Black leaders decided that they could not oppose the president's foreign policy while supporting domestic policies that they welcomed. Mary McLeod Bethune may have been continuing her anti-colonial efforts outside of Europe, according to one researcher. In her 2013 doctoral dissertation about the NCNW and Bethune, Ashley N. Robertson argues that Bethune had never been adequately recognized for her anti-colonial activism on behalf of African people in Haiti, Cuba, and Liberia. Bethune received Haiti's highest honor in 1949, the Haitian Medal of Honor and Merit, as well as Liberia's Star of Africa three years later. "Bethune utilized her powerful positions as a way to create solidarity among African women throughout the diaspora," Robertson writes. Robertson believes that one of Bethune's main activities during her years with the NCNW was to attempt to create solidarity among all people of African descent. Interestingly, she did this in part through her work with the CAA—the anti-colonial organization for which Alphaeus worked—and through her efforts with the United Nations. By 1948, the nation's racial equality movement and the anti-colonial movement—both of which promoted equality and opposed rampant oppression—were at odds in the minds of many Americans. By this time, Bethune, Eunice, and their colleagues in the NCNW were hopeful that a newly formed body called the United Nations could be the vehicle that would help promote racial equality around the world.

THE POSTWAR PERIOD brought dramatic changes throughout the world, and few could be considered more significant than the establishment in 1945 of the United Nations. In April of that year, fifty-one delegates from around the world met in San Francisco to form the charter for the new peace-keeping body whose goal was to prevent another world war. The San Francisco meetings were designed to give structure to the agency and determine how it would run. President Truman appointed Mary McLeod Bethune to attend the signing of the charter as his consultant on interracial affairs and understanding; she also represented the NAACP with Du Bois and NAACP head Walter White. As such, she was the only Black woman at the signing. Bethune invited Eunice, who attended parts of the UN charter meetings as a representative of the NCNW. This invitation would prove to be a pivotal event in Eunice's life, and it would mark the beginning of a long association with the United Nations, an affiliation that she valued.

THE FACT THAT the federal government maintained surveillance of Alphaeus could not have surprised Addie Hunton. Military Intelligence had Addie and two other women on their radar when they traveled to France during World War I to provide support for the two hundred thousand Black troops there as part of American Expeditionary Forces. The officials were alerted when one of Addie's colleagues committed the possible "crime" of telling troops they should protest their abysmal living conditions overseas. Her later work with the NAACP and her activities to promote Pan-Africanism also drew the attention of federal officials, and Lutz writes that the FBI opened a file on her in 1933. She had delivered her last major speech at the NAACP's 1932 convention when she repeated her pleas for Blacks in the United States to consider themselves as part of a world community—one where racial inequality was still a reality. By the early 1940s, Addie, who had been ill on and off through much of the last decade, curtailed many of her activities, although she had been scaling them down for much longer because of exhaustion or illness. Addie Hunton died on June 21, 1943, in Brooklyn. She is buried in Cypress Hills Cemetery in Brooklyn, next to her husband, William. The state of Addie's health had long been somewhat of a mystery; she was ill frequently, based on reports over the years in the Black press, but the nature of her illness remained unclear. Typical was this cryptic brief item in the *Chicago Defender* "Notes" column that Addie "had been ill [and] is on the road to recovery." At times, it was implied that Eunice had taken care of her during these illnesses. Eunice, too, had continual bouts of illness, although none was severe enough for her to miss work for an extended time. (For instance, one short newspaper story noted that Eunice had been in a "sanitarium" after abdominal surgery following a "lingering illness of ten weeks.") Other items in Black newspapers noted that on occasions, Eunice visited Mary McLeod Bethune at her home in Florida, apparently to recuperate.

The immediate postwar years brought changes in many civic and cultural organizations, including the women's club movement. By 1949, the NCNW "had begun to drift," according to historian Lutz. The informative *Aframerican Women's Journal* had been renamed *Women United*, and its content now began focusing on domestic issues like fashion and the raising of families. Most important, the group's founder and longtime president, Bethune, stepped down, prompting many in the movement to speculate about who would replace her. The society-gossip columnist of the *Pittsburgh Courier*, "Toki," donated much of her column in October 1949 on this speculation, mentioning about a dozen Black leaders as possibilities. She included in this group Eunice Carter: "Edith Sampson and Eunice Carter—both women are attorneys and brilliant," she writes. Ultimately it was one of the other people "Toki" named—educator and activist Dorothy Height—who took over as NCNW president.

SINCE SHE BEGAN working for Dewey in 1935, Eunice was fiercely loyal to him. This loyalty may have come about because he made it clear he appreciated and admired her hard work; or because the two were aligned politically in their right-of-center Republicanism; or because their work made up a large part of the lives of both. Whatever the reason, Eunice was devoted to Dewey, and perhaps she felt that his public praise helped her serve as a role model for other Black citizens. Addie Hunton and other clubwomen believed that visible role models played a pivotal role in the quest for racial equality, and Dewey did appoint religious and racial minorities to key positions at a time when others would not.

His overt boasting about his hiring record seems self-serving and even comical when viewed today: "I determined when I became district attorney all elements of the population should be represented," he said in a 1939 interview with the *Afro-American*. "I have more Jews working in the department than has ever been true before," he said. "There are more colored persons in outstanding positions than has been true of any other administration. . . . In fact, a colored woman [Eunice] is the head of the largest bureau in this office." In the story, Dewey is effusive about Eunice's impressive familial and academic background, and he noted that she ran the busiest department in his office. Her office, he said, handles misdemeanors in three different courts, a number that is three times higher than similar divisions around the country. "She commands the respect of the bench in this city," he added. And, for some reason, he mentioned that Eunice earned $6,000 a year (about $112,000 in 2020 dollars).

He went on to say that two other Black attorneys—James Yergen and Frank Rivers, the latter whom Dewey would one day appoint to a judgeship—worked in his office. Dewey again mentioned Rivers's impressive academic credentials—he earned degrees from Yale University and Harvard Law School. (Interestingly, the story noted that Rivers was the highest-paid attorney in Dewey's office—earning $1,000 a year more than Eunice.)

The story in the *Afro-American* portrayed the thirty-seven-year-old Dewey in glowing terms, describing him as an "alert, vigorous and youthful" man who is handsome and "even better looking than his pictures . . . virile with the punch and forcefulness of a go-getter." Later in the story, under the subhead, "Equal under the Law," the story says that Dewey believes that the administration of justice should not be "polluted by racial injustice" and that during his years as a prosecutor "a number of incidents have occurred in which Mr. Dewey saved colored defendants who had been unjustly accused of a crime." The article cited the case of a Black man who had been framed on a gun charge. Shortly after he took office, Dewey took steps to drop the case and even "sent the policeman who framed [him] to jail." Dewey evidently believed his equal-opportunity hiring record would help him politically. How much of a role his professed commitment to equality played in Eunice's loyalty to him both in the workplace and politically is not known. What is clear, however, is that Dewey was not reluctant to utilize Eunice's race in his quest for political office.

Dewey's loss in the 1938 gubernatorial race to Herbert Lehman gave him a boost politically; his near-win against an incumbent Democratic governor in Democrat-dominated New York indicated to most high-level Republicans that he could win that job in the future. Still, while Dewey had name recognition thanks to the mob prosecution, he lacked the decades of government and political experience of some of his rivals. In 1942, he did win a hard-fought nomination for governor after Wendell Willkie, a lifelong Democrat who switched parties in 1939, opted to sit out the race.

But Willkie, who swooped in to take the Republican Party's 1940 presidential nomination from Dewey, refused to endorse Dewey for governor. (Willkie, an interventionist, believed that the nation should get involved in World War II, and he made it clear that he would not endorse anyone who didn't support President Franklin Roosevelt's foreign policy in the wake of Pearl Harbor. Dewey, like many of his Republican colleagues, was an isolationist.)

As a close colleague and friend of Dewey's, Eunice could not help but enter the fray and support Dewey and, in fact, help campaign for him—action she took in 1942 at a time when many of her friends, including Mary McLeod Bethune, were Democrats and internationalists. Characteristically, Dewey campaigned tirelessly against his rival for governor, New York Attorney General John J. Bennett Jr., even though polls gave Dewey a wide lead. Promising voters that he would focus on his job as governor rather than eyeing the presidency during his time in Albany, Dewey maintained a rigorous speaking schedule and was obsessive about details. But Dewey always had his eye on the next campaign.

Correspondence between Dewey and Eunice during his quest for the presidential nomination and his victorious campaign for governor indicate that the two had a warm and friendly relationship. Letters and memos also suggest that Eunice helped him demonstrate that he was dedicated to racial equality. Dewey made his first appearance as a presidential candidate on the Republican ticket in Minneapolis in late 1939. In front of the ten thousand spectators who jammed an auditorium, he declared that the New Deal was the policy of "fear and defeatism." At the end of his speech, the crowd gave Dewey a standing ovation. But more important, West Coast Republicans responded favorably, prompting him to decide to officially kick off his presidential nomination campaign tour the next year in California and make his way through many of the far western and mountain states. Eunice was impressed by his showing in Minneapolis, writing him as he headed west: "Dear Chief, I can tell you of the deep sense of satisfaction and pride with which I listened to that superlative opening speech of yours. To me, it was 'tops.'" She added that she wanted him to know that he could always rely on her support.

Dewey made his first major speech at a rally before the Republican Assembly broadcast from the Hollywood Bowl. In a memo to him and the campaign, Eunice suggested a way he could get the notice of Black newspapers on the West Coast—stories that could help him win the Black vote there, she believed. "The Negroes on the Pacific Coast . . . know little of

Thomas E. Dewey and the Negro. Our [predominantly Black] publications in the East do not reach them readily. California will probably have two colored delegates," she wrote. Eunice wrote that people in California are used to "the dramatic and spectacular and respond to stimuli of this kind more quickly than any other people in the country." She enclosed instructions for what she called a "publicity stunt" in Los Angeles that involved herself being photographed there: "Have Eunice H. Carter leave [New York] on sleeper plane April 19th to reach Los Angeles on April 20th. All Negro newspapers notified. Pictures boarding plane." She wrote that the "story" for the press would be meetings with herself and Black Republican leaders in California with an account of "influential [Black] figures who have rallied to Dewey support." (She added that Los Angeles Assistant City Solicitor and "Negro Republican Leader" Bert McDonald "can be depended on for publicity in Los Angeles.") The Republican Party did not pick Dewey as its presidential nominee in 1940, but he handily won the governor's race in 1942 and moved to Albany in 1943. Eunice and the rest of the prosecutor's staff remained in New York under the direction of Dewey's successor, prosecutor Frank Hogan. (Hogan, who had been an attorney with Eunice on Dewey's mob-busting team and became a close friend of Dewey's, would serve as prosecutor from 1942 until 1974.) Although the two no longer worked together, memos and letters between Eunice and Dewey reflect a warm and ongoing relationship. When Eunice sent Dewey a telegram about Addie's death, he responded immediately with a telegram of condolence. But one of the most revealing personal notes between Eunice and her longtime boss may have been written shortly after his victorious first race for governor. In her elegant and flowing handwriting, Eunice sent him a warm congratulatory letter two weeks after the election:

> Dear "Boss": Because I knew that your mail was staggering, I waited until some of the tumult and the shouting died to tell you how happy I am for you because of your recent election as Governor of our State.
>
> There is no doubt in my mind that your administration will be one of the most eminently successful ones of all times. My hope for you is that the burdens of office will not weigh too heavily upon you—that you will enjoy tackling them, realizing that they, as important as they are, are a preparation, a prelude to even greater tasks.—Sincerely yours, Eunice H. Carter.

Whether Eunice meant the term "a prelude to even greater tasks" metaphorically or literally is not known. Was she saying that she expects him to one day become president, or was she saying that she hopes his future successes would bring him peace and fulfillment overall?

Politically, Dewey did go on to greater things—after assuming his first term as New York governor in 1943, he would be reelected twice before leaving that post in 1955. In the 1940s, Dewey did seek "greater tasks" politically but fell short both times. He ran unsuccessfully for president in 1944 and 1948. Despite these losses, however, he would become a household name outside of New York for decades to come and, ironically, an iconic figure in journalism. But not in the way he planned.

EUNICE KEPT WORKING in the prosecutor's office after Dewey moved to the governor's mansion in Albany and was now in charge of the juvenile justice program. But according to her grandson, much changed after her friend and mentor left—and it wasn't for the better. Stephen Carter writes that Eunice may have wanted the prosecutor's job, but it went to Hogan, a Democrat who was three years younger than she. Hogan soon raised the salary of Frank Rivers, from $7,500 to $10,000. Rivers, James Yergen, and Eunice were still the only Black attorneys in the prosecutor's office, and Eunice's salary remained at $6,500. Hogan also moved her out of the Special Sessions Bureau and into a program she developed for adolescent offenders. The move was at best a lateral one, Stephen Carter implies, because she was moved out of a full bureau. He adds that Hogan never promoted her.

Stephen Carter implies that his grandmother had higher ambitions— she might have wanted a judgeship. In addition to getting what prosecutor Hogan labeled as a well-earned raise in pay, Frank Rivers was appointed by his former boss Dewey to a judgeship in New York City Court, a job Eunice would have wanted, Stephen Carter writes. Yet she wrote a letter to Dewey when he was governor, praising him for appointing Rivers judge. In a handwritten note, she thanked him for his appointment of Rivers, writing, "It's good to know that you are still blazing a trail by making such appointments when they are merited." And Dewey responded, thanking her for the note about Rivers. Still, Stephen Carter writes, Eunice remained loyal to Dewey, sometimes blaming the lack of a promotion on the actions of her brother, Alphaeus, whom she believed may have indirectly hurt her career because of his legal problems.

IN 1945, EUNICE LEFT public employment and the prosecutor's office and entered private practice in 1946. Two years later, she became business partners with journalist and businessman Ernest E. Johnson to form

Carter-Johnson Associates, a public relations firm geared toward minorities, which shared office space with her law firm. The business union lasted about a year before dissolving for unknown reasons. It is unknown how successful she was in private practice this second time, but Stephen Carter implies that she actively sought business. Of course, there were few Black female attorneys in the country when she earned her law degree two decades before. Gradually, more women and more minorities were earning law degrees and working as attorneys, but the number of Black female lawyers in the United States was very low even by 1950. That year, according to one study, the United States had 6,615 women lawyers, 83 of whom were Black, and 174,550 male lawyers. The 1947 *Ebony* story about Black female lawyers in the United States drove home the point that their numbers were tiny. The story also noted that more than their male counterparts, Black women lawyers often worked for social justice causes. Black women lawyers are highly influential in their communities, the story continued, and are often leaders and officers in groups such as the NAACP, the Urban League, and the NCNW. A caption under Eunice's photo notes that she is chairperson of the NCNW (and the caption reinforces the idea that Eunice remained loyal to one political party—it identifies her as a "staunch Republican"). Eunice already belonged to several attorney organizations, including the National Association of Women Lawyers, the National Lawyers Guild, the New York Women's Bar Association, and the Harlem Lawyers Association.

Stephen Carter writes that the years of the late 1940s were troubled in some ways for his grandmother. (She had turned fifty in 1949.) But it is evident that in some ways, her decades of hard work were paying off. She and her husband moved from their longtime Harlem home on Edgecombe Avenue in 1947 to a townhome on Jumel Terrace north of Harlem. And their son, Lisle Jr., who had served in the Army, was discharged in 1946 and moved in with them. The stately home allowed Eunice, who enjoyed entertaining, to exercise her hospitality—she now had a prestigious address, and she continued to serve an essential role in Harlem society. Perhaps even more important, Lisle Jr. had graduated from St. John's University law school and became an attorney, much to his mother's delight. She took great pride in his legal successes. In 1950, Lisle Jr. and several colleagues opened up the law firm of Carter, Smith, Watson and Wright, and shared office space with Eunice's firm at her Manhattan office at 516 Fifth Avenue.

Eunice's work with the NCNW and international causes had significantly intensified by 1947, and she was cultivating an image by then as the

NCNW's authority on global as well as legal issues. She was particularly active in causes related to the United Nations, and her work with different organizations sometimes was complementary. By 1949, Eunice became an "elder statesperson" of sorts in some of these social justice causes, and she accelerated her international travel schedule for the NCNW.

Throughout her career and life, Eunice no doubt learned that her work and dedication to some causes could make her unpopular to some colleagues, friends—and in the case of Alphaeus—relatives. She learned the art of compromise—or at least compartmentalization—much to the dismay of some people who loved and respected her. For example, by the time she entered private practice, many of her colleagues in the NCNW had switched their allegiance to the Democratic Party. And her political and philosophical differences with Alphaeus led to a permanent split between them. In 1948, Eunice once again may have alienated many of those to whom she was close with her work promoting international causes. That year, the United Nations voted in favor of the Genocide Convention, a treaty that defined genocide—the destruction of a national, ethnic, racial, or religious group—as an international crime that would allow for international legal prosecution. But twenty countries had to ratify it before it could become law. And it was here, as it turned out, that Eunice took what turned out to be a controversial stand in supporting the treaty.

Interestingly, the United States and the American Bar Association took a stand against this human rights treaty. US officials in the South said they did not believe such a pact should be internationalized, and they maintained it could violate state's rights, as it would allow federal courts to hear cases of alleged genocide in individual states (mostly in the South). The American Bar Association said it believed the pact could violate some constitutional protections. Eunice became one of two New York lawyers who went against the American Bar Association stand. In testimony to the US Senate, she said women and children and members of minority groups were particularly vulnerable to acts of genocide, which made the pact particularly necessary. But a portion of Eunice's comments were also seen as letting the South off the hook when it came to acts of racial violence. She said in testimony that the lynching of individuals is not related to the extinction of mass groups of people, thus indicating that under the treaty, individuals could not be held accountable for racial violence in the United States. These comments infuriated her brother, Alphaeus, and others. (The United States became the ninety-eighth nation to ratify the Genocide Pact forty years later in 1988, when President Ronald Reagan signed it during a ceremony in Chicago.)

Eunice gave up her law practice in 1952. She spent much of her time with civic organizations, including the International Council on Women, a peace and human rights group whose goal is to bring together women from all over the world. She represented that group in 1953 before the UN Commission on the Status of Women, urging that citizenship rights for men and women be equal. Eunice had begun to travel extensively for her work with the NCNW and other organizations. In a 1949 radio interview conducted by Eleanor Roosevelt, Eunice, then chairperson of the NCNW board, outlined much of her international travel. She had planned to go to Legnano, Italy, as the NCNW representative at a meeting of the International Council on Women, and then to Geneva, Switzerland, for a meeting of organizations that consult with the UN Economic and Social Council, one of that organization's largest bodies. In the 1950s, she traveled to Germany, first as part of an NCNW delegation asked to study the conditions of women in occupied Germany and then as an aide to a German government task force on women in public life.

When Mrs. Roosevelt asked Eunice the purpose of the Economic and Social Council, she answered succinctly: the United Nations has granted eighty organizations worldwide "consultative" status to convey public opinion about social and economic issues. Eunice added that much of her work over the last few years had been for the United Nations and the Council. Within five years of that radio interview, Eunice was elected to chair the International Conference of Non-Governmental Organizations of the United Nations.

The *Chicago Defender* and the *Pittsburgh Courier*, which had for decades covered many of Eunice's personal and professional activities, were filled with information about her travels from the mid-1940s until the early 1960s. "Eunice H. Carter Among Delegates to Paris Talks," reads the headline in the *Chicago Defender* in a September 1947 story describing her trip with fourteen other women to attend the first International Assembly of Women in Paris. Under the headline, "American Women of Color Are Traveling Abroad," *Defender* society columnist Rebecca Stiles Taylor writes that Eunice and two other clubwomen were in Athens, Greece, for a meeting of the International Council of Women of the World.

In keeping with her parents' involvement with the NAACP and YMCA-YWCA, Eunice had long been active with local YWCAs in Harlem and Manhattan, and later was a cochair of the YWCA's Committee on Development of Leadership in Other Countries. She became chairwoman of the Friends of the NAACP. In 1964, she was voted the vice president of the eastern division of the Pan-Pacific Women's Association.

On a personal level, Eunice never reconciled with her brother, Alphaeus, and Stephen Carter writes that neither she nor Lisle Jr. helped Alphaeus with his legal troubles. Lisle Carter Sr. died in 1963 at age seventy after maintaining his dental practice for forty years. Eunice did live to see some of the successes of her son, Lisle Jr., who had a distinguished career as an attorney and educator. The first president of the University of the District of Columbia, Lisle Carter Jr., was an Army veteran, legal counsel to the National Urban League, and one of the highest-ranking Black members of the Department of Health, Education, and Welfare. He was also a professor at Cornell University and chancellor of the Atlanta University Center, a consortium of Black colleges. Like his grandparents and uncle, Lisle Carter was active throughout his life in many social justice and civic organizations. He had five children.

Eunice Hunton Carter died of cancer on June 25, 1970, in Knickerbocker Hospital in Manhattan, twelve days after the death of her brother, Alphaeus. While the two did not have a close relationship as adults, they had at least one characteristic in common: their devotion to their work, whether it was a paid job or causes they supported.

Dorothy Hunton, Alphaeus's widow, writes in her memoir about him, "work was his life, and life was his work, and neither would be separated from each other." The same was true for Eunice.

10

The Aftermath

LIKE ALL GOOD crime sagas, the story of Thomas E. Dewey, Eunice Hunton Carter, and Charles "Lucky" Luciano contains a plot twist at the end, along with a dash of irony. The unpredictable ending brings with it an upside-down logic, where the incarcerated become free and the free, to some degree, remain incarcerated in prisons of their own making.

The story ends with Luciano walking free and presidential hopeful Dewey on the front page after Election Day—but, of course, not because he was victorious.

The sensational 1936 trial of Luciano and his codefendants marked the perfect coda to an era that brought with it Prohibition's end, the struggle of a nation to regain its footing after a devastating economic disaster, and the glamorization and growth of the nation's underworld. As one writer noted, the public viewed the gangsters of the era as "an aristocracy of crime" where "almost every thug was at least a king." There is little question that the drama of the trial and the resulting victory for Dewey and his men, and one woman, propelled these mob busters to hero status. No wonder the lead crime buster, Dewey, was able to reject lucrative offers to star as himself in movies about the trial. On a more practical level, however, his victory allowed the thirty-four-year-old Dewey to pursue political ambitions that he had been harboring for nearly a decade. And it launched to national significance the legal talents of Eunice, one of the few Black female attorneys of the era and the first Black female assistant prosecutor in New York.

But fame isn't necessarily what it's cracked up to be. As one mob historian notes, working against brutal criminals and gang bosses created a prison of its own for Dewey and his team. For security reasons, Dewey, in particular, was forced to live in a world similar to a gangster's. He traveled with armed security guards, made essential telephone calls from secret locations, and was always looking over his shoulder. And the long hours he worked as a prosecutor didn't help his marriage. His wife, Frances, and two sons saw little of their husband and father during much of his career, both as a prosecutor and a politician. Frances made it clear that she did not share her husband's enthusiasm for politics, telling friends that she did not enjoy "life in a fishbowl," nor did she enjoy talking politics.

Further, she suffered from illnesses such as poor appetite, bronchitis, and chronic allergies (prompting one friend to note that she was probably allergic to politics). As an assistant prosecutor, Eunice also became well aware of the dangers of a job where she worked fighting brutal criminals. Her only child spent much of his childhood in his father's native Barbados, and there was speculation about the reason for this. Eunice once said that it was for health reasons, but some people believed that he was sent out of the country for security reasons related to Eunice's job. Eunice's grandson speculates that his grandparents' long workdays made it difficult for them to raise a small child.

In the short run, many members of Dewey's special prosecutor's team became successful at prosecuting gangsters and dirty politicians after the trial, when Dewey was elected New York prosecutor. One of his most high-profile prosecutions involved Democratic operative and Tammany Hall leader Jimmy Hines, who was found guilty in 1939 of protecting from arrest members of a crime ring operated by mobster Dutch Schultz. Hines led New York's Eleventh Assembly District and acquired power by dispensing favors and selling his influence to gangsters. A previous trial before 1939 ended in a hung jury. The later conviction was another feather in Dewey's cap, in part because it represented the Tammany political machine's further decline in influence and Dewey's targeting of corrupt politicians.

The excitement and glamor of the Luciano trial may have brought fame to the prosecutors, but its aftermath revealed what some believed were questionable legal tactics of Dewey. Some of these were first introduced nearly a year after the dramatic verdict when in March 1937, several prostitutes who served as the prosecution's key witnesses recanted their testimony. Florence "Cokey Flo" Brown said she had never met Luciano despite having testified she did, adding that she was able to identify him because she had seen his picture in newspapers. Others, including Nancy

Presser, said they lied when they said they knew Luciano because they were offered suspended sentences if they testified as they did. Brown said she was drunk at the time of the trial. Judge Philip J. McCook, ruling on a request from Luciano's attorneys for a new trial based in part on the recanted testimony, said he did not find the recantations credible.

Still, these recantations were not the only criticisms of Dewey's prosecutorial tactics in the Luciano case. Some legal scholars and elected officials questioned the objectivity of the trial's so-called "blue-ribbon" jury that was made up primarily of wealthy Whites. Members of such a panel, according to Dewey, were far more knowledgeable and more qualified than a conventional jury. New York's judicial council, after studying years of decisions by such juries and finding unusually high conviction rates, decided in 1938 that such special juries were unfair. The state Senate voted to abolish "blue-ribbon" juries in criminal cases that year at the objection of Dewey. The crime-busting prosecutor got his way, though, and the measure was not approved by the state government. Blue-ribbon juries in New York weren't struck down for another twenty-five years.

Another tactic Dewey relied on during the Luciano trial—the liberal use of wiretaps—was also roundly criticized in the aftermath of the trial. At the time, federal law required a court order for wiretaps, but New York's laws were much looser. Labor unions, in particular, sought legislation that would limit the use of evidence obtained by them and require police officials to obtain court orders to execute them. At New York's 1938 state constitutional convention, groups including the American Labor Party and the American Civil Liberties Union argued that law-enforcement officials often abused wiretaps, and those groups backed their limited use. Democrats supported this effort. Republicans and Dewey did not. The latter claimed such limitations on wiretaps would shackle law enforcement. Ultimately, Dewey and the Republicans prevailed, although at Dewey's suggestion, a weak compromise was reached that evidence from such taps can be used without search warrants if circumstances prevented police officers from obtaining search warrants.

BY FAR, THE MOST notorious and shocking coda to the sensational mob trials of 1936 involved the commuting of "Lucky" Luciano's thirty-to-fifty-year prison sentence. In a twist that few of the police, prostitutes, bookers, gangsters, attorneys, or even spectators of the trial could have predicted, Governor Thomas E. Dewey ruled in 1946 that Lucky Luciano be released from prison after serving ten years of his sentence. He was deported to Sicily.

Much has been written about the reasons Dewey, as governor of New York, gave for this action, but variations of the same story emerge. By 1946, the New York harbor had become a strategic link to Europe during World War II as enormous numbers of troops and equipment sailed from the New York docks to Europe. Many of the thousands of dockworkers there were immigrants, and many came from Italy. Naval intelligence officials began to worry about sabotage—they feared some of the dock workers could be sympathetic to Mussolini, or that through them, the fascist dictator would infiltrate the American docks. Complicating the matter was the fact that the mob controlled the New York docks.

In 1942, when Herbert Lehman was still New York governor, naval officials felt they had no choice but to meet with mob leaders, including the notorious Meyer Lansky and Luciano attorney Moses Polakoff. The mob agreed to help the navy and keep the docks safe—if Luciano were freed at the end of the war. Mob leaders kept their part of the bargain. Luciano's attorney filed for a commutation of his sentence in 1946, the state parole board agreed to it after an investigation, and Dewey, now New York governor, signed off on it. Cheered on by a crowd of well-wishers at a Brooklyn pier, Luciano on February 9, 1946, boarded the *Laura Keene* and headed to his new home of Sicily. He stopped in Cuba, attempting to set up operations there, but US officials pressured Cuban officials to send him on to Italy. Luciano had not been pardoned, and he was warned that if he returned to the United States, he would be treated like an escaped criminal. Luciano spent the rest of his life in Italy, although he did want to return to the United States. He died in Naples in 1962 at age sixty-five. But he did eventually return to his adopted country: he was buried in St. John Cemetery in Queens, New York, in a plot not far from his old nemesis, mob boss Salvatore Maranzano, whom Luciano ordered murdered three decades earlier.

Dewey rarely, if ever, discussed the details of Luciano's commutation, and he brings it up only briefly in his memoir, *Twenty Against the Underworld*, writing about it on two pages of the five-hundred-page book. Dewey stresses that it was Lehman and not he who was governor when the idea of freeing Luciano was initiated. And when the parole board gave its recommendation for release to Governor Dewey four years later, Dewey said he felt compelled to honor it. Because of what he felt was inaccurate gossip behind the reasons for the commutation, Governor Dewey ordered an exhaustive study of the issue. The results of what became a 2,882-page study indicated that Luciano "had indeed rendered all the assistance of which he was capable and that it had been of real value to the war effort," Dewey wrote in his memoir.

The effect, if any, on Dewey's long-term political career will never be known. But two years after the commutation, he was propelled into the public eye and imbedded into popular culture.

Shortly after he began his first term as governor in 1943, he was selected as the Republican nominee for president against the incumbent Franklin D. Roosevelt. Dewey lost—but it was by the closest margin of any of Roosevelt's four victories. A popular governor, Dewey was viewed as a progressive. In his first term, he increased state aid for education, established a commission to eliminate religious and racial discrimination in hiring, and liberalized unemployment insurance regulations. Later he signed legislation creating the State University of New York and ordered pay raises for the state workers and teachers. Dewey made it clear in all his campaigns, and particularly his presidential bids, that he sought and valued Black voters. In his 1944 presidential bid, he met with Black leaders. He continually brought up the fact that he had appointed Eunice and several other Black people to key jobs in his prosecutor's office and with the state. A long front-page story in the *Pittsburgh Courier* described his swing through the Midwest touting his record with minorities. The newspaper wrote that Dewey and Republicans are "banking heavily upon wooing the Negro vote away from Roosevelt by bringing Dewey face to face in intimate friendly contact with Negro political leaders." Still, near the end of the story, the reporter wrote that "missing in Dewey's presentation of his policies was any mention of the general problems of Negro people." (Earlier that year, however, Dewey did outline a platform that would promote federal legislation against lynching, establish a federal fair-employment commission, and investigate racial discrimination in the armed forces.)

When Dewey became the Republican nominee for president in 1948, he was the clear favorite. Roosevelt's vice president, Harry Truman, became president following Roosevelt's death three months after the beginning of his fourth term, but incumbent President Truman faced headwinds—high inflation was wracking the economy, there was wide labor unrest, and his own party was divided about whether they wanted him as their candidate. The meticulous and energetic Dewey, who in previous campaigns tended to the most minor detail, was seen as the sure winner.

But in one of the biggest upsets in presidential election history, Dewey and his running mate, California Governor Earl Warren, lost. Truman got 49.6 percent of the popular vote and 303 electoral votes to Dewey's 45.1 percent of the popular vote and 189 electoral votes. For decades, political analysts have pondered why the favored Dewey lost the race. Some believed that Dewey and Republicans, thinking their win was a certainty, played it safe and softened strong stands on issues. Others think that it was a coalition of labor, farmers, Blacks, and Jewish voters who handed Truman the victory. The now-famous photograph of a grinning Truman holding the *Chicago Tribune* proclaiming "Dewey Defeats Truman" was taken two days after the election, when Truman, on his way from Missouri to Washington, saw the paper in St. Louis and posed with it. The photo must have seemed particularly ironic to Dewey, and not only because it was spectacularly inaccurate. For most of his political career, he had managed to curry favor with reporters and finesse editors and publishers to get the kind of coverage he wanted.

Dewey declined to run for a fourth term as New York governor, ending his political career. After returning to the practice of law, he became a political power broker, influencing nominations of senators, governors, and presidential candidates. He was a crucial voice in persuading Republicans to nominate Dwight D. Eisenhower over Ohio Senator Robert A. Taft at the 1952 Republican National Convention. Dewey turned down an offer from President Richard Nixon in 1968 to become chief justice of the US Supreme Court, saying he was too old. Thomas E. Dewey died of a heart attack on March 16, 1971, in Bal Harbour, Florida, less than an hour after completing eighteen holes of golf. He was sixty-eight.

LIKE DEWEY, Eunice, as she grew older, also achieved the status of "elder statesperson" in society. Eunice served in this role when it came to domestic and international social justice and gender and racial equality causes. Two stories about her published in the late 1940s illustrate how she was seen in this role, and both speak to her power. And both are telling in other ways. Eunice was selected as one of thirteen Black women named by *Ebony* magazine in 1949 as "Women Leaders." The magazine published large photos of each woman, along with a summary of their accomplishments and a one-word summary of their titles or professions (i.e., "educator," "organizer," "public official").

Interestingly, Eunice's label in the story was not "attorney" or "businesswoman," but instead "Republican." "[She] has been prominent in New York GOP politics for 15 years," the story states. "In her job as assistant D.A. the former social worker spent ten years . . . helping to uncover and smash the city's biggest rackets."

An article two years earlier in the *Pittsburgh Courier* demonstrates, probably unintentionally, the balancing act of women when they try to succeed in their work and domestic lives. The twelve-paragraph story, which ran under the headline, "Women of Merit," was ostensibly written to trumpet the professional successes of Eunice and some others: "Recently I had the pleasure of interviewing one of New York's most prominent attorneys," the story begins. "No, no, not He, this time it happens to be She." Despite the inference early on that Eunice does defy stereotypes, the story by today's standards labels her in the second paragraph. "And she is Mrs. Lisle Carter, wife of Dr. Lisle Carter, a very well-known dentist of N.Y.C. Of course, you know her as Unice [*sic*] Carter. Aside from being a very capable attorney, Mrs. Carter, just as any other home executive, has that all important responsibility of handling a household. . . [and] with the aid of an assistant supervises her three-story home in Jummell [*sic*] Terrace, in the Washington Heights section of Manhattan quite beautifully." The story then goes on to describe her as "regal," "delightful," and "charming."

The *Courier* story does list her accomplishments in the fifth paragraph and describes them in detail. After noting the pride she takes in her son Lisle Jr., who was a law student at the time, it also lists her club and civic work, noting that "space limitations" in the newspaper prevent the naming of all of them.

But the story also illustrates how women were viewed as successful when they were adept in both their careers and their roles as wives and mothers. The identification of Eunice at first as "Mrs. Lisle Carter" was not unusual for the era, although it seems ironic today, just as her obituary in the *New York Times* refers to her as "Mrs. L. C. Carter" (making it difficult to find her obituary in a search of the newspaper using the name "Eunice Carter").

Eunice's and Dewey's identities were forged by their work and the fulfillment it gave them. They were both most comfortable in their offices, as well as in workplaces that extended beyond conventional office spaces. Ultimately, Eunice strove for success outside of her job through her dedication to social justice and equality causes and women's clubs. Dewey found tremendous fulfillment as a public servant; he certainly would have earned more money in a successful law practice than as the longtime governor of one of the most populous states in the country. And he could not have been motivated only by money in his two quests for the highest office in the country.

Both of their "families" consisted of those with whom they worked, and they thrived on the camaraderie and validation of these surrogate families. Both shared the collective and glamorous identity as "crime fighter" early in their careers, but both went on to battle social injustice on a grander and more substantial scale. Finally, both dedicated their later years to working for causes they held dear. It was the sense of community they felt in these public spheres that forged their identities.

In his biography of Dewey, Richard Smith offers a telling anecdote about his subject's personality. When he was sixty-seven, in 1970, his wife Frances died after a debilitating illness. Dewey was devastated. After an extensive period of mourning, he began seeing the socialite Kitty Carlisle Hart. That relationship brightened his life considerably, and he wanted to please her. At one point, he and Hart—who jokingly called herself "an old-line Socialist"—began discussing presidential politics, and she harshly criticized then President Richard Nixon. For the first time in their relationship, Dewey disagreed with her and was not accommodating. He cut her off with one sentence: "I'm a party man," he said.

Eunice Carter was a "party woman" in more ways than one. She remained loyal to one political party after many of her friends and relatives had abandoned it, but she also continued working steadfastly for causes she deemed important. In an essay about Harlem that she wrote when she was twenty-six, she acknowledges that winning the fight against racial injustice was very difficult—but absolutely necessary: "It takes rare courage to fight a fight that more often than not ends in death, poverty or prostitution of genius. . . . But it is to those who make this fight despite the tremendous odds . . . that we must look for the breaking of the bonds now linked together by ignorance and misunderstanding."

ACKNOWLEDGMENTS

The story of Eunice Hunton Carter and Thomas Dewey spans many decades and venues. We could not have told their story without the help of friends, relatives, colleagues, librarians, and archivists who provided valuable support and encouragement throughout our years of research and writing.

We want to thank the staff of the Mob Museum in Las Vegas for first "introducing" us to Eunice Carter through its exhibit of the 1936 mob trials in New York. The personnel there knew she was an important figure in justice and law enforcement, and we are glad that many thousands of museum visitors can hear her story.

We are particularly grateful to those who helped us access the letters, original writings, memorabilia, and other primary documents that helped this story come alive. This includes Samantha Meredith and others at the Black Mecca Museum and the Chatham-Kent Black Historical Society in Chatham, Ontario; Kenneth Chandler at the National Archive of Black Women's History in Landover, Maryland; archivists at the Moorland-Springarn Research Center at Howard University; Nanci Young, Dominique Tremblay, and Michele LaFleur at Smith College; Melinda Wallington at the University Rochester River Campus Libraries; Patricia Glowinski at the Municipal Archives of the City of New York; and the librarians and archivists at Alden Library at Ohio University. We also want to thank Biography International, an organization whose members provided encouragement and guidance.

We also sincerely appreciate the painstaking research help of graduate students Claire Rounkles at Ohio University and Anna Alden at the University of Rochester.

Little has been written outside of anthologies about the Hunton family and their important work fighting oppression around the world. We are very grateful, therefore, to Christine Ann Lutz for her comprehensive and compelling dissertation, "The Dizzy Steep to Heaven: The Hunton Family, 1850–1970," and to Eunice Carter's grandson, Stephen L. Carter, for his engaging biography of his grandmother, *Invisible: The Forgotten Story of the Black Woman Lawyer Who Took Down America's Most Powerful Mobster*, which helped us understand her relationship with her own family.

And we want to thank, also, Fredric Nachbaur of Fordham University Press for his guidance and his enthusiasm for this project.

Finally, thank you so much to our friends and family who encouraged us, provided assistance, and in general were patient enough to live for several years with Carter and us: Doug Daniel, Patrick Washburn, Nick Hirshon, Liqun Liu, and, of course, Tim Doulin.

Sources

Most of the original material in this book comes from the following archives:

Black Mecca Museum, Chatham-Kent Black Historical Society, Chatham, Ontario

Howard University, Moorland-Springarn Research Center, *Jesse Edward Moorland Papers*, Washington, DC

Municipal Archives, City of New York, Manhattan District Attorney's Papers, Luciano Series III Trial and Related Material

National Archive of Black Women's History, National Council of Negro Women Collection, Landover, Maryland

Smith College, Neilson Library and Special Collections Libraries, Northampton, Massachusetts

University of Rochester River Campus Libraries, Rare Books, Special Collections and Preservation, Thomas E. Dewey Collection, Rochester, New York

NOTES

1. Heirs to the Struggle

Epigraph: *Survey* 6, no. 6 (March 1, 1925): 684.

Recollection of the day the women left for France: See Hunton and Johnson, *Two Colored Women*, 8–9.

Background about Black citizens and thoughts about serving their country: See Brown, *Private Politics and Public Voices*, 105; and Williams, "World War I in the Historical Imagination W. E. B. Du Bois," 3–22.

Black soldiers and manual labor: See Hunton and Johnson, *Two Colored Women*. See also Williams, "African Americans and WWI," and Rief, "Thinking Locally, Acting Globally," 203–222.

Hunton's biography of her husband: A. Hunton, *William Alphaeus Hunton*.

Hunton and Johnson's respect for the Black soldiers and their intent to "record impressions": Hunton and Johnson, *Two Colored Women*, 6.

Tasks of Johnson and Hunton in France: Hunton and Johnson recount these tasks throughout *Two Colored Women*. For a summary, see Brown, *Private Politics and Public Voices*, 84.

Numbers of welfare workers sent to France: See Brown, 93; see also Chandler, "Addie Hunton," 270–283.

Du Bois's essay: W. E. B. Du Bois, "An Essay Toward a History of the Black Man," *The Crisis* 18, no. 2 (June 1919): 63–87.

Investigation of the three women welfare workers: Lutz, "The Dizzy Steep to Heaven," 217. Her information came from War Department memos and surveillance records.

On Hunton's background: See MacLachan, "Addie Waites Hunton," 556. Johnson's background is mentioned in Chandler, "That Biting, Stinging Thing," 501.

Incident of restrictions placed on Black soldiers to hear a band: Hunton and Johnson, *Two Colored Women*, 21. Hunton and Johnson recount similar anecdotes throughout their book.

Warm treatment by the French: Hunton and Johnson, 128.

German leaflet: Hunton and Johnson, 38.

French "racial consciousness": Hunton and Johnson, 111.

Hunton and Johnson's "faith" in the soldiers: Hunton and Johnson, 110.

"Salvation" of music: Hunton and Johnson, 153.

Black soldiers and the victory parade: Hunton and Johnson, 133.

Incident on the women's trip home: Hunton and Johnson, 21.

Optimism of women about soldiers gaining "broader view of life": Hunton and Johnson, 177.

Soldiers being exposed to culture and art: Hunton and Johnson, 177–178.

Jim Crow "internationalized" during war: Brown, *Private Politics and Public Voices*, 86. For more information on *Plessy v. Ferguson*, see the History website at https://www.history.com /topics/black-history/plessy-v-ferguson.

Welfare program in France seen as a challenge to White supremacy: Chandler, "That Biting, Stinging Thing," 505.

Racism exacerbated by World War I: Du Bois, "An Essay." In the same article Du Bois said he believes that Black soldiers were glad they served in the war despite the racism in their own country.

On details about the Great Migration: See Williams, "African Americans and WWI."

Information about Addie Hunton's background and birth date: Hine, *Black Women in America*. Several other sources have cited her birthday as 1875, but details about her life indicate that it would be earlier, most likely 1866. In his biography of his grandmother, Eunice, Stephen Carter indicates that Addie Hunton was born between 1866 and 1875, although the date of 1875 is on her tombstone. Carter also writes that Hunton's father spelled his name "Waits," but she used "Waites" most of her life. See Carter, *Invisible*, 18–19. See also Becker, "Addie D. Waites Hunton."

Addie on "turning point" in their lives": A. Hunton, *William Alphaeus Hunton*, 27.

Details of Huntons' courtship: A. Hunton, 38.

William and "culture shock": A. Hunton, 13.

Details of William's youth: A. Hunton, 1–3.

The Huntons and Pan-Africanism: See Lutz, "Addie W. Hunton,"16; and Richard Mares, "Black Women Communists and Pan Africanism: An Interview with Minkah Makalini," African American Intellectual History Society, March 25, 2017, accessed November 15, 2020, https:// www.aaihs.org/black-women-communists-and-pan-africanism-an-interview-with-minkah -makalani/.

William's life in Ottawa: A. Hunton, *William Alphaeus Hunton*, 11.

History of the YMCA: See the "The Story of our Founding" on the YMCA website, accessed November 15, 2020, http://www.ymca.net/history/founding.html.

Background of Brown's YMCA activity: See Mjagkij, *Light in the Darkness*, 1–3.

William's ambivalence about taking the YMCA job for which he was well-suited: Hunton, 13. His salary was noted in Mjagkij, 35–36.

William as "Pioneer Prophet": Addie Hunton mentions that W. E. B. Du Bois gave him this appellation in her introduction to *William Alphaeus Hunton*.

William and "God's will" to move: A. Hunton, 11.

Co-workers saddened by his departure: A. Hunton, 17.

Reasons Addie Waites Hunton wrote her husband's biography: A. Hunton, 17.

Alphaeus Hunton quote: D. Hunton, *Alphaeus Hunton*, 177.

Addie on rereading William's letters: A. Hunton, *William Alphaeus Hunton*, 17.

Moorland's memorial speech: Transcript from William Hunton's memorial service, St. Mark's Church, Brooklyn, New York, January 7, 1917. Jesse E. Moorland Papers, box 126-62, folder 1188. Howard University, Moorland-Springarn Research Center, Washington, DC.

William as unlike other men his age: A. Hunton, *William Alphaeus Hunton*, 38.

William downplaying his hardships: A. Hunton, 20. She gives specific examples of these hardships on pages 70–71.

William's letter from Jefferson City: A. Hunton, 73.

William suggesting that he and his wife not travel together in the South: A. Hunton, 74.

Addie's recollection of her train trip with their baby: A. Hunton, 74.

William on "practical Christianity": A. Hunton, 21.

William's promotion: Mjagkij, *Light in the Darkness*, 37.

Addie's duties while traveling with William: Mjagkij, 39.

Addie's views of her husband's character: Mjagkij, 39–40, 123.

William's travel schedule: He wrote of his itinerary in many letters, especially to Moorland. Some of these can be found in Jesse E. Moorland Papers, box 126-63, folders 1200–1212. For instance, in a letter to Moorland dated October 7, 1902, he writes he would be in Atlanta from October 14–17; Normal, Alabama, Oct. 22–24; Cleveland from Oct. 22–24; and Chattanooga on Oct. 25 (folder 1209). His letter mentioning his hectic schedule was written to Moorland from Atlanta on October 1, 1901 (folder 1207).

William's letter from Ottawa: A. Hunton, *William Alphaeus Hunton*, 43–44.

Moorland involved with Department of Colored Troops during World War I: See Chandler, "That Biting, Stinging Thing Which Ever Shadows Us," 500.

Rosenwald pledge: A. Hunton, *William Alphaeus Hunton*, 68–70, and Mjagkij, *Light in the Darkness*, 78–79.

William's relationship with Moorland: William Hunton conducted extensive correspondence with Jesse Moorland, most of which are archived in the Jesse E. Moorland Papers. Addie Hunton quotes her husband talking about Moorland, and she often mentions him in her biography of her husband in other contexts. Hundreds of letters between William A. Hunton and Moorland are stored in the Jesse E. Moorland Collection at Howard University, Moorland-Springarn Research Center, Washington D.C.; most are written by Hunton to Moorland. His mention of his baby "kicking and rolling on the floor" is dated August 16, 1896, from Normal, Alabama (box 126-63, folder 1196); the letter lamenting his baby's death is dated October 3, 1896 (folder 1196); the letter mentioning Addie Hunton's pregnancy is dated June 13, 1899 (folder 1199); the letter about the birth of Carter is dated July 20, 1899 (folder 1200); he mentions her temperature in a letter dated August 23, 1901 (folder 1206).

Recruiters stressing interdenominationalism: Mjagkij, *Light in the Darkness*, 55–56.

William making peace with YMCA and racism and Du Bois criticism: Brown, *Private Politics and Public Voices*, 86–87, and Mjagkij, *Light in the Darkness*, 78–79. Mjagkij mentions William Hunton's "self-help" philosophy on pages 2–4.

Addie's relationship with Moorland: See Lutz, "The Dizzy Steep to Heaven," 85.

Addie's mention of death "stalking" her family and the death of two of their babies: A. Hunton, *William Alphaeus Hunton*, 126. William Hunton's poem is reprinted on p. 127; he mentions his baby William Jr. in a letter from Ottawa during his visit on page 44.

Addie's mention of the lynching near Atlanta: A. Hunton, 132. She also notes here that she and William questioned the wisdom of bringing a child into such a cruel world, but she quickly added that baby Eunice brought the couple great joy.

2. Free But Not Equal

Description of Stanton Hunton: *Fauquier County, Virginia Register of Free Negroes, 1817–1865*, abstracted and indexed by Karen King Ibrahim, Karen Hughes White, and Courtney Gaskins. From Afro-American Historical Association of Fauquier County, "Genealogies," pages 24 and 25, section 1208 in binder: Families 1201–1121, Black Mecca Museum, Chatham-Kent Black Historical Society, Chatham, Ontario.

Slave and mistress linked by blood: A. Hunton, *William Alphaeus Hunton*, 2. Hunton discusses the life of Stanton Hunton on pages 1–11. But there are varying stories about Stanton Hunton's lineage. Christine Lutz notes that Elizabeth Hunton may have been Stanton's aunt; see Lutz, "The Dizzy Steep to Heaven," 55. Lutz also writes that Stanton's father may have been William Hunton, the brother of his owner. In his biography of his grandmother, Eunice Carter, Stephen L. Carter writes that Stanton's mother was almost certainly a slave. See Carter, *Invisible*, 15–17. Stephen L. Carter also questions the story of Stanton's mistress allowing him to buy his freedom. He speculates, instead, that she sold him to William Gaines, who because of Gaines's financial difficulties, allowed Stanton to buy himself.

The effect his birthplace of Canada had on William: Addie Hunton discusses this throughout her *William Alphaeus Hunton*; see esp. 6–11.

History of Chatham's growth: Walton, "*Blacks in Buxton and Chatham*," 7, 11.

Newspaper urging Blacks to immigrate to Canada: Walton, 12.

Black population of Chatham from 1851 to 1861: Walton, 125. He obtained this number from census data.

Numbers of skilled and unskilled workers: Walton, 62.

Journey of Stanton from Washington to Chatham with his brother: A. Hunton, *William Alphaeus Hunton*, 2. Also, the Black Mecca Museum features a fictionalized "oral history" recording of Stanton, in which he describes his life in Chatham, and his marriage. See the Chatham-Kent Black Historical Society and Black Mecca Museum website, accessed November 15, 2020, https://ckbhs.org/.

Stanton Hunton as owner of a building: Stanton oral history, Black Mecca Museum.

Religious make-up of Chatham's Black residents: Walton, "*Blacks in Buxton and Chatham*," 74.

Stanton Hunton's faith in religious traditions and value self-reliance: A. Hunton, *William Alphaeus Hunton*, 7.

Occupations of Stanton Hunton's children: Stanton oral history, Black Mecca Museum.

Details of John Brown's visit to Chatham and Stanton's memory of it late in his life: Hunton, *William Alphaeus Hunton*, 3–4. Christine Lutz writes about the number of Blacks and Whites who attended the Chatham meeting, 83. Robin Winks also writes about his visit to Chatham, and Canada's response to the raid at Harper's Ferry in his *Blacks in Canada*, 267–269.

Census figures of those who left Chatham and Buxton after the Civil War: Walton, "*Blacks in Buxton and Chatham*," 320 and 257–258.

Racism in Chatham and racial epithets: Walton, 198–199, 254.

Nebulous feelings of identity among former slaves: Lutz, "*The Dizzy Steep to Heaven*," 77–80.

Hunton family's loyalty to the British and William's trip to London: The exhibit featuring Stanton Hunton in the Black Mecca Museum makes reference to his loyalty to England; Addie Hunton writes of her husband's London visit in *William Alphaeus Hunton*, 95.

William's character shaped by Stanton and his birthplace: Hunton, 5.

Hunton infants who died: Addie Hunton makes a brief reference to her son who died in infancy in *William Alphaeus Hunton*. Stephen Carter writes of a daughter, Bernice, who died, in *Invisible*, 7.

William's malaria: Letter, William Hunton to Jesse Moorland, May 9, 1899, Jesse E. Moorland Papers, box 126-63, folder 1199, Howard University, Moorland-Springarn Research Center, Washington, DC.

Addie's activities after moving to Atlanta: These are recounted in several biographical sketches, including Herb Boyd, "Addie Waites Hunton: A Crusader for Justice and Women's Rights," *New York Amsterdam News*, Feb. 11, 2016; and Hutson, "Addie D. Waites Hunton," 337–338.

Mary Church Terrell biography: See Barnett, "Mary Church Terrell," 583–585.

Background of NACW: Extensive primary sources about the formation, activities, and members of the NACW are available in archives at the NCNW in the National Archive of Black Women's History. This archive houses history files about that organization in its Mary McLeod Bethune Papers: The Bethune Cookman College Collection, 1922–1955, accessed November 15, 2020, https://www.nps.gov/mamc/learn/historyculture/mamc_nabwh.htm. Linda S. Moore offers For the number of women in women's clubs and other organizations, see Moore, "Women and the Emergence of the NAACP," 480.

NACW as middle-class organization: Lutz, "The Dizzy Steep to Heaven," 111.

Black women in "no-woman's" land: See Jones, *Labor of Love*, 44.

Black women and "true womanhood": See Giddings, *When and Where I Enter*, 6–7.

Background of *The Crisis* and *Voice of the Negro*: See the NAACP website (www.naacp .org/campaigns/the-crisis-magazine/) and Bullock, *Afro-American Periodical Press*, 118–134, respectively.

Articles in the first year of *Voice of the Negro*: See *Voice of the Negro*, vol. 1, 1904, in *The Black Experience in America*. The following appeared in the magazine during its first year of publication: Henry A. Rucker, "Why Colored Men Cannot be Democrats," September 1904, 386–390; Fannie Barrier Williams, "The Negro and Public Opinion," January 1904, 31; Kelly Miller, "The Negro as a Political Factor," January 1904, 19, and February 1904, 37.

Addie Hunton's writings: On the character of Black women, "Negro Womanhood Defended," *Voice of the Negro*, July 1904, 280–282. On the activities of the NACW, "The National Association of Colored Women," *The Crisis*, May 1911, 17–18; on the Atlanta chapter of the NACW, "The Southern Federation of Women," *Voice of the Negro*, December 1905, 850–854.

Extent of Addie's travels: Lutz, "The Dizzy Steep to Heaven," 172.

Numbers of YMCA student associations under Hunton and Moorland: This was taken from the William Hunton entry in Logan and Winston, *Dictionary of Negro Biography*, 339.

William Hunton working with limited resources: Addie Hunton provides many excerpts of letters from her husband discussing this in her *William Alphaeus Hunton*; see also Mjagkij, *Light in the Darkness*, 5.

William Hunton's travels overseas: A. Hunton, *William Alphaeus Hunton*, 94–96. She talks about the great applause he routinely received on pages 94–103.

Schools in Atlanta: Lutz, "The Dizzy Steep to Heaven," 133. See also Carter, *Invisible*, 8–9.

Moorland's loans to Hunton: See William Hunton to Jesse Moorland, October 6, 1903, and Moorland's telegram in response, October 19, 1903, Jesse E. Moorland Papers, box 126-63, folder 1211, Howard University, Moorland-Springarn Research Center, Washington, DC.

The most tragic event of the Huntons' lives: See A. Hunton, *William Alphaeus Hunton*, 132. For details of the riot see Ernie Suggs, "29 Reasons to Celebrate Black History Month, No. 8: The 1906 Atlanta Riot," *Atlanta Journal–Constitution*, January 4, 2017. See also Stephen Carter, *Invisible*, 3–9.

Riot triggering William's colitis: A. Hunton, *William Alphaeus Hunton*,133.

Addie on taking "final leave" of Atlanta: A. Hunton, 133.

Brooklyn as magnet for immigrants and Blacks: See William P. Moore, "Progressive Business Men of Brooklyn," *Voice of the Negro*, July 1904, 304–308, in *The Black Experience in America*.

Addie working for YWCA: See Lutz, "The Dizzy Steep to Heaven," 165–166.

Description of the Cosmopolitan Society: A. Hunton, "The Cosmopolitan Society of Greater New York," *Voice of the Negro*, May 1907, 185–186.

William honored by the YMCA: William Hunton thanks YMCA members for this honor in a memo to YWCA officials, Jesse E. Moorland Papers, box 126-62, folder 1186. Moorland mentions the honorary degree from Howard in his remarks at Hunton's memorial service, transcript, Jesse E. Moorland Papers, box 126-62, folder 1186.

Hunton family trip to Europe: See Lutz, "The Dizzy Steep to Heaven," 163–164. Lutz mentions that Addie Hunton may have planned the trip because she was lonely; see also Carter, *Invisible*, 22–23. Hunton talks about it briefly in *William Alphaeus Hunton*, but mentions nothing about being lonely. She notes that the family returned because of her husband's illness (*William Alphaeus Hunton*, 134). Dorothy Hunton, widow of Alphaeus Hunton, writes in her biography of her husband that Eunice and Alphaeus became fluent in German during that trip and also visited Switzerland. See D. Hunton, *Alphaeus Hunton*, 12.

William's trip to Long Island: A. Hunton, *William Alphaeus Hunton*, 134.

Addie's volunteering with the NAACP: Lutz, "The Dizzy Steep to Heaven," 167–169.

Addie's reprinting of get-well wishes: A. Hunton, *William Alphaeus Hunton*, 145–151.

Visits from William's siblings: A. Hunton, 139.

William's and Addie's trips to Saranac Lake and John Brown's grave: Hunton, *William Alphaeus Hunton*, 155. Also, Stephen Carter, *Invisible*, 26–27.

Correspondence between William Hunton and Moorman late in William's life: All of these are in Jesse E. Moorland Papers, box 126-63. Addie Waites Hunton's letter to Jesse E. Moorland asking for a loan was written on December 4, 1914, folder 1216. Letters from her to Jesse E. Moorland reflecting her stress are dated December 17, 1915 and January 15, 1915, and March 11, 1915; all are in folder 1216; Addie Waites Hunton mentioned in a letter dated December 14, 1914 that she had a savings account for her children, folder 1216; the letters from Jesse E. Moorland to Shipp are dated April 30, 1914 and May 1, 1914, folder 1215. Shipp's letter to Jesse E. Moorland is dated May 5, 1915 and is in folder 1215. Jesse E. Moorland's letters to YMCA secretaries seeking donations are dated February 11, 1915, folder 1211. Porter's letter to Jesse E. Moorland is dated February 9, 1915, folder 1215.

Decision by Addie to leave Saranac Lake: William Hunton mentioned this in a letter to Moorland, April 15, 1915, box 126-63, folder 1211.

Du Bois letter to Moorland: Du Bois to Moorland, November 11, 1916, box 126-63, folder 1215.

The couple's "years of unbroken companionship": Hunton, *William Alphaeus Hunton*, 145.

3. One Vision in Her Eye, One Cry in Her Soul

Details about memorial service and notes of condolence: Jesse E. Moorland Papers, box 126-62, folder 1188, Howard University, Moorland-Springarn Research Center, Washington, DC.

Transcript of Moorland's eulogy: Jesse E. Moorland Papers, box 126-62, folder 1188.

Letter from Moorland to Du Bois: The letter is dated November 18, 1916. Jesse E. Moorland Papers, box 126-62, folder 1188.

Addie's summary of condolence letters: A. Hunton, *William Alphaeus Hunton*, 156–169.

Sanders' words, as quoted by Addie Hunton: A. Hunton, 176.

Addie's note to John Hope: See Lutz, "The Dizzy Steep to Heaven," 195. Addie Hunton does not elaborate about the "investments," but it is possible they came from an inheritance from her father, who was a successful businessman.

Addie's activities in 1907 and 1914: Hutson, "Addie D. Waites Hunton," 337–338.

Activities and goals of the NACW: See Walker, "The Black Woman," 348–350.

Sexual exploitation after World War I: Giddings, *When and Where I Enter*, 85–87.

Similarities and differences between Black and White women's clubs: Giddings, 95–96.

Social welfare and civil rights going hand-in-hand: Gordon, "Black and White Visions of Welfare," 567.

Study of club women's marital status: Gordon, 567.

Addie's speech to the Negro Christian Student Conference: Transcripts of the conference speeches are reprinted in Negro Christian Student Conference, *New Voice in Race Adjustments*, 215–219. Figures on attendance are on page 2.

Special issue of *The Crisis:* The August 1915 edition published essays about a variety of topics within the women's suffrage movement. Addie Hunton's essay appeared on pages 188–189.

Addie's comments about the relationship between William and his two children: A. Hunton, *William Alphaeus Hunton*, 152.

Addie's recollection of her time in France: Hunton and Johnson, *Two Colored Women*.

Eunice's relationship with Ovington: See Lutz, "The Dizzy Steep to Heaven," 272.

First Black students at Smith College: See the online exhibit, "History of the Black Students Alliance at Smith College," accessed November 15, 2020, https://libex.smith.edu/omeka/exhibits/show/black-students-alliance.

Eunice's activities at Smith College: Margaret Blake, "Eunice Hunton Carter, 1921, attorney," *Smith Alumnae Quarterly*, November 1935, 26. For an accounting of the number of Black people who attended college at the time, see Gordon, "Black and White Visions of Welfare," 569–570.

Details about "False Gods": These are taken from the play's program for the play, which is in a folder about Carter at the Smith College Special Collections, Young Library. The review in the *Smith College Weekly*, "False Gods Proves Artistic Achievement," is dated June 15, 1921. The *Chicago Defender* story about her graduation, "Two New York Women Win Honors at Smith," is dated June 25, 1921.

Information about Black newspapers: The history and style of the *Chicago Defender* is discussed in Washburn, *African American Newspaper*, 81–83; the expansion of these papers and their circulation and content is reviewed in Roberts and Kilbanoff, *The Race Beat*, 12–13; the papers as "indispensable tools" can be found in Pride and Wilson, *History of the Black Press*, 29. The gossipy stories about Hunton and Carter appeared in the *Pittsburgh Courier*: "Addie

Hunton-Floyd Sued For Divorce, Gossips Say," October 25, 1924; and "Eunice Carter In Sanitarium," December 9, 1933.

Eunice's story about spending Christmas alone: See Eunice Hunton, "Who Gives Himself," *Opportunity*, December 1924, 374.

Eunice's first jobs after college: Blake, *Smith Alumnae Quarterly*. Her story also referred to the social service agency as often "confused" and "inadequate."

Eunice's law school record and her entrance into the bar: See Berry, *50 Most Influential Women in Law*, 135–138. The *Chicago Defender* story, "New York Women Pass Bar Examination," appeared in the May 20, 1933 edition.

Background of *Opportunity*: See Johnson, "Rise of the Negro Magazine," *Journal of Negro History* 13, no. 1 (1928): 7–21.

Eunice's contributions to *Opportunity*: "Replica," *Opportunity: Journal of Negro Life*, September 1924, 276. "Digression," *Opportunity: Journal of Negro Life*, December 1923, 381; "Who Gives Himself," *Opportunity: Journal of Negro Life*, December 1924, 374.

Changing focus of *Opportunity* and the literary party held by Du Bois: See Lewis, *W. E. B. Du Bois*, 157–159.

Eunice and the "Czarinas": See Carter, *Invisible*, 46–49. Carter also writes throughout much of his biography of his grandmother that Eunice Carter tried hard to please her mother, and that her mother sometimes shaped her major life decisions.

Eunice's wedding announcement: "Dr. L. C. Carter Marries Popular School Teacher," *Chicago Defender*, December 6, 1924. Background about Lisle Carter is from his obituary in the *Pittsburgh Courier*, March 9, 1963.

Background of Harlem Renaissance: See Johnson, "A Generation of Women Activists," 223–240. For information about the population of West Indies immigrants in Harlem, see Bair, "Crusader," 169–171. Rev. Adam Clayton Powell called Harlem a "symbol" and literary critic Alain Locke called it a "race capital."

Opinions of Blacks and service in World War I: Rief, "Thinking Locally, Acting Globally," 211.

Number of lynchings: The number that year varies by source, but clearly it was high. These statistics were taken from Salem, "Black Women and the NAACP," 54–70. Salem writes of the "religious fervor" on page 66.

Eunice's essay in *Survey*: See Eunice Roberta Hunton, "Breaking Through," *Survey* 6, no. 6 (March 1, 1925): 684.

Number of female Black attorneys: J. Smith, *Rebels in Law*, 15, 277, 286; see also Ruth Whitehead Whaley's contribution, "Women Lawyers Must Balk Both Color and Sex Bias," which was written in 1949 and reprinted in *Rebels in Law*, 49–51.Whaley's "Seventy Carry on Battle for Sex and Race Equality in Courts," *Ebony*, August 1947, 18–21, notes that Black women lawyers of the era were more likely to work in government than private practice and that judges often passed over women jurists when making judicial appointments.

Charlotte Ray as first Black woman attorney: Many sources confirm this. See, for example, J. Smith, *Rebels in Law*, 277.

Howard as primary law school for Black students: Segal, *Blacks in the Law*, 1–3.

Background of Pan-African movement: See Lutz, "Addie W. Hunton," 115–116.

Clubwomen's organized actions to promote peace: See Plastas, "A Band of Noble Women." Terrell's Zurich speech is mentioned on page 33. Plastas also discusses the relationship between Black female reformers like Addie Hunton and others and their participation in the Women's International League for Peace and Freedom.

Du Bois summary of Addie's talk at the first Pan-African Congress: See Du Bois, "The Pan-African Congress," *The Crisis* 17, no. 6 (April 1919): 273–274.

Addie's goals for her work after the war: See Chandler, "Addie Hunton," 277.

Addie's attendance at International Council of Women of the Darker Races: Rief, "Thinking Locally, Acting Globally," 216–217.

Background of the WILPF and its conference: See Plastas, "A Band of Noble Women," 3–5; and Rief, "Thinking Locally, Acting Globally," 203–204.

Addie's interest in Haiti and the study for the WILPF: Lutz, "Addie W. Hunton," 118.

Addie's work with the WILPF and Terrell's reasons for leaving the organization: See Blackwell-Johnson, *No Peace Without Freedom*, 43, 68–69, 73–74. Rief, in "Thinking Locally, Acting Globally," explains at length some of the conflicts within the group, noting that Black club women were influential in the attention the WILPF brought to American foreign policy toward Black sovereign nations.

Representing themselves in the newly formed International Council of Women of the Darker Races: See Rief, "Thinking Locally, Acting Globally," 218. Lutz, *"The Dizzy Steep to Heaven,"* 242, offers information about the group's first conference.

Recognition that change in the United States must not be separated from change worldwide: Blackwell-Johnson, *No Peace Without Freedom*, 113.

Growth in clout of the NCNW: Rief, "Thinking Locally, Acting Globally," 218.

4. The Business of Reaching New Heights

Eunice's religion and legal career: See Berry, *50 Most Influential Women in Law*, 135–138.

Background on Alphaeus Hunton: See his obituary, "Dr. W. A. Hunton, Expert on Africa," *New York Times*, January 16, 1970; and D. Hunton, *Alphaeus Hunton*.

Background of Blacks and women's suffrage: See "African American Women Leaders in the Suffrage Movement," Turning Point, accessed November 15, 2020, https://suffragistmemorial .org/african-american-women-leaders-in-the-suffrage-movement; Brent Staples and some others believe that the history of women's suffrage, with its focus on Stanton and Susan B. Anthony, glosses over the contributions of Black women, as well as the racism exhibited by some in the movement. See Staples, "How the Suffrage Movement Betrayed Black Women," *New York Times*, July 28, 2018.

Eleanor Roosevelt's involvement with anti-lynching legislation: See Social Studies Help Center, http://www.socialstudieshelp.com, and Gallagher, *Black Women*, 8.

Du Bois essay on Blacks voting: *The Crisis*, May 1928, 168. Villard's essay, "The Plight of the Negro Voter," appeared in *The Crisis*, November 1934, 323.

Information about African Americans running for office in the early 1900s: Gallagher, *Women and Politics*, 27–29.

Socialist Party's appeal and the run of Johnson: Gallagher, 27–28.

Perception of racism in the Republican Party: Gallagher, 34–35. Failure of the NACW to pass a resolution endorsing Republicans: "The Stand of Colored Women," *The Crisis*, September 1920, 235. Examples of racism in Democratic Party: Gallagher, 34, 37.

Women "hammering away" at White privilege: Gallagher, 24.

Eunice's senior thesis: This is on file at the Neilson Library and Special Collections Libraries, Smith College, Northampton, MA.

New York Age endorsement of Eunice: Gallagher, *Women and Politics*, 6.

Results of 1934 New York election: "Democrats Sweep Polls in New York," *New York Age*,

November 10, 1934; and "Democrats Win Assembly Control," *New York Times*, November 7, 1934. The item in *The Crisis*, "Runs Good Race," is dated December 1934, 366.

Background of Harlem riot: See Fogelson and Rubenstein, *Mass Violence in America*; and "Police Shoot Into Rioters: Kill Negro in Harlem Mob," *New York Times*, March 20, 1935.

Coverage of Harlem riot: See "Harlem Riot Guilt to be Sifted Today," *New York Times*, March 25, 1935; information on the Hamidic League can be found in Bair, "Crusader," 169–171.

Opposition to the makeup of the Harlem Commission: "Mayor's Committee Under Fire," *New York Amsterdam News*, March 30, 1935.

"Cause" of the riot as economic inequality: Roy Wilkins's comments are quoted in *Time* magazine, "Mischief Out of Misery," April 1, 1935, 13; Stewart is quoted in a 2019 interview with Jerry Jazz Musician, accessed November 15, 2020, https://jerryjazzmusician.com/2019/05/interview-with-jeffrey-stewart-author-of-the-new-negro-the-life-of-alain-locke/.

Summary of Commission's findings: See a summary of the findings in "Excerpts From Riot Commission Reports," *Washington Post*, accessed November 16, 2020, https://www.washingtonpost.com/archive/politics/1992/05/04/excerpts-from-riot-commission-reports/8549a43f-7c40-41db-ae06-b01671ca56ab/.

Eunice buttonholing politicians: See Powell, *Ninety Times Guilty*, 89–90.

Addie's work with the NAACP in the 1920s: See Lutz, "The Dizzy Steep to Heaven," 260. Lutz discusses the school for Haitian children on page 246.

Bethune's relationship with Eleanor Roosevelt: Correspondence from Bethune regarding National Council of Negro Women business illustrates the friendship and collegiality between Mrs. Roosevelt and Bethune. See, for example, the NCNW Records, series 4, box 1, folder 20; and series 5, box 6, folders 9, 10, 14 (for correspondence and some clippings about their meetings). National Council of Negro Women Collection, National Archive of Black Women's History, Landover, Maryland.

Addie's support of and work with Bethune: Lutz, "The Dizzy Steep to Heaven," 251. Lutz also discusses Addie's poor health and possible depression on page 279.

Addie "fighting for her life:" See Hull, *Give Us Faith*, 323.

Eunice's comments in *Survey*: Eunice Roberta Hunton, "Breaking Through," *Survey* 6, no. 6 (March 1925): 684.

Eunice's comments about visits with her son: "I earn 5,500 per year," *The Afro-American*, March 5, 1938. Lutz brings up the possibility that Carter's son spent some of his childhood in Barbados for safety reasons, 285.

Background on Thomas E. Dewey: See Smith, *Thomas E. Dewey*, 74–84; and Dewey, *Twenty Against the Underworld*, 13–58. Dewey discusses his religious upbringing on page 43; his paternal grandfather on pages 20–25; and his college life and his move to New York on pages 56–58. Mary M. Stolberg discusses his grades in college and law school, and his inability to be courted by the biggest law firms in *Fighting Organized Crime*, 65–70. See also the *New York Times* obituary, "Thomas E. Dewey is Dead at 68," March 17, 1971.

5. From Squash Racquet to Racket Squasher

References to Oral History transcripts stored in the Thomas E. Dewey Collection refer to oral history interviews conducted by Harlan Phillips as background for Dewey's autobiography, *Twenty Against the Underworld*.

Hoover's role in fighting the mob: See Kenneth Akerman, "Five Myths About J. Edgar Hoover," *Washington Post*, November 14, 2011; and Christopher Elias, "A Lavendar Reading of J. Edgar Hoover," *Slate*, September 2, 2015, accessed November 15, 2020, http://www.slate.com /blogs/outward/2015/09/02/how_collier_s_suggested_j_edgar_hoover_was_gay_back_in_1933.html.

Politicians capitalizing on fears of organized crime: See Stolberg, *Fighting Organized Crime*, 3–7.

Dewey growing his famous moustache: See his *New York Times* obituary, "Thomas E. Dewey is Dead at 68," March 17, 1971.

Dewey's relationship with Medalie: Stolberg, *Fighting Organized Crime*, 66–70.

Background on Tammany Hall and its approach to politics: See, for example, Ackerman, *Boss Tweed*. For information about Tammany Hall and New York's district attorneys, see Raab, *Five Families*, 44–46.

Young Republicans' disdain of Tammany Hall and their efforts for reform: Stolberg, *Fighting Organized Crime*, 68–69.

Dewey's appointment by Medalie: Stolberg, *Fighting Organized Crime*, 69.

Dewey's perfectionism: See Smith, *Thomas E. Dewey and His Times*, 114. See, also, Stolberg, *Fighting Organized Crime*, 71.

Medalie's advice to Dewey regarding Waxey Gordon and Gordon's lifestyle and failure to pay taxes: See Stolberg, *Fighting Organized Crime*, 72, and Dewey, *Twenty Against the Underworld*, 125.

Paper trail left by Gordon: See Smith, *Thomas E. Dewey and His Times*, 134, and Dewey, *Twenty Against the Underworld*, 122. Dewey writes at length about the Waxey Gordon investigation in his autobiography on pages 117–139. He talks about his prosecution on page 125.

Dewey's move to Medalie's offices: Dewey, *Twenty Against the Underworld*, 138, and Smith, *Thomas E. Dewey and His Times*, 140.

Background of the newly formed grand jury and LaGuardia's memo: See "Fight Against Fear," *Time*, February 1, 1937, 16–21.

Dodge seeking special prosecutor: See "Fight Against Fear," *Time*, February 1, 1937; see also "Racket Grand Jury Balks Over Corbin, But Dodge Is Firm," *New York Times*, June 5, 1935, and "Grand Jury Submits List Of Prosecutors," *New York Times*, May 28, 1935.

Dewey's life as an attorney in private practice: Powell, *Lucky Luciano*, 48.

Selection of Corbin and scathing report of grand jury: Stolberg, *Fighting Organized Crime*, 59–61.

Lehman's initial selection of special-prosecutor candidates: "Lehman Calls 4 Lawyers to Parley As All Decline to Head Racket Inquiry," *New York Times* June 28, 1935; and "Dodge Offers Racket Inquiry Post to Dewey," *New York Post*, July 1, 1935. Lehman's meeting at his home: "Dodge Withholds Comments on Order; La Guardia Pledges Cooperation of Police," *New York Times*, June 25, 1935.

Lehman's announcement of Dewey as special prosecutor: See "Dewey Chosen By Lehman to Head Racket Inquiry; Acceptance Held Certain," *New York Times*, June 30, 1935; and "Dewey Picked For Racket Quiz," *New York Post*, June 29, 1935. The *Long Island Daily Press*, "Lehman Gives Dewey Job of Proving Vice," June 30, 1935, noted other lawyers declined the job.

Dewey recalling that Lehman was "ungracious": Dewey, *Twenty Against the Underworld*, 151.

The *New York Times* noting that Dewey's omission was a surprise: "Dodge will Obey Governor's Order," *New York Times*, June 26, 1935. The editorial, "Mr. Dewey as Prosecutor" was published on July 1, 1935. Dodge said he was seeking people "of mature age" in "Racket Grand Jury Balks over Corbin but Dodge is Firm," *New York Times*, June 5, 1935.

Dewey having his work cut out for him: See Dewey, *Twenty Against the Underworld*, 152. His "demands" to work independently were discussed in "Dewey to Demand Full, Free Inquiry," *New York Times*, July 1, 1935. The flattering editorial, "Mr. Dewey as Prosecutor," was published on the same day.

Dewey's "foxy face" and role as "racket squasher: *Time*, "Fight Against Fear."

Background of the term "rackets": See R. Smith, *Thomas E. Dewey and His Times*, 126–127.

Salaries of Dewey and his staff: Smith, 153. The size and details of his staff can be found in Smith, 154 and 155, and Stolberg, *Fighting Organized Crime*, 86.

Dewey's questioning about what criminals thought of him: R. Smith, *Thomas E. Dewey and His Times*, 150–151.

Dewey hiring Eunice after their first meeting: He said this in "Dewey has 3 in His Office," (Baltimore) *Afro-American*, September 2, 1939.

Coverage of appointment of Eunice Carter: "Naming of Mrs. Carter, Negro, as Aide Viewed as Move to Break Policy Racket," *New York Times*, August 6, 1935; "Eunice Carter on Important Staff," *Pittsburgh Courier*, August 10, 1935; *Opportunity: Journal of Negro Life*, September 1935; and "Mrs. Carter seen as Only Negro Appointee," *New York Amsterdam News*, August 10, 1935.

Comments from Dewey's staff about public relations: These come from the oral history conducted by Harlan Phillips. Steinberg's interview is in the Thomas E. Dewey Collection, series 13, box 7, folders 9 and 13; Herlands' interview is in series 13 box 7, folders 3, 64 and 65; Gelb's interview is in series 13, box 7, folders 2 and 5. University of Rochester River Campus Libraries, Rare Books, Special Collections and Preservation, Rochester, New York.

Description of special prosecutor's offices: Time, "Fight Against Fear"; "Police Guard Dewey's Office," *Long Island Press*, August 2, 1935; and "Dewey Picks Suite to Keep Inquiry Secret," *New York Post*, July 16, 1935.

Dewey's radio speech on July 30, 1935: A transcript of this can be found in the Thomas E. Dewey Collection, series 9, box 1, folder 4. University of Rochester River Campus Libraries, Rare Books, Special Collections and Preservation, Rochester, New York.

Letters of support to Dewey from news executives: These letters can be found in the Thomas E. Dewey Collection: Marty J. Berg to Dewey, July 31, 1935, series 1, box 88; William M. Hewitt to Dewey, August 7, 1935, series 1, box 88; Arthur Brisbane to Dewey, July 31, 1935, series 1, box 88; Dewey to Arthur Brisbane, August 3, 1935, series 1, box 88; Arthur Hays Sulzberger to Dewey, July 16, 1935, series 1,box 88; Ira Wolfert to Dewey, July 29, 1935, series 1, box 88. Steinberg's comments came as part of the Phillips oral history, transcript in series 13, box 7, folder 9.

Dewey's comments about press manipulation in his autobiography: See Dewey, *Twenty Against the Underworld*, 179–180.

Wire stories about Dewey's speech: All of the wire stories that were published outside of New York were written under the byline of Paul Harrison and appeared in small- and mid-sized newspaper markets. All were published during the first two weeks of August 1935. The wide reach of the stories indicated the public interest nationally in Dewey's investigation.

Eunice Carter's curiosity about prostitutes' mob links: This is discussed in nearly all accounts of the prosecution of the mob in the 1930s under Dewey. He talks about it—and his skepticism of the link at first—in *Twenty Against the Underworld*, 187–189; it is also discussed in Smith, *Thomas E. Dewey and his Times*, 181–183; and Stolberg, *Fighting Organized Crime*, 121–124.

Background of Dutch Schultz and his dealings with law-enforcement officials: See Stolberg, *Fighting Organized Crime*, 93–95; Dewey also discusses Schultz in his *Twenty Against the Underworld*, 271–278.

6. "I Must Save My Sister"

Dewey "working around" the established system: Stolberg, *Fighting Organized Crime*, 95–97.

Background of loan-shark activities: "Mayor Orders War to End Gang Power, Chiefs are Hunted," *New York Times*, October 30, 1935.

Dewey's insistence on using multiple witnesses in usury cases: See Stolberg, *Fighting Organized Crime,* 97, and R. Smith, *Thomas E. Dewey and His Times*, 176–178.

Details of loan-shark arrests and Dewey's manipulation of judicial system: R. Smith, 176, and Stolberg, 96–97.

Details of new grand juries and praise of Dewey and jurors: See Stolberg, 97, and "Lehman to Set Up Two Grand Juries in Dewey Inquiry," *New York Times*, July 8, 1936.

Robbin's comments on the importance of usury convictions: The transcript for these comes from the manuscript of Dewey's memoir, *Twenty Against the Underworld*, and is stored in series 13, box 7, folders 6 and 29, Thomas E. Dewey Collection, University of Rochester River Campus Libraries, Rare Books, Special Collections and Preservation, Rochester, New York.

Eunice's reading of "tip" letters: City of New York, Manhattan District Attorney's Papers, Correspondence–Prostitution (a–z), Luciano Series I Investigation Files, box 1, folder 1-17, New York City Municipal Archives.

Details of prostitutes' lives and their earnings: See R. Smith, *Thomas E. Dewey and His Times*, 182–183, and Dewey, *Twenty Against the Underworld*, 188–189.

Prostitutes viewed as unreliable witnesses: See Volkman, *Gangbusters*, 53.

Individual stories of some prostitutes: See Powell, *Lucky Luciano*, 48. He also discusses at length their drug addiction.

Luciano's desire to run the mob like a "chain store": See, for example, Shae Cox, "When Luciano's Luck Ran Out," Mob Museum, June 10, 2019, accessed November 15, 2020, https://themobmuseum.org/blog/when-lucianos-luck-ran-out/. Smith, Dewey, and others note this in their memoirs and histories of the mob.

Background of well-known madams: See, for instance, Karen Abbott, "The House that Polly Adler Built," *Smithsonian*, April 12, 2012, accessed November 15, 2020, https://www.smithsonianmag.com/history/the-house-that-polly-adler-built-65080310/.

Luciano's criminal background: See Stolberg, *Fighting Organized Crime,* 116–118, Cox, "When Luciano's Luck Ran Out," and Raab, *Five Families*, 30–31. Raab details Luciano's early criminal activities and discusses his nickname.

Luciano's contact with high-profile mobsters: Stolberg, *Fighting Organized Crime,* 119. She also writes about the early nineteenth-century history of New York City gangs on 118–119.

"Image" of each New York ethnic gang: Raab, *Five Families*, 25.

Luciano's assassination of Maranzano and Masseria: See Stolberg, *Fighting Organized Crime,* 118–120, and Raab, *Five Families*, 30–31.

Luciano's wealth, generosity and penchant for luxury: See Raab, *Five Families*, 50–51 and Powell, *Lucky Luciano*, 72.

Set-up of the Commission: Raab, *Five Families*, 33. Raab also discusses this in the documentary, *Lucky Luciano: Father of the Mob*, American History Channel, accessed November 15, 2020, https://www.ahctv.com/tv-shows/mafias-greatest-hits/full-episodes/lucky -luciano.

Hot Springs as gangster "hideout": See Whalen, *Murder Inc.*, 110.

Instructions from Dewey and Deputy Chief Inspector McAuliffe to eighty squads of policemen on the eve of the raids: City of New York, Manhattan District Attorney's Papers, "Raid—Instructions to Police," "Raid—List of Apartments," "Raid—List of Property Taken," "Raid—List of Prostitution and Bookers," "Raid—Index Cards of Information Seized in Vice Records." These are found in Luciano Series I Investigation Files, box 3, folder 35-45, New York City Municipal Archives.

Details of the raids and arrests: See "Dewey's Vice Raids Stagger Leaders of Underworld," *Long Island Daily News*, February 3, 1936; Raphael Avellar, "72 Girls Freed, Each Gets $150 As Dewey Aids," *New York World Telegraph*, June 12, 1936; "Lucky Luciano Keeps Fighting," *Long Island Daily Press*, April 7, 1936; "Seven Jurors Seated at Luciano Trial," *New York Post*, May 12, 1936.

Newspaper coverage of Luciano's arrest in Hot Springs, Arkansas: "Luciano, In Jail, Maps Court Fight," *New York Herald Tribune*, April 20, 1936; "Luciano Due Today; Faces $350,000 Bail," *New York Herald Tribune*, April 18, 1936; "Luciano Is Returning; 6 Lawyers Outwitted," *New York Post*, April 17, 1936; "Dewey Agents Seize Luciano at Hot Springs," *New York Herald Tribune*, April 2, 1936.

Gelb's comments on Luciano's anonymity: Oral history transcripts, Harlan Phillips interviewing Sol Gelb, June 24, 1958, series 13, box 7, folder 6, 9, Thomas E. Dewey Collection, University of Rochester River Campus Libraries, Rare Books, Special Collections and Preservation, Rochester, New York.

Dewey's description of Luciano from crime magazine: Dewey, *Twenty Against the Underworld*, 186.

Newspapers' description of Luciano: "Dewey Agents Seize Luciano At Hot Springs," *New York Herald Tribune*, April 2, 1936; "50,000 Bribe to Free Luciano Finds No Taker," *New York Herald Tribune*, April 7, 1936; "Lucania Is Named By A Vice Witness," *New York Times*, May 19, 1936; "Lucky Luciano Keeps Fighting," *Long Island Daily Press*, April 7, 1936; Russ Symontowne, "Two Girls Unmask Luciano Gang's Grip on Bordello Profits," *New York Daily News*, May 14, 1936; John Crosson, "Luciano Goes On Trial Today As Vice Lord," *New York Daily News*, May 11, 1936; Russ Symontowne, "Two Girls Unmask Luciano Gang's Grip on Bordello Profits," *New York Daily News*, May 14, 1936; Russ Symontowne, "Names Luciano One of Unholy Three of Vice," *New York Daily News*, May 17, 1936; Russ Symontowne, "Cringing Vice Witness Tells of Iron Rule," *New York Daily News*, May 19, 1936; "3 Plead Guilty in Luciano Trial," *New York World-Telegram*, May 11, 1936; "Vice Ring 'Seizure' Is Laid to Lucania," May 14, 1936, *New York Times*; Russ Symontowne, "Law Dooms 6 to Die; Nails 3 Luciano Aids," May 12, 1936, *New York Daily News*.

7. Getting Lucky: The People v. Charles Luciano

Setting of the trial and initial jury selection: Most of the New York newspapers covered this in detail. See, for example, "Three Admit Guilt as Vice Trial Opens," *New York Times*, May 12, 1936, and "3 Plead Guilty in Luciano Trial," *New York World-Telegraph*, May 11, 1936. "Luciano Goes on Trial Today As Vice Lord," *New York Daily News*, May 11, 1936; "Law Dooms 6 to Die;

Nails 3 Luciano Aides," *New York Daily News*, May 12, 1936. Interestingly, the *New York Times*, which referred to Luciano as "Charles Lucania" throughout the trial, listed the names of jurors, all the defendants, and all the attorneys involved in the case.

Details about the "blue-ribbon" jury selection: See "Jury Completed for Luciano Vice Trial," *New York Daily News*, May 13, 1936. Wolcott Gibbs and John Bainbridge explained that blue-ribbon jurors tend to convict; see Gibbs and Bainbridge, "Profiles: St. George and the Dragnet," *New Yorker*, May 25, 1940, 30 .

Hotel arrangements of jurors: See the memos sent to jurors impaneled on May 8, 1936, Luciano Series III Trial and Related Material, box 30, folder 2, New York City Municipal Archives. Gibbs and Bainbridge note in their *New Yorker* story how the prosecution witnesses were treated to movies and shopping before the trial.

Attempt to get "executive" jurors: These scheduling conflicts were outlined in a May 8, 1936, memo from Paul Lockwood to the prosecution team, box 30, folder 2, New York City Municipal Archives.

Disposition of jurors called: Lockwood's memo, followed Dewey's instructions about the accommodations for jurors.

Details of lack of previous prosecution of prostitutes who were arrested: This is available in grand jury minutes, including summaries of grand jury testimony and lists of witnesses by defendant, Luciano Series V Bound Material Grand Jury Minutes, boxes 1–16, New York City Municipal Archives.

"Their Battle Begins Now": See *New York Daily News*, May 12, 1936, for these photos and headline; but some of the testimony here is taken from accounts in the New York newspapers, which covered the trial extensively. See, for example, Russ Symontowne "Trial of Lucania Will Start May 11," *New York Herald Tribune*, April 25, 1936; "Dewey Traces Vice to Take Of 12 Million," *New York World Telegram*, May 13, 1936; John Crosson, Russ Symontowne, "Witness Names Lucky Vice Czar," *New York Daily News*, May 22, 1936; Raphael Avellar, "Vice Ring Slit Girls' Tongues for Talking," *New York World Telegram*, May 25, 1936; Russ Symontowne, "Aid's Bride Reveals Luciano's Debt Grip on Vice Underlings," *New York Daily News*, May 29, 1936; Raphael Avellar, "First Witness in Vice Trial Enters Denials," *New York World Telegram*, June 1, 1936.

Luciano as "Rockefeller" of prostitution: Gibbs and Bainbridge, "Profiles," 27.

Other details of trial and testimony: Much of this was taken from material witnesses and house of detention reports, expenses incurred in the prosecution's investigation, interoffice memos, medical reports and correspondence concerning material witnesses in custody in Luciano Series II Extraordinary Grand Jury, boxes 1 and 2, folders 7–17, New York City Municipal Archives.

Dewey praising Presser decades later: See Dewey, *Twenty Against the Underworld*, 221.

Luciano's statement on his eagerness to take the stand: "Luciano Says He's Eager to Take Stand," *New York World Telegram*, May 31, 1936.

Dewey's closing: Dewey writes about this at length in his *Twenty Against the Underworld*, 207–253; Selwyn Raab also discusses it in the documentary "Lucky Luciano: Father of the Mob," American History Channel, https://www.ahctv.com/tv-shows/mafias-greatest-hits/full -episodes/lucky-luciano.

Dewey transforming himself in cross examination: See Gibbs and Bainbridge, "Profiles," 24, 30.

Media coverage of Luciano's conviction and sentencing: "Luciano Convicted With 8 in Vice Ring on 62 Counts Each," June 8, 1936, *New York Times*; "Luciano and 8 Found Guilty, All

Face Life in Prison," June 8, 1936, *New York Daily News*; "Luciano and Lieutenants in Vice Ring, Each of Whom Faces 1,865 Years in Prison," *New York World-Telegram*, June 8, 1936. For praise for Dewey, see, "Luciano Convicted," *Daily News*, June 9, 1936.

Luciano's sentencing seen as severe: See Whalen, *Murder, Inc.*, 122.

Court details of Dewey's roundups of prostitutes and his strategy of isolating them until they talked: Luciano Series III Trial and Related Material, box 30, folder 2 New York City Municipal Archives. Testimony of the defense bringing this up at the trial is also in box 30, folder 2.

Hickman Powell's relationship with Dewey as reporter and assistant: See Powell, *Ninety Times Guilty*.

Dewey's fame after trial: See, for example, Whalen, *Murder, Inc.*, 120. Dewey's ever-present crime persona is noted in Gibbs and Bainbridge, "Profiles," 24.

8. "Making History for the Race"

Dewey pondering an electoral run: See Smith, *Thomas E. Dewey and His Times*, 229. Smith writes about the constant security and Frances Dewey's health problems on page 227.

Number of registered Democrats and Republicans in New York City and the dominance of Democrats: R. Smith, 227–237. Smith also discusses the ambivalence of Dewey about running for prosecutor.

Dewey's campaign efforts: R. Smith, 232. Smith writes about his swearing-in on page 353.

Dewey's first activities as prosecutor: R. Smith, 354–356.

Dewey's appointment of second woman: "Dewey Names Second Woman Staff Member," *New York Herald Tribune*, January 21, 1938.

Afro-American story about Eunice: "I Earn $5,500 a Year," *Afro-American*, March 5, 1938.

Eunice's possible relationship with Fletcher Henderson: See Carter, *Invisible*, 196–197.

Speculation about lesbian affair: See Hull, *Give Us Faith*, 253–254.

Background of Lisle Carter: See his obituary in the *Pittsburgh Courier*, March 9, 1963.

Lisle Jr.'s relationship with his parents: See Carter, *Invisible*, 155–156, 199.

Details of Smith honorary degree: "Four Women Get Honors at Smith," *New York Times*, June 21, 1938.

Opportunity stories about Eunice: See "In the News," *Opportunity*, August 1936, 230; and "Eunice Hunton Carter," *Opportunity*, September 1938, 261.

Eunice "making history for the race": "Woman Aide to Dewey is Commended," *Chicago Defender*, April 16, 1938.

Appointment of two other Black attorneys: R. Smith, *Thomas Dewey and His Times*, 245.

Special edition of *Life*: A series of stories on the topic of race was published in the *Life* magazine: "Negroes: The U.S. Also Has a Minority Problem," October 3, 1938, beginning on page 49. The "20 Most Distinguished Negroes" listing appeared on page 58. See also "Negroes Like Roosevelt and the New Deal Most," *Life*, June 27, 1938, 12–13.

NCNW declining to endorse Republicans: See Gallagher, *Women and Politics*, 8, 24, 34. Du Bois comments about Republicans and Blacks appeared in an editorial in *The Crisis*, May 1928, 168; see also Villard, "The Plight of the Negro Voter," *The Crisis*, November 1934, 323.

The New Deal and new federal agencies: Much has been written about the federal relief efforts of the New Deal. For a summary, see Hopkins, "The Road Not Taken," 306–316.

Roosevelt's "Black Cabinet": Ross, "Mary McLeod Bethune and the National Youth Administration," 1–28. Ross notes that Roosevelt's efforts drew criticism from some people who believed that his efforts to cultivate a Southern block of congresspersons forced him to temper some of his equal rights efforts.

NCNW's initial goals: These are spelled out in a history of the organization written by archivists at the National Archive of Black Women's History as part of National Council of Negro Women Collection, National Archive of Black Women's History, Landover, MD.

Bethune and Eleanor Roosevelt's friendship: See Abdul Rob, "Mary Bethune: From Educator to Presidential Aide," Demontfort University, Leicester, England, accessed November 15, 2020, https://www.blackhistorymonth.org.uk/article/section/science-and-medicine/mary-mcleod-bethune-educator-to-presidential-aide/.

Bethune urging Black people to switch political allegiance: Ross, "Mary McLeod Bethune and the National Youth Administration," 1–28.

Summary of NCNW national meeting: "Women Meet in Washington, Decry Role Offered Them in Welfare Set-Up," *Chicago Defender*, April 9, 1938.

Bethune letter to Mrs. Roosevelt: This letter is dated August 5, 1941, National Council of Negro Women Collection, series 4, box 2, folder 1, National Archive of Black Women's History, Landover, MD.

Aframerican Women's Journal content: Most copies of the journal can be found in the National Council of Negro Women Collection in series 13 folders. The January 1941 issue is in series 13, box 1, folder 17. The Convention issue in 1944 is in series 13, box 1, subgroup 1.

"Heavy lifters" in the NCNW: Black Women Oral History Project, Interviews, 1976–1981. Interview of Dorothy Irene Height by Polly Cowan, Schlesinger Library, Radcliffe Institute, Harvard University, accessed December 13, 2018, https://id.lib.harvard.edu/ead/sch01406/catalog.

Story about Addie: "A Dreamer of the South," *Aframerican Women's Journal*, Summer and Fall 1940, 33, in National Council of Negro Women Collection, series 13, box 1, folder 6, National Archive of Black Women's History, Landover, Maryland.

Letter outlining the honoring of Eunice: Daisy George to Bethune, February 9, 1955, National Council of Negro Women Collection series 4, folder 28, box 6.

9. "A Prelude to Greater Tasks"

Support of Dewey by Edwin Jaeckle and other Republicans: See R. Smith, *Thomas E. Dewey and His Times*, 266–269.

Dewey's nontraditional campaigning and his focus on individuals and Black voters: R. Smith, 266–267. Smith also notes that most big unions supported Lehman on page 272.

Sulzberger note to Dewey: See A. H. Sulzberger to Dewey, September 30, 1938, series 10, box 36, folder 7, Thomas E. Dewey Collection, University of Rochester River Campus Libraries, Rare Books, Special Collections and Preservation, Rochester, New York.

Results of the New York governor's race and Dewey's status as rising star: R. Smith, *Thomas E. Dewey and His Times*, 277–278.

William Hunton's relationship with his children: See A. Hunton, *William Alphaeus Hunton*. Stephen L. Carter discusses the relationship between Eunice Carter and her parents in his *Invisible*, 11–12.

Background on Alphaeus Hunton: See his obituary, "Dr. W. A Hunton, Expert on Africa," *New York Times*, January 13, 1970; a summary of his life is also given in the description of the holdings of the William Alphaeus Hunton Jr. papers at the New York Public Library, http://archives.nypl.org/scm/20646.

Stories about Pan-Africanism in *Aframerican Women's Journal*: The magazine featured stories and items about internationalism in the early 1940s; examples of these can be found in the National Council of Negro Women Collection series 13 folders, National Archive of Black Women's History, Landover, MD.

Appeal of Marxism: See D. Hunton, *Alphaeus Hunton*, ii.

Background of Alphaeus Hunton and the international Black identity movement: See Lutz, "The Dizzy Steep to Heaven," 290–291; for information about the role of Black people in the anti-colonial movement, see, for instance, Roark, "American Black Leaders," 254–270.

Alphaeus' talents as an organizer: Lutz, "The Dizzy Steep to Heaven," 294.

Paul Robeson's background as an activist: See Gilbert King, "What Paul Robeson Said," *Smithsonian Magazine*, September 13, 2011, accessed November 15, 2020, https://www.smithsonianmag.com/history/what-paul-robeson-said-77742433/.

Alphaeus's estrangement from his mother and sister: Lutz, "The Dizzy Steep to Heaven," 297. She also discusses the CAA's two successful events after World War II, 310–311.

Reversal of the nation's anti-colonial sentiment: See Roark, "American Black Leaders," 254.

Details of the "Peekskill Riot:" See Lutz, "The Dizzy Steep to Heaven," 313. See also King, "What Paul Robeson Said."

Reversal of the NAACP stand and that of many newspapers: Roark, "American Black Leaders," 258–265.

Government activity against Alphaeus Hunton: See Carter, *Invisible*; and Lutz, "The Dizzy Steep to Heaven," 316–317. See also Hunton's obituary, "W. A. Hunton, Expert on Africa," *New York Times*, January 16, 1970; and D. Hunton, *Alphaeus Hunton*, ii.

President Truman's attending the NAACP convention and his civil rights stand: See Roark, "American Black Leaders," 268.

Bethune as unsung leader in anti-colonial movement: See Robertson, "The Drums of Africa Still Beat in my Heart."

Bethune, Du Bois, and White at the United Nations: See "Bethune-Cookman College founded," AAREG, October 3, 1904, accessed November 15, 2020, https://aaregistry.org/story/civil-rights-pioneer-mary-mcleod-bethune/Bethune. Also, nearly all biographical information about Bethune includes the fact that she was the only Black woman present at the signing of the UN charter. Eunice Carter's initial participation in the UN conference is discussed in Berry, *50 Most Influential Women*, 136.

FBI file and surveillance of Addie Hunton: See Lutz, "The Dizzy Steep to Heaven," 217 and 264–265. Lutz notes Addie Hunton probably gave her last major speech, 266.

NCNW "drifting": Lutz, 324.

Eunice mention in "Toki" column: "Toki Types," *Pittsburgh Courier*, October 1, 1949.

Dewey interview in the (Baltimore) *Afro-American*: "Dewey has 3 in his office, *Afro-American*, September 2, 1939.

Details of Dewey's first gubernatorial and Presidential run: See Smith, *Thomas E. Dewey and His Times*, 343–404.

Accounts of Dewey's successes in Minneapolis: See "Dewey Plans Extension of Tour in West," *Albany Times Union*, December 14, 1939. His speech was also covered in the *Detroit Lakes* (Minnesota) newspaper on December 14, 1939.

Eunice's letter of support after Dewey's Minneapolis rally: This is undated, but believed to be written sometime in early 1940, as he was en route to California. Thomas E. Dewey Collection, series 10, box 36, folder 7, University of Rochester River Campus Libraries, Rare Books, Special Collections and Preservation, Rochester, New York.

Eunice's "publicity" stunt memo: Eunice Carter to Dewey, April 9, 1940, Thomas E. Dewey Collection, series 10, box 36, folder 7.

Correspondence between Dewey and Eunice: Eunice letter thanking Dewey for appointing Rivers is dated September 13, 1943; Dewey replied the next day in a note to Eunice. Eunice's telegram to Dewey about her mother's death is dated June 22, 1943, and his response is dated June 23, 1943; and her handwritten letter to him congratulating him on his win in the first governor's race is date November 17, 1942. Thomas E. Dewey Collection, series 10, box 36, folder 7.

Number of Black female lawyers in 1950: See Smith, *Rebels in Law*, 286. The *Ebony* story, "Lady Lawyers, 70 Carry on Battle for Sex and Race Equality in Courts" was published in August 1947, 18–21.

Details of Eunice's testimony about the United Nations and the Genocide pact: Lutz, "The Dizzy Steep to Heaven," 325–236. Details of the pact and its signing decades later by the United States are discussed in Steven V. Roberts, "Reagan Signs Bill Ratifying U.N. Genocide Pact," *New York Times*, November 5, 1988.

Eunice's work with the United Nations and its Commission on the Status of Women: See, for example, Lutz, "The Dizzy Steep to Heaven," 35. For a discussion of her work in Germany, see Rebecca Stiles Taylor, "Federated Clubs: American Women of Color are Traveling Abroad," *Chicago Defender*, April 21, 1951.

Radio interview with Mrs. Roosevelt: Eunice Carter was interviewed on June 3, 1949, as part of "The Eleanor and Anna Roosevelt Program." The transcript is available in the Franklin Delano Roosevelt Presidential Library, file: 80-5(72), track 4.

Examples of newspaper coverage of Eunice: "Eunice H. Carter Among Delegates to Paris Talks," *Chicago Defender*, September 13, 1947; and Taylor, "Federated Clubs."

Eunice's involvement with the YMCA/YWCA and the NAACP: This is mentioned in most biographical profiles; see also Herb Boyd, "Eunice Hunton Carter: a Unique Attorney and Crime Fighter," *New York Amsterdam News*, December 13, 2018.

Accomplishments of Lisle Carter Jr.: These are reviewed in his obituary by Lauren Wiseman in the *Washington Post*, September 25, 2009. Eunice Carter's obituary: "Mrs. L. C. Carter, Once Dewey Aide," *New York Times*, January 26, 1970.

Their life was their work: See D. Hunton, *Alphaeus Hunton*, ii.

10. The Aftermath

Gangsters as "aristocracy" of crime: Wolcott Gibbs and John Bainbridge, "Profiles: St. George and the Dragnet," *New Yorker*, May 25, 1940, 24.

Dewey offered to star as himself in films: See R. Smith, *Thomas E. Dewey and His Times*, 250.

Dewey living in same world as gangsters: See Whalen, *Murder Inc.*, 122.

Dewey's wife disdaining politics and her illness: Smith, *Thomas E. Dewey and His Times*, 226–227.

Reasons Eunice's son lived in Barbados: She discusses this in an interview, "I Earn $5,500 Per Year," (Baltimore) *Afro-American*, March 5, 1938. See also Carter, *Invisible*, 154–157.

Details on the Hines case: See Hines's obituary, "Jimmy Hines Dead; Ex-Tammany Chief," *New York Times*, March 26, 1957; and Gibbs and Bainbridge, "Profiles," 28.

Presser and Brown recanting their testimony: Details of this are discussed in Stolberg, *Fighting Organized Crime*, 158–159; and in Smith, *Thomas E. Dewey and His Times*, 224–225.

Unfairness of blue-ribbon juries: See Stolberg, 219–220.

Debate over wiretaps: See Stolberg, 221, and Smith, 253–255.

Background of Luciano commutation: See, for instance, Whalen, *Murder Inc.*, 123–124, and Smith, *Thomas E. Dewey and His Times*, 571–572.

Details of Luciano's voyage and his death: Powell, *Lucky Luciano*, xii-xiii.

Dewey's discussion of Luciano's commutation: See Dewey, *Twenty Against the Underworld*, 269–270.

Background of Dewey's later career: See "Thomas E. Dewey is Dead at 68," *New York Times*, March 17, 1971, and a summary of Dewey's career from archivists in the Thomas E. Dewey Collection, University of Rochester River Campus Libraries, Rare Books, Special Collections and Preservation, Rochester, New York.

Stories about Dewey's campaign plank regarding minorities: See John F. Davis, "Dewey Begins Drive to Woo Negro Vote, *Pittsburgh Courier*, August 12, 1944; and Fred Atwater, "GOP Platform Bids for Negro Vote; Governor Dewey Sidesteps Queries," *Chicago Defender*, July 8, 1944.

Details of "Dewey Defeats Truman": See Dewey's *New York Times* obituary, "Thomas E. Dewey is Dead at 68;" and Elizabeth Nix, "'Dewey Defeats Truman': The Election Upset Behind the Photo," History.com, November 1, 2018, accessed November 15, 2020, https://www.history.com/news/dewey-defeats-truman-election-headline-gaffe.

Later stories about Eunice: See "Women Leaders," *Ebony*, July 1949, 19–22; and "Women of Merit" *Pittsburgh Courier*, March 22, 1947. Eunice's *New York Times* obituary, "Mrs. L. C. Carter, Once Dewey Aide," appeared on January 26, 1970.

Dewey's relationship with Kitty Carlisle Hart: See R. Smith, *Thomas E. Dewey and His Times*, 635.

Eunice's essay in *Survey*: "Breaking Through," *Survey* 6, no. 6 (March 1, 1925): 684.

BIBLIOGRAPHY

Ackerman, Kenneth. *Boss Tweed: The Rise and Fall of the Corrupt Pol Who Conceived the Soul of Modern New York*. New York: Carroll and Graf, 2005.

Bair, Barbara. "The Crusader." In *Encyclopedia of the American Left*. Champaign: University of Illinois Press, 1992.

Barnett, Evelyn Brooks. "Mary Church Terrell (1863–1954)." In Logan and Winston, *Dictionary of American Negro Biography*, 583–586.

Becker, Thea G. "Addie D. Waites Hunton." *American National Biography*. Vol. 4. New York: Oxford University Press, 1999. https://doi.org/10.1093/anb/9780198606697.article.1500354.

Berry, Dawn B. *The 50 Most Influential Women in Law*. Los Angeles: Lowell House, 1997.

The Black Experience in America: Negro Periodicals in the United States, 1840–1960. New York: Negro Universities Press, 1969.

Blackwell-Johnson, Joyce. *No Peace Without Freedom, No Freedom Without Peace: African-American Women Activists in the Women's International League for Peace and Freedom, 1915–1970*. Carbondale: Southern Illinois University Press, 2004.

Brown, Nikki. *Private Politics and Public Voices: Black Women's Activism from World War I to the New Deal*. Bloomington and Indianapolis: Indiana University Press, 2006.

Bullock, Penelope L. *The Afro-American Periodical Press, 1838–1909*. Baton Rouge and London: Louisiana State University Press, 1991.

Carter, Stephen L. *Invisible: The Forgotten Story of the Black Woman Lawyer Who Took Down America's Most Powerful Mobster*. New York: Henry Holt, 2018.

Chandler, Susan. "Addie Hunton and the Construction of an African American Female Peace Perspective." *AFFILIA* 20, no. 3 (Fall 2005): 270–283.

Chandler, Susan K. "'That Biting, Stinging Thing Which Ever Shadows Us': African-American Social Workers in France during WWI." *Social Service Review* 69, no. 3 (September 1995): 498–514.

Dewey, Thomas E. *Twenty Against the Underworld*. New York: Doubleday, 1974.

Fogelson, Robert, and Richard Rubenstein, eds. *Mass Violence in America: The Complete*

Report of Mayor La Guardia's Commission on the Harlem Riot of March 19, 1935. New York: Arno Press, 1969.

Gallagher, Julie A. *Women and Politics in New York City*. Urbana, Chicago, and Springfield: University of Illinois Press, 2012.

Giddings, Paula J. *When and Where I Enter: The Impact of Black Women on Race and Sex in America*. New York: Morrow, 1982.

Gordon, Linda. "Black and White Visions of Welfare: Women's Welfare Activism, 1890–1945." *Journal of American History* 78, no. 2 (September 1991): 559–590.

Hickman, Charles Grutner, and Ed Becker. *Lucky Luciano: The Man Who Organized Crime in America*. New York: Barricade Books, 1939.

Hine, Darlene Clark. *Black Women in America*. Vol. 2. New York: Oxford University Press, 2005.

Hopkins, June. "The Road Not Taken: Harry Hopkins and New Deal Relief Work." *Presidential Studies Quarterly* 29, no. 2 (June 1999): 306–316

Hull, Gloria T., ed. *Give Us Faith: The Diaries of Alice Dunbar-Nelson*. New York: W. W. Norton, 1984.

Hunton, Addie W. *William Alphaeus Hunton: A Pioneer Prophet of Young Men*. New York: Association Press, 1938.

Hunton, Addie W., and Kathryn M. Johnson. *Two Colored Women with the American Expeditionary Forces*. Brooklyn, NY: Eagle Press, 1920. Reprinted as *Two Colored Women in World War I France* by Big Byte Books, 2014.

Hunton, Dorothy. *Alphaeus Hunton: The Unsung Valiant*. Richmond Hill, NY: Dorothy Hunton, 1986.

Hutson, Jean Blackwell. "Addie D. Waites Hunton." In Logan and Winston, *Dictionary of American Negro Biography*, 337–338.

Johnson, Lauri. "A Generation of Women Activists: African American Female Educators in Harlem, 1930–1950." *Journal of African American History* 89, no. 3 (Summer 2004): 223–240.

Jones, Jacqueline. *Labor of Love, Labor of Sorrow: Black Women and the Family from Slavery to Present*. New York: Basic Books, 2009.

Lewis, David Levering. *W. E. B. Du Bois: The Fight for Equality and the American Century, 1919–1963*. New York: Henry Holt, 2000.

Logan, Rayford W., and Michael R. Winston, eds. *Dictionary of American Negro Biography*. New York: W. W. Norton, 1982.

Lutz, Christine A. "Addie W. Hunton." In *Portraits of African American Life Since 1865*, edited by Nina Mjagkij, 115–116. Wilmington, DE: SR Books, 2003.

———. "The Dizzy Steep to Heaven: The Hunton Family, 1850–1970." PhD diss., Georgia State University, 2001.

MacLachan, Gretchen E. "Addie Waites Hunton." In *Black Women in America: An Historical Encyclopedia*, edited by Darlene Clark Hine, 556. Brooklyn, NY: Carlson Publications, 1993.

Mjagkij, Nina. *Light in the Darkness: African Americans and the YMCA, 1852–1946*. Lexington: University Press of Kentucky, 1994.

Moore, Linda S., "Women and the Emergence of the NAACP." *Journal of Social Work Education* 49, no. 3 (June 2013): 476–489.

Negro Christian Student Conference. *The New Voice in Race Adjustments: Addresses and Reports Presented at the Negro Christian Students Conference, Atlanta, Ga., May 14–18, 1914*. Edited by A. M. Trawick. New York: Student Volunteer Movement, 2014.

Plastas, Melinda. *"A Band of Noble Women: The WILPF and the Politics and Consciousness of Race in the Women's Peace Movement, 1915–1945."* PhD diss., State University of New York, Buffalo, 2001.

Powell, Hickman. *Lucky Luciano: The Man Who Organized Crime in America*. New York: Barricade Books, 2000 [1939].

———. *Ninety Times Guilty*. New York: Arno Press, 1974.

Pride, Armistead S., and Clint C. Wilson II. *A History of the Black Press*. Washington, DC: Howard University Press, 1997.

Raab, Selwyn. *Five Families: The Rise, Decline, and Resurgence of America's Most Powerful Mafia Empires*. New York: Thomas Dunne Books, 2005.

Rief, Michelle. "Thinking Locally, Acting Globally: The International Agenda of African American Clubwomen, 1880–1940." *Journal of African American History* 89, no. 3 (Summer 2004): 203–222.

Roark, James L. "American Black Leaders: The Response to Colonialism and the Cold War, 1943–1953." In *The African-American Voice in U.S. Foreign Policy Since World War II*, edited by Michael L. Krenn. New York and London: Garland Publishing, 1998, 254–270.

Roberts, Gene, and Hank Klibanoff. *The Race Beat*. New York: Vintage Books, 2006.

Robertson, Ashley N. "'The Drums of Africa Still Beat in My Heart': The Internationalism of Mary McLeod Bethune and the National Council of Negro Women, 1895–1960." PhD diss., Howard University, 2013.

Ross, Joyce B. "Mary McLeod Bethune and the National Youth Administration: A Case Study of Power Relationships in the Black Cabinet of Franklin D. Roosevelt." *Journal of Negro History* 60, no. 1 (January 1975): 1–28.

Salem, Dorothy C. "Black Women and the NAACP, 1909–22." In *Black Women in America*, edited by Kim Marie Vaz, 54–70. Thousand Oaks, CA: Sage, 1995.

Segal, Geraldine R. *Blacks in the Law*. Philadelphia: University of Pennsylvania Press, 1983.

Smith, J. Clay. *Rebels in Law: Voices in History of Black Women Lawyers*. Ann Arbor: University of Michigan Press, 1998.

Smith, Richard N. *Thomas E. Dewey and His Times*. New York: Simon and Schuster, 1982.

Stolberg, Mary M. *Fighting Organized Crime: Politics, Justice and the Legacy of Thomas E. Dewey*. Boston, MA: Northeastern University Press, 1995.

Volkman, Ernest. *Gangbusters: The Destruction of America's Last Mafia Dynasty*. Winchester, MA: Faber and Faber, 1998.

Walker, Ernestein. "The Black Woman." In *The Black America Reference Book*, edited by Mabel M. Smythe, 348–350. Englewood Cliffs, NJ: Prentice-Hall, 1976.

Walton, Jonathan W. *"Blacks in Buxton and Chatham, Ontario, 1830–1890: Did the 49th Parallel Make a Difference?"* PhD diss., Yale University, 1979.

Washburn, Patrick. *The African American Newspaper*. Evanston, IL: Northwestern University Press., 2006.

Whalen, Robert Weldon. *Murder Inc. and the Moral Life: Gangsters and Gangbusters in LaGuardia's New York*. New York: Fordham University Press, 2016.

Williams, Chad. "World War I in the Historical Imagination W. E. B. Du Bois." *Modern American History* 1 , no. 1 (March 2018): 3–22.

Winks, Robin. *The Blacks in Canada: A History*. Montreal: McGill-Queen's University Press, 1971.

INDEX

Abbreviations: *AWH* Adelina Waites Hunton, *EHC* Eunice Hunton Carter, *TED* Thomas E. Dewey, *WAH Jr* William Alphaeus Hunton, Jr., *WAH Sr* William Alphaeus Hunton, Sr.

Marilyn S. Greenwald is a professor emerita in the E. W. Scripps School of Journalism at Ohio University. Her teaching and research interests include biography writing, news reporting, and reviewing the arts. She is the author of *Pauline Frederick Reporting: A Pioneering Broadcaster Covers the Cold War* (Potomac, 2015) and *A Woman of the Times: Journalism, Feminism, and the Career of Charlotte Curtis* (Ohio University Press, 1999), which was a notable book of the *New York Times*.

Yun Li is a reporter at CNBC covering the US financial markets. Her work has appeared in Reuters, Bloomberg News, and other outlets. She holds a master's degree in journalism from the E. W. Scripps School of Journalism at Ohio University.

SELECT TITLES FROM EMPIRE STATE EDITIONS

Britt Haas, *Fighting Authoritarianism: American Youth Activism in the 1930s*

David J. Goodwin, *Left Bank of the Hudson: Jersey City and the Artists of 111 1st Street*. Foreword by DW Gibson

Nandini Bagchee, *Counter Institution: Activist Estates of the Lower East Side*

Susan Celia Greenfield (ed.), *Sacred Shelter: Thirteen Journeys of Homelessness and Healing*

Susan Opotow and Zachary Baron Shemtob (eds.), *New York after 9/11*

Andrew Feffer, *Bad Faith: Teachers, Liberalism, and the Origins of McCarthyism*

Colin Davey with Thomas A. Lesser, *The American Museum of Natural History and How It Got That Way*. Forewords by Kermit Roosevelt III and Neil deGrasse Tyson

Wendy Jean Katz, *Humbug! The Politics of Art Criticism in New York City's Penny Press*

Lolita Buckner Inniss, *The Princeton Fugitive Slave: The Trials of James Collins Johnson*

Mike Jaccarino, *America's Last Great Newspaper War: The Death of Print in a Two-Tabloid Town*

Angel Garcia, *The Kingdom Began in Puerto Rico: Neil Connolly's Priesthood in the South Bronx*

Jim Mackin, *Notable New Yorkers of Manhattan's Upper West Side: Bloomingdale–Morningside Heights*

Matthew Spady, *The Neighborhood Manhattan Forgot: Audubon Park and the Families Who Shaped It*

Robert O. Binnewies, *Palisades: The People's Park*

Elizabeth Macaulay-Lewis, *Antiquity in Gotham: The Ancient Architecture of New York City*

For a complete list, visit www.fordhampress.com/empire-state-editions.